CICERO
LAELIUS, ON FRIENDSHIP
&
THE DREAM OF SCIPIO

ARIS AND PHILLIPS CLASSICAL TEXTS

CICERO

On Friendship & The Dream of Scipio

Edited with an introduction, translation and notes by

J. G. F. Powell

Aris & Phillips is an imprint of Oxbow Books

First published in the United Kingdom in 1990. Reprinted 2005, 2015 by
OXBOW BOOKS
10 Hythe Bridge Street, Oxford OX1 2EW

and in the United States by
OXBOW BOOKS
908 Darby Road, Havertown, PA 19083

Paperback Edition: ISBN 978-0-85668-441-8

A CIP record for this book is available from the British Library

For a complete list of Aris & Phillips titles, please contact:

UNITED KINGDOM
Oxbow Books
Telephone (01865) 241249
Fax (01865) 794449
Email: oxbow@oxbowbooks.com
www.oxbowbooks.com

UNITED STATES OF AMERICA
Oxbow Books
Telephone (800) 791-9354
Fax (610) 853-9146
Email: queries@casemateacademic.com
www.casemateacademic.com/oxbow

Oxbow Books is part of the Casemate Group

CONTENTS

PREFACE

In preparing this edition, I have tried to keep in mind an "ideal reader", not very different, perhaps, from some of the Classical Studies undergraduates whom I have taught at Newcastle: a reader whose experience of Latin literature, and especially of the Latin language, is limited, but who has an eager appetite for the study of the Ancient World, and who desires, in pursuit of that interest, to achieve as full as possible an understanding of these particular texts. I believe that such a reader is, in principle, capable of understanding any matter that comes within the province of classical scholarship (philology and textual criticism included), provided that it is explained clearly enough, and provided that the explanation does not presuppose prior knowledge that he or she does not possess. On the other hand, I accept that there are some matters in which, generally speaking, such a reader is less likely to be interested than in others. Accordingly, in conformity with the requirements of this series, I have commented on textual and linguistic matters only when that seemed necessary for the understanding of the text; and in such cases, as elsewhere, I have tried to ensure that the discussion is intelligible to those without long training in Latin scholarship.

At the same time, I hope that this edition may not be without interest for more advanced scholars. Both the works under consideration raise questions of sources, structure and literary aims. Although these questions have often been discussed in specialised literature, it seems opportune to examine them afresh and in some detail, and in particular to question some opinions with regard to them that seem to have acquired an undeserved currency. Further, the process of preparing commentaries on these texts, and especially (some may be surprised to learn) of translating them, has revealed many individual problems that do not appear to have been satisfactorily dealt with hitherto. I have read as much previous literature on the *Laelius* and *Somnium* as I could find, and have referred to it when it seemed to me appropriate. Any professional scholar who finds the bibliographical material inadequate for his purposes should consider the class of readers for which the book is primarily intended, while any reader who is unable to follow up the references to untranslated ancient texts or to foreign books and articles may be assured that (unless through my own inefficiency) they do not conceal any major points of information or argument that are not otherwise elucidated. It should also be said that I do not aim to provide a full and comprehensive treatment of all the general issues raised by these texts: if those issues could all be covered within the format of a relatively compact edition such as this, the texts would be far less worth reading than they are. In particular, a full discussion of the history of the concept of friendship, in Graeco-Roman civilisation or in any other, is outside the scope of this work. There are in my opinion some types of question which the wise commentator should leave his readers to consider for themselves.

The text of both the *Laelius* and the *Somnium Scipionis* printed here is my own. It does not differ radically from the texts of previous editions, but I have incorporated some of the results of my own work on the manuscripts. Throughout, I have followed my own judgement in the choice of readings, and, in the Appendix, I have attempted to justify my choices with reference to the available manuscript evidence, the sense of the respective passages, and Latin usage. However, some minor points have been left undiscussed, and a full critical apparatus is not included. Those who wish for one must wait until the publication of my Oxford Classical Text of *De Republica*, *De Legibus*, *Cato Maior de Senectute*, and *Laelius de Amicitia*. In one respect I may be thought to have taken a radical line: as in my Cambridge edition of the *Cato Maior* (Cambridge Classical Texts and Commentaries, 28, C.U.P. 1988), I have entirely reconsidered and revised the punctuation and paragraphing of the text. I believe that only in this way can one properly exhibit to the reader the structure of the argument and the detailed progression of thought. The accumulated conventions of editors on this matter have no authority whatsoever; the only true criterion is the logic of the text itself. The conventional chapter and section numbers (products of the seventeenth and sixteenth centuries respectively: cf. J.Glucker, "Chapter and Verse in Cicero", *Grazer Beiträge* 11 [1984] 103-12) have been retained in their traditional places, but the reader must not be surprised to see them in the middle of paragraphs, and sometimes even in the middle of sentences. The *Somnium Scipionis* is unfortunately burdened with two sets of section numbers: sections 1-21 of the *Somnium* itself correspond to *De Republica* 6.9-29. To avoid confusion I have given the former first in each case, followed by the latter in brackets.

The translation aims to keep as close as possible to the sense of the original, and to convey that sense in such a way that it can be perceived with the minimum of difficulty by a non-Latinate English reader. If it also succeeds in conveying something of the literary qualities of the original, so much the better. It is not (it goes without saying) meant as a "crib" or a "construe": the Latinate reader will find that in many places I have chosen to preserve the logic of the Latin at the expense of the precise syntax. I have often found that the adoption of a particular turn of phrase in the translation can obviate the necessity for further comment; but on the other hand, there are some occasions when no translation can serve on its own to elucidate the meaning fully, and in such cases the commentary must be referred to by the non-Latinate reader. This applies in particular to the peculiarly Roman moral or evaluative terms such as *virtus*, *humanitas*, *constantia*, or *fides*, which have no single equivalents in English, but must be translated variously according to the context.

The convention of this series is that the commentary is on the translation, with English lemmata. I have tried genuinely to keep to this: I have, I hope, resisted the temptation to write the commentary as if it were on the Latin and then to substitute an English lemma at the last moment. I am aware that this convention makes the commentary less easy to use for those who read the text in the original, but the slight inconvenience is not hard to overcome.

The "ideal reader" characterised at the beginning, and indeed any intelligent reader who is curious about ancient life and thought, should find much of interest in these two pieces of Ciceronian philosophy. They are among the most accessible and enjoyable of his works. They are largely free of the bombast that some find repellent in his political speeches. The humane idealism of the *Laelius* stands as a monument to what was best in Roman civilisation, even though the reality of Roman life did not always resemble the ideal very closely, and even if Cicero may occasionally appear slipshod or hypocritical in his presentation of it. The *Somnium Scipionis* is an extract from what would probably be thought of as Cicero's greatest literary work, if it had survived entire. The *Somnium* gives a fascinating insight into Graeco-Roman views of man's place in the cosmos; and, brief though it is, it has been immensely influential in later times.

Most of the work for this edition was carried out in the Department of Classics at Newcastle University, a place where the maxim κοινά τὰ φίλων is daily put into practice in scholarly matters. I owe various debts to various colleagues, but I am particularly grateful to Professor David West for his help in reading and criticising a draft of the whole volume. I am indebted to Dr. R. W. Sharples for the opportunity to read an unpublished paper of his on the *Laelius*, to Dr. R. Mayer for bibliography on friendship, to Dr. K. Lomas for the history of the Blossii of Cumae, to Prof. T. P. Wiseman for references on *scaena* (*Lael.* 96), and to my mother for useful comments on the translation and for help with the proofs. I am grateful to the University of Newcastle for allowing me a term's leave in the autumn of 1989 in order that I could complete this book, and to Corpus Christi College, Oxford, for temporary membership of the Senior Common Room during that term.

J.G.F.P.
Newcastle upon Tyne
April 1990

BIBLIOGRAPHICAL NOTE

There are in existence countless editions of both the *Laelius* and the *Somnium Scipionis*. It would serve no useful purpose to list them here. I mention only those which I have found particularly helpful in the course of preparing the commentary. *Laelius*: Seyffert-Müller (1876), Reid (1883), Laurand (1928), Combès (1971); and the two fascicles which are (at the time of writing) all that has appeared of the commentary of K.A.Neuhausen (Heidelberg 1981-5). *Somnium*: Ronconi (ed. 2, 1967), Bréguet's Budé edition of the *De Republica* (1980), and Büchner's commentary on the *De Rep.* (1986).

Scholarly books and articles are referred to at appropriate points in the introduction and commentary. The abbreviations used for ancient references and for the titles of periodicals are in most cases the standard ones, though the reader should be warned that I refer to Cicero's *Cato Maior de senectute* as *Cato Maior* or *CM*. The following modern works, references to which recur, are cited by abbreviated title:

Astin, *Scipio* — A.E.Astin, *Scipio Aemilianus* (Oxford 1967)

Beare, *Roman Stage* — W.Beare, *The Roman Stage* (London 1950)

Becker, *Technik und Szenerie* — E.Becker, *Technik und Szenerie des ciceronischen Dialogs* (Osnabrück 1938)

Boyancé, *Études* — P.Boyancé, *Études sur le Songe de Scipion* (Paris 1936)

Bringmann, *Untersuchungen* — K.Bringmann, *Untersuchungen zum späten Cicero* (Göttingen 1971)

Broughton, *MRR* — T.R.S.Broughton, *The Magistrates of the Roman Republic* (New York 1951-60)

Büchner, *Ciceros Somnium Scipionis* — K.Büchner, *Ciceros Somnium Scipionis: Quellen, Gestalt, Sinn*, Hermes Einzelschriften 36 (1976)

Diels-Kranz — H.Diels and W.Kranz, *Die Fragmente der Vorsokratiker*, ed. 6 (Berlin 1951)

Fantham, *Imagery* — E.Fantham, *Comparative Studies in Republican Latin Imagery* (Toronto 1972)

Festugière, *RHT* — [A.J.] Festugière, *La Révélation d'Hermès Trismégiste* (4 vols., Paris 1944-54)

Fortenbaugh, *Quellen zur Ethik Theophrasts* — W.W.Fortenbaugh, *Quellen zur Ethik Theophrasts* (Amsterdam 1984)

Gottschalk, *Heraclides* — H.Gottschalk, *Heraclides of Pontus* (Oxford 1980)

Hellegouarc'h, *Vocabulaire* — J.Hellegouarc'h, *Le Vocabulaire latin des relations et des partis politiques sous la république* (Paris 1963; ed. 2, 1972)

Long-Sedley — A.A.Long and D.N.Sedley, *The Hellenistic philosophers* (Cambridge 1987)

OCD — *Oxford Classical Dictionary*

OLD   *Oxford Latin Dictionary*, ed. P.G.W.Glare (Oxford 1982)

Otto, *Sprichwörter*   A.Otto, *Die Sprichwörter und sprichwörtlichen Redensarten der Römer* (Leipzig 1890, repr. Hildesheim 1962)

Rawson, *Cicero*   E.Rawson, *Cicero* (London 1975, repr. Bristol 1983)

RE   Pauly-Wissowa, *Realencyclopädie der classischen Altertumswissenschaft* (Stuttgart 1893-)

Skutsch, *Ennius*   O.Skutsch, *The Annals of Quintus Ennius* (Oxford 1985)

Staveley, *Voting and Elections*   E.S.Staveley, *Greek and Roman Voting and Elections* (London 1972)

Stockton, *Cicero*   D.Stockton, *Cicero: a Political Biography* (Oxford 1971)

Stockton, *Gracchi*   D.Stockton, *The Gracchi* (Oxford 1979)

SVF   J. von Arnim, *Stoicorum Veterum Fragmenta* (Leipzig 1905)

T. & T.   L.D.Reynolds ed., *Texts and Transmission: a survey of the Latin classics* (Oxford 1983).

LAELIUS DE AMICITIA: INTRODUCTION

l. General introductory remarks Cicero's *Laelius de amicitia* is concerned with a subject that should be of universal human interest. It is attractive as a literary work in its own right, and it offers a considerable range of evidence for Roman social and political life and thought.

As a treatise on moral philosophy, it must be admitted, it leaves something to be desired. It is neither detailed nor comprehensive in its treatment of moral issues. Judged purely as a work of analysis, it does not compare very well with Aristotle's discussions of friendship in the *Nicomachean* and *Eudemian Ethics*. In some of its preoccupations, it reflects ancient philosophical debates which, however lively they were in the philosophical schools of Cicero's time, may perhaps, at least on first acquaintance, seem arid and artificial to a modern reader. But the *Laelius* is not meant as a work of pure philosophy. It combines a modicum of philosophical analysis with practical common-sense advice, and above all with rhetorical celebration of the value of friendship (in the best possible sense of that word). The term "rhetorical" should not be misunderstood to imply that there is anything artificial about the sentiments expressed. Cicero presents an ideal of friendship, affectionate but without misplaced sentiment, based on natural affinity of character and on common pursuits and opinions: this ideal appears to be perfectly genuine, and, taken by itself, contains nothing which a twentieth-century reader would regard as outdated or unfamiliar.

Some readers may, at first glance, be troubled by the fact that Cicero writes almost entirely about aristocratic male Romans. It is true that some of his observations are not directly applicable to a modern democratic society. It is also true that he only discusses friendship between males, and the modern reader may naturally jump to the conclusion that he, and others of his time, could only envisage such an idealised intellectual companionship in an all-male setting. Such a conclusion would, however, be wrong. Stoic philosophers, both Greek and Roman, talked of marriage in almost exactly the same terms as those in which Cicero describes ideal friendship; but it must be remembered that in most ancient philosophical literature the subjects of friendship, love and marriage were clearly demarcated, and it is not surprising that Cicero says nothing of the latter two topics. It may further be noted that while Cicero had himself found great satisfaction in his friendship with Atticus, his experiences of family life around the time of writing had not been so satisfactory. But in any case, the Roman social background (interesting though it is in itself) is not essential to most of the points that Cicero makes about friendship. He speaks of friendship as a universal human attribute, not as something confined by a particular social context. In fact, his view of friendship as an essential part of human nature is incompatible with the idea that variations in social custom make a significant difference to the quality of friendship.

2. The topic of friendship in the ancient philosophical tradition, and in Cicero's earlier works The idea of a philosophical or moralistic treatise on friendship, written by a somewhat disillusioned senior politician, and cast in the form of a fictional dialogue set eighty or ninety years in the past relative to the time of writing, may perhaps strike a modern reader as a little unfamiliar. Cicero's own preface goes some way towards explaining the genesis of the work (§§4-5). He claims that the topic had been suggested to him by his great friend Atticus, and that he thought he could do the public some good by writing about it. He says, further, that he chose the form of a dialogue set in the past, as he had done in the *Cato Maior de senectute*, in order to give an appearance of additional authority to the opinions contained in it.

First of all, however, it needs to be explained why the topic of friendship should have suggested itself to Cicero (or Atticus) at all as being a suitable subject for such a work. The immediate explanation lies in the Greek philosophical tradition. Friendship (φιλία) was one of a number of practical moral themes that were regularly treated by Greek philosophers in their capacity as teachers of general ethics and the "art of living". As with other aspects of this ethical strand in Greek philosophy, the first impetus towards reflective discussion of friendship came from Socrates and the Socratic writers. Plato, in the *Lysis*, makes his Socrates discuss the term φίλον in its various aspects: the word is confusingly ambiguous in Greek, since it can be either active in meaning ("friendly" or "loving") or passive ("dear"). The Platonic Socrates's mind-bending display of logical analysis seems to have had little direct influence on the later tradition, except that it does seem to have started the debate on whether friendship arises from similarity or from dissimilarity (see below, commentary on §27). More down-to-earth is the discussion on friendship to be found in Xenophon's *Memorabilia*, purporting to be a reminiscence of a conversation of Socrates. Parts of this were directly adapted by Cicero (without acknowledgement): notably the maxim that friendship can only exist among the good (§18, Xen. *Mem.* 2.6.16; this later became a philosophical commonplace), the observation that most people are careless about acquiring and keeping friends (§62, Xen. *Mem.* 2.4.4), and the enumeration of the advantages of a good friendship (§22, Xen. *Mem.* 2.4.5-7).

In Aristotle's *Ethics* (*Nicomachean Ethics*, books 8 and 9; *Eudemian Ethics*, book 7), the moral and practical aspects of friendship are subjected to an acute philosophical analysis. The connection of friendship with individual character is stressed, and friendship is divided into three types, or rather one true type (friendship between good men) and two inferior forms of relationship (association for profit and for pleasure) which may also be called "friendship", but with some qualification. The relation between the three types is presented rather differently in the *Nicomachean* and *Eudemian* versions. Against the background of this classification, a number of more specific moral problems are discussed. There are marked similarities between some of Cicero's observations and those of Aristotle: it is not clear whether Cicero had direct access to these Aristotelian texts, but it may be that Aristotle's ideas reached Cicero through the mediation of later Peripatetic writers. For further remarks on this point, see below, Introd. §8. (There is a considerable bibliography on Platonic and Aristotelian ideas of friendship: see most recently A.W.Price, *Love and Friendship in Plato and Aristotle* [Oxford 1989] and literature there cited.)

From the catalogues of works in Diogenes Laertius, and elsewhere, we have evidence for no less than seven treatises entitled περὶ φιλίας, by various Greek philosophers: Simmias of Thebes, an associate of Socrates and Plato (D.L. 2.124), Speusippus and Xenocrates in the early Academy (D.L. 4.4 and 12), Theophrastus the successor of Aristotle (D.L. 5.45, Gellius 1.3), the later Peripatetic Clearchus (fr. 17-18 in F.Wehrli, *Die Schule des Aristoteles* [Basel 1967-9] vol. III, = Athenaeus 8.349f and 12.535e) and the Stoics Cleanthes (D.L. 7.175) and Chrysippus (Plutarch, *Stoic. Repugn.* 1039b). All these works are entirely lost except for one or two fragments, and the extent of Cicero's debt to them, if any, is quite impossible to assess. The views of the Epicureans on friendship do not appear to have been embodied in distinct treatises, but a number of surviving Epicurean maxims concern the topic, and we can learn a good deal about the views of the school from what Cicero himself tells us (cf. below). (For the maxims on friendship, see *Kyriai Doxai* 27 = *Gnomologium Vaticanum* 13; *GV* 23, 28, 34, 39, 52, 56-7, 78; Long-Sedley II, 141-2; J.Bollack, *Actes*, VIIIème Congrès Budé [Paris 1969] 221-36; in general, A.-J.Voelke, *Les rapports avec autrui dans la philosophie grecque d'Aristote à Panétius* [Paris 1961] 91-98; J.M.Rist, *CPh* 75 [1980] 121-9. For Cicero's attitudes to Epicurean doctrines of friendship, see R.Hirzel, *Untersuchungen zu Ciceros philosophischen Schriften* [Leipzig 1877] I, 169; II, 678. I have not seen A.Grilli, "Sull'amicizia epicurea nel *Laelius*", *Elenchos* 5 [1984] 221-4.)

That Cicero knew a number of philosophical treatises on friendship seems to be indicated by his reference to the genre in *Ad Fam.* 3.8.5 (a letter to Appius Claudius); but the only reasonably plausible connection that can be made between the *Laelius* and a Hellenistic work on friendship comes from the comment of Aulus Gellius (1.3) that Cicero "appeared to have read" Theophrastus's treatise on friendship when he composed the *Laelius*, and that he "transferred" some points from it. Gellius compares section 61 of Cicero unfavourably with a passage of Theophrastus on a corresponding topic (the question of what one is to do if the demands of friendship conflict with moral principles); the passage of Theophrastus that he quotes is unlike anything in Cicero. We also happen to know from other sources that Cicero's precept to "judge before making friends, not make friends before judging" comes from Theophrastus (see on §85). But apart from this, there is no way of telling what, or how much, Cicero owes to him. It is to be noted that Theophrastus's work on friendship ran to three books; so it probably provided a wide choice of material from which Cicero might have selected. (A full study of the material from Cicero and elsewhere that *might* be traced to Theophrastus was made by G. Heylbut, *De Theophrasti libris* περὶ φιλίας [Diss. Bonn 1876]. See also Fortenbaugh, *Quellen zur Ethik Theophrasts* 66-76, 111-3, 285-303.)

Cicero had referred to friendship in three of his earlier philosophical works: the *De Legibus*, the *De Finibus Bonorum et Malorum*, and the *De Natura Deorum*. In all these instances he was concerned, as in the *Laelius*, with the debate as to whether friendship was a natural phenomenon, to be desired for its own sake, or something which is primarily sought for the sake of the advantages that it brings. In the *De*

Legibus (1.33-35 and 1.49), written probably in the late 50's BC, he wrote of friendship as a manifestation of the natural social bond between human beings which also gave rise to laws and political organisations. However, the *De Legibus* contains no extended discussion of friendship; in fact the manuscripts at 1.34 contain an annotation, *"de amicitia locus"* ("section on friendship"), suggesting either that some such discussion has been lost, or more likely (since it is reasonably clear that Cicero left the work unfinished) that Cicero himself intended to insert one, but never in fact did. In the *De Finibus Bonorum et Malorum*, one of the series of larger works written in 45 BC, there is a longer section on friendship. The Epicurean speaker Torquatus discusses it from the point of view of the school which he represents, speaking in high praise of friendship itself, but stressing the utilitarian account of its origins and justification (*Fin.* 1.66-70). Cicero in his own person rejects this view (2.82-85), arguing, as he does in the *Laelius*, that friendship means nothing unless it is desired for its own sake. The topic is also alluded to briefly elsewhere in the *De Finibus* (3.55; 3.70; 5.65-8; 5.74; 5.81). In the *De Natura Deorum* (1.121-2), the topic of friendship is enlisted as a parallel for the relationship between men and gods, the same point being made against the Epicureans as in the other two works.

Philosophic ideas on friendship had also spread into the tradition of rhetoric and public speaking. Study of human character, psychology and behaviour was considered vital for the successful orator: for Aristotle, this was one of the three main sources of persuasiveness in rhetoric (*ethos*; the others being *pathos* [emotion] and *logos* [reasoning]). Aristotle included in his treatise on rhetoric, under the general heading of *ethos*, a discussion of friendship and the qualities of character that conduce towards it (*Rhet.* 2.4). Cicero seems fairly clearly to have drawn on this in the *Laelius* (§§65-6). Among Cicero's own treatises on rhetoric, we find the topic of friendship mentioned in the early *De Inventione*, where Cicero refers to the two sides of the philosophical dispute about its *raison d'être*, and says that either may be considered right for rhetorical purposes (*Inv.* 2.167; cf. also [Cic.] *Ad Herenn.* 3.4; 3.10; 3.14). Among the generalised ethical subjects which Cicero lists as suitable for rhetorical practice (*Partitiones oratoriae* 62) we find the question *quibus officiis amicitia colenda sit* - "what are the duties of friendship?" or "what services should be performed in order to maintain friendship?". The practical use of such exercises may be illustrated, by way of example, from Cicero's *Pro Plancio*, where the orator justifies himself for opposing a friend of his: in *Planc.* 5 he produces the conventional definition of friendship as community of aims (cf. *Lael.* 20), while in sections 80-81 of the same speech he expatiates on the topic of gratitude for favours received. (For the influence in Cicero's speeches of philosophical ideas on friendship, see A.Michel, *Rhétorique et philosophie chez Cicéron* [Paris 1960] 608-12; cf. also G.Boissier, *Cicéron et ses amis* [Paris 1921]; R.Sansen, *Doctrine de l'amitié chez Cicéron* [Lille 1975]. Compare also the rhetorical "thesis" referred to by Cicero in *Ad Att.* 9.4. For the use of the topic in rhetorical exercises, note in addition that Jerome, *In Michaeam* 2.7 [*Corpus Christianorum, Series Latina* 76, p. 509] quotes a maxim on friendship from an unspecified *controversia*.)

It is clear from all this that a number of the basic points made in the *Laelius* were simply part of Cicero's standard repertoire of ideas and arguments. It is probable that in writing this treatise, Cicero was to a large extent simply reproducing and elaborating on ideas which had been in his mind for many years (*saepissime ... cogitanti* in §26 may be more than a merely conventional phrase). We should not necessarily envisage him as doing any very large amount of *ad hoc* research among the Greek philosophical writings mentioned above, though of course he may have read or re-read one or two of them before starting to write the *Laelius*. Still less should we imagine him using any particular Greek book as his "source" or "model"; that would have been quite unnecessary. Though it is clear that most of the individual ideas in the *Laelius* derive ultimately from Greek sources, the composition and arrangement is Cicero's own. On the philosophical content, see further below, Introd. 8.

*   *   *

The anterior question, why friendship was such a popular subject among ancient philosophers in the first place, cannot here be treated fully. The answer may have something to do with the nature of ancient society; but probably it has more to do with the overriding themes of ancient ethics. Socrates and his successors were concerned above all with the search for that "wisdom" or "virtue" which would enable the superior man to take complete control of his own life, in so far as that was believed possible. In view of that, friendship would create a particular problem: instinct told the philosophers that friendship was a good thing, but how was it to be reconciled with the ideal of self-sufficiency? For modern thinkers, whose inherited morality is much more altruistic, friendship is intrinsically less of a problem, whatever particular moral questions may arise from it. (See A.-J. Voelke, *Les rapports avec autrui ...*, cited above, §2; O.Gigon, *Grundprobleme der antiken Philosophie* [Bern 1959] 302-14; L.Dugas, *L'amitié antique d'après les moeurs populaires et les théories des philosophes* [Paris 1894]; J.-C. Fraisse, *Philia. La notion d'amitié dans la philosophie antique* [Paris 1974], rev. A.A.Long, *CR* 29 [1979] 80-2. I have not seen E.Piscione, "Il primato dell'amicizia nella filosofia antica", *Sapienza* 37 [Naples 1984] 377-95.)

3. The circumstances of composition   So much for the background of thought against which Cicero conceived the *Laelius*: what of Cicero's own position at the time of writing? The *Laelius* comes chronologically very near the end of the main series of Cicero's philosophical works, which were composed in the two years 45-44 BC. It is absent from the list of philosophical works in the *De Divinatione*, published not more than a few weeks after the assassination of Caesar on the Ides of March, 44 BC; thus it may be deduced that it was not only not yet written, but not even projected at that time. On the other hand, a passage of the *De Officiis* (2.31), published in November 44, refers back to the *Laelius* as by then already written. Therefore the *Laelius* was conceived and written between March and November of 44.

There have been attempts to argue for a more precise dating from certain passages in the letters. *Att.* 16.11, which provides the latest possible date for the first two books of the *De Officiis*, mentions another unspecified "book" to which Cicero is presently putting the final touches; some have taken this to be the *Laelius*, but this is not certain. In *Att.* 16.13a.2, Cicero asks Atticus for historical information about C.Fannius, who is one of the speakers in the *Laelius*. It has often been supposed that he wanted the information for the purposes of this dialogue, but that is quite implausible. This letter is subsequent to *Att.* 16.11 and therefore to *De Officiis* I-II, in which the *Laelius* is mentioned as already completed; and the point of enquiry is the date of Fannius's tribunate, which is not mentioned anywhere in the *Laelius*. Otherwise, various arguments from silence have been tried. Some have thought that the correspondence with C. Matius in August 44 (*Fam.* 11.27-8), ought to have included some reference to the *Laelius*, if the dialogue was already written at that time; or, conversely, that Matius's letter (11.28.2) does indeed contain a covert reference to it. Others have noted the absence of any mention of the treatise in *Att.* 16.13.1 (written July 44), where the *Cato Maior* is referred to. But such arguments carry little weight. A number of scholars have adhered to a speculative and ill-founded theory of a double recension, according to which a first version of the *Laelius* was drafted by Cicero in April or May, but the text we have dates from November and allegedly represents a second version, substantially altered in the light of current political events (see bibliography below, Introd. §6). The question of precise dating is indeed relevant if one wishes to trace connections between the *Laelius* and the political situation at the time of writing (cf. below), but these apparent connections are either too tenuous to be of help at all, or could equally well apply to any point of time between the available limits. There are some parallels between the *Laelius* and the *First Philippic*, which was composed in September 44, but it is not possible to establish the priority of one or the other. Altogether it seems necessary to admit that we do not know precisely when the *Laelius* was completed, within the period March-November 44. (On the question of dating, see Bringmann, *Untersuchungen* 215, a generally clear discussion which unfortunately seems to ignore the *terminus ante quem* provided by *Off.* 2.31. The topic of Cicero and Matius has inspired a number of studies: H.Dahlmann, *Neue Jahrbücher für Antike und deutsche Bildung* 1 (1938) 225-38, A.Heuss, *Historia* 5 (1956) 53-73, B.Kytzler, ibid. 9 (1960) 96, R.Combès, *REL* 36 (1958) 176-86; cf. Bringmann, *Untersuchungen* 270-7; K.L.Singh in P.MacKendrick, *The Philosophical Books of Cicero* (London 1989) 218ff. The idea that the correspondence with Matius provided the impetus for Cicero to compose, or revise, the *Laelius* seems unprovable.)

For Cicero, this period was predominantly one of uncertainty. He had spent the year 45, and the first months of 44, in retirement, being practically excluded from politics during Caesar's dictatorship. It is to this period that the majority of his philosophical works belong. After the death of Caesar, he had returned to public life, hoping that there would be a restoration of normal Republican government; but these hopes were soon dashed as the "Liberators" lost the political initiative to Antony, and there was fear of a renewal of civil war. Cicero kept away from Rome, and travelled round his various country houses in Italy; he considered going to Greece, and in August actually embarked at Syracuse; but he heard that there was a prospect of a settlement, and so decided to return to Rome. There he immediately came into political conflict with Antony; this issued in the set of speeches which he himself later named the *Philippics*. (For more detailed information on the background of this period, see Rawson, *Cicero* 260-77; Stockton, *Cicero* 280ff.)

During this time, Cicero no doubt sought distractions from the unpredictable and dangerous political situation. He added to the sum of his philosophical writing, composing the *De Officiis* for his son, who was (ostensibly) studying philosophy in Athens. But the greatest reassurance undoubtedly came from his friendship with Atticus. The two men corresponded unceasingly on political and personal matters, and the naturally impulsive and indecisive Cicero relied heavily on the advice of the equable and detached Atticus. It is no great surprise that he chose to celebrate this friendship in a philosophical treatise dedicated to Atticus himself. Either just before or just after the Ides of March - certainly before the publication of the *De Divinatione*, which took place soon after the Ides - Cicero had written and dedicated to Atticus the *Cato Maior de senectute*, a dialogue on how to cope with old age. During the summer of 44 he wrote a work entitled *De Gloria*, also destined for Atticus; that treatise, however, has not survived. Old age, glory and friendship were all topics that concerned Cicero personally: old age because he was himself approaching it (he was sixty-two in 44 BC), glory because the pursuit of glory had been one of the main preoccupations of his life, and friendship because of his highly valued friendship with Atticus. These three works stand apart from the series of larger philosophical writings: the *Cato* and *Laelius*, at least, are not works of academic philosophy (though they rely on a philosophical background), but constitute a more intimate and personal expression of Cicero's own ideals and preoccupations.

As for Cicero's claim to benefit the public by writing the *Laelius*, it is in part simply repeated from contexts which apply to the whole series of philosophical works, such as *Div.* 2.1. He saw the writing of didactic treatises as an alternative method of serving the interests of his country, when deprived of the opportunity to do so in politics. In particular, however, Atticus had apparently said that he found the *Cato Maior* to be of practical benefit (*Att.* 16.11.3), and Cicero also no doubt hoped that the *Laelius*, and particularly the warnings it contains against civil war, might have some effect on the morale of his contemporaries. There are a number of more or less clear allusions to issues that were important at the time of writing. The "obituary" of Scipio in sections 11-14 is couched in terms that occasionally recall the *First Philippic* and may also conjure up the memory of Caesar (cf. commentary). In §§40-43, Laelius is made to speak in strongly disapproving terms of Tiberius Gracchus (to whose tribunate some traced the origin of the civil strife of the last century of the Republic), and, by a sort of dramatic irony, virtually to prophesy the civil war. The theme of the breaking of friendships for political reasons, from which the *Laelius* takes its starting point, must have been of close concern to many Romans in the forties BC. It is hard to avoid thinking of Cicero himself in his dealings with Antony: in the *First Philippic* he still claims that there is friendship between them, while in the *Second* Cicero is Antony's declared political enemy. The violent denunciations in this speech provide an ironic contrast with the exhortations to moderation in the *Laelius*. (On the relationship of the *Laelius* to the contemporary political situation, see Bringmann, *Untersuchungen* 206-28 and 268-70; P.Pucci, *Maia* 15 [1963] 342-58; K.Heldmann, *Hermes* 104 [1976] 72-103.)

4. The literary form of the *Laelius* The literary form of this work is best understood from a glance back at the *Cato Maior*, to which it was explicitly intended to be a companion-piece. The dedication to Atticus, and the fact that the two dialogues are on particular themes of practical ethics, have already been mentioned. In addition, the speakers in both dialogues are noble Romans of the past; both works are named after the principal speaker, who is chosen in each case for his appropriateness to the subject; Laelius, the main speaker in the dialogue that bears his name, is a subordinate speaker in the *Cato Maior*; Laelius's friend Scipio Aemilianus is the third speaker in the *Cato*, while the *Laelius* is set just after Scipio's death, which event forms the starting-point of the discussion; and in the latter dialogue, Laelius makes a reference to the conversation supposedly reported in the *Cato* (*Lael.* 11). Both dialogues consist largely of continuous exposition by the main character, prompted by an enquiry from the subsidiary speakers. The dialogues are both set out in dramatic form, and not as narrations. There are a number of detailed parallels of expression and thought between the two works; these are collected by P.R.Coleman-Norton, *CW* 41 (1947-8) 210-16.

The antecedents of this type of dialogue, thus characterised, are not very easy to trace, owing to the loss of most Greek philosophic dialogues written after Plato and Xenophon. The influence of those two authors, and particularly perhaps of the latter, is very clear; but it is possible (though not by any means proved) that there may have been closer parallels still among the dialogues of Aristotle and his successors. Cicero's older contemporary Varro wrote a series of dialogues, in Latin, with titles (e.g. *Catus de liberis educandis, Messalla de valetudine*) in precisely the form of Cicero's *Cato Maior de senectute* and *Laelius de amicitia*, known collectively as the [*libri*] *Logistorici*. Very little survives of any of these; but the chief uncertainty concerns their date. If they were written before 44 BC, then Cicero might have been imitating them; but Varro outlived Cicero by a number of years, and may have written the *Logistorici* later in imitation of the *Cato* and *Laelius*. For further discussion of these matters, with bibliography, the reader is referred to my edition of the *Cato Maior*, pp. 5-9.

The similarity of the *Cato* and *Laelius*, as described above, is very striking; but there are some differences between the two works. The main speech of the *Cato* is formally constructed, with a fourfold division of the subject, announced early in the proceedings and faithfully adhered to in what follows. The *Laelius* is much more informal and conversational. There is no announcement of headings for discussion. The subject of friendship is approached obliquely, not immediately as is the topic of old age in the *Cato*. After the main subject has been reached, *Laelius* makes quite a short speech, and says he has finished; the other speakers then overcome his reluctance to proceed. After another fairly short section, *Laelius* asks for the other speakers' approval before continuing; and the remainder of the exposition is very informally structured (cf. below, Introd. §6). There is a difference in style and tone as well: in the *Cato*, despite the Ciceronian urbanity and the Ciceronian philosophical views, Cato has something of the brusque authority that we expect of him, while in the present dialogue Laelius shows much more modesty and reluctance in putting forward his opinions, and his style of speaking is more flowing and periodic.

5. The persons of the dialogue and the historical setting Gaius Laelius, the main speaker, was an obvious choice for the part, especially when one considers that

Cicero had already employed him as a major character in the *De Republica* (a fact that is alluded to in the *Laelius* itself) and as a subsidiary interlocutor in the *Cato Maior*. The tradition of his friendship with Scipio Aemilianus was already well established (cf. Astin, *Scipio* 81), and Cicero had referred to it a number of times in his previous writings. Perhaps the most striking of these was the famous letter to Pompey (*Fam.* 5.7.3) which he wrote at the end of 63, offering to play Laelius to Pompey's Scipio.

Laelius's father, also named Gaius Laelius, was the first of his family to enter public life. The elder Laelius was closely associated with Scipio Africanus the Elder, and played an important part in the Second Punic War, during which, among other things, he commanded the fleet at Carthago Nova in 209, and was in command of one wing at the battle of Zama. Subsequently he had a senatorial career, culminating in the consulship of 190. Around this time was born the Laelius of our dialogue, who thus inherited noble rank from his father, as well as a connection with the family of the Scipios. Scipio Aemilianus was born in 185. He was the son of L.Aemilius Paulus, but he was adopted by the son of Africanus, P.Scipio, who was in bad health and presumably childless. The friendship between Scipio and Laelius may have dated from their adolescence, though if so, it is perhaps odd that Polybius makes no mention of it in his account of Scipio's early life (in fact, Polybius himself claims to have been Scipio's best friend at this period). In the Third Punic War, Laelius served as Scipio's legate at the siege of Carthage in 147. Subsequently he became praetor in 145 and consul in 140: there is no need to assume, as some do, that Laelius needed Scipio's persuasion to achieve these senatorial offices, though he may well have benefited from Scipio's support.

This dialogue itself is one of our main sources for Laelius's political career. In it are mentioned his opposition to the bill of C.Licinius Crassus in 145, and his activities in the wake of the Gracchan crisis. We learn that he was on the *consilium* (co-opted advisory panel) of the consuls of 132 when they made enquiry into the sedition of Tiberius Gracchus; together with Scipio, he opposed Gracchus's supporter Carbo in 131 or 130. We do not learn from Cicero (in this case Plutarch is our source of information) that Laelius, as consul in 140, had apparently put forward some sort of agrarian proposal very like that subsequently introduced by Tiberius Gracchus, but had withdrawn it owing to senatorial opposition (see Astin, *Scipio* 307-10). According to Plutarch, it was this piece of political moderation that earned Laelius his nickname *Sapiens*; cf. on §1. It seems clear that what Laelius and his sort objected to in Tiberius Gracchus was not the content of his measures, but the fact that he was prepared to provoke violence and to overstep the limits of constitutional procedure. A man like Laelius – with whom, no doubt, Cicero himself felt considerable sympathy – would be

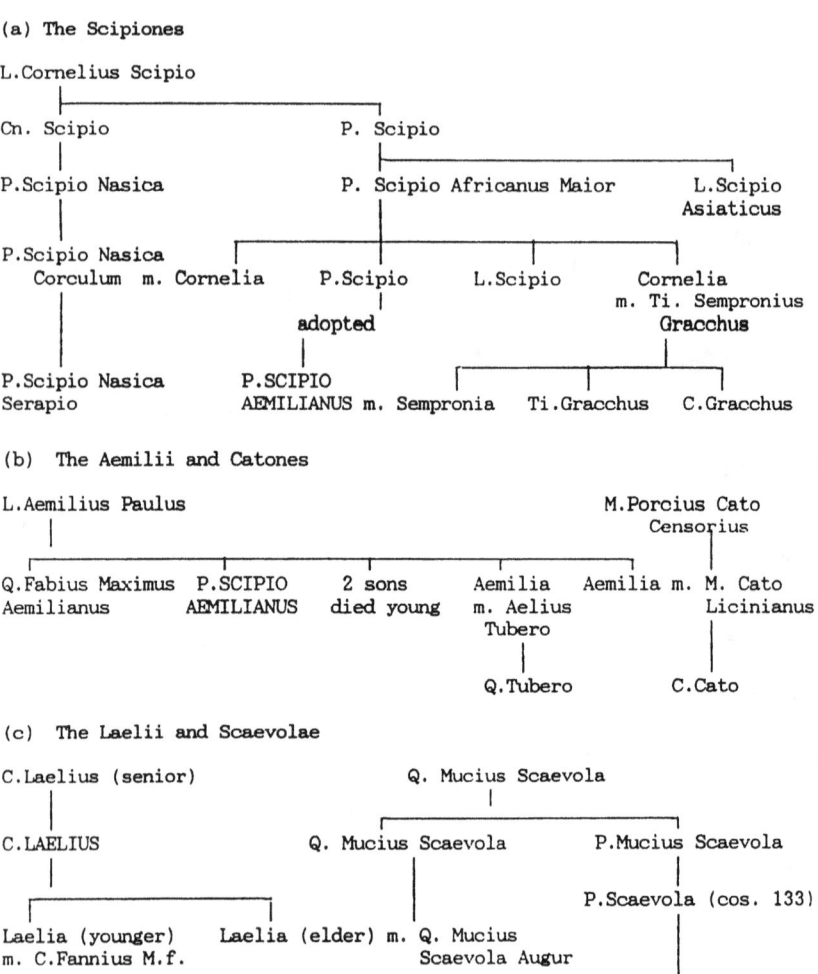

Fig. 1 Family trees

bound to come out on the side of order. After the death of Scipio Aemilianus in 129 BC, soon after which this dialogue is set, we hear nothing more of Laelius, and even the date of his death is uncertain.

Cicero clearly had great admiration for Scipio and Laelius. He imagined them as the centre of a highly civilised and cultured circle of friends, in which poets and Greek men of learning consorted with Roman aristocrats. The atmosphere of this circle is encapsulated in the *De Republica*. Doubtless Cicero introduced a measure of idealisation. Talk of the "Scipionic Circle", as if the reality corresponded exactly with Cicero's picture, is perhaps hazardous; particularly since a great deal more seems often to be implied, when scholars use that term, than is warranted even by Cicero's presentation. There is no ground, in Cicero or elsewhere, for supposing that Scipio and his friends ever formed a coherent political faction or a centre of active cultural Hellenisation (see Astin, *Scipio* 294-306; J.E.G.Zetzel, *HSCP* 76 [1972] 173-9, and further literature there cited). But there is no doubt that the latter half of the second century was a period of considerable cultural activity in the Roman world, and that this was encouraged by the interests of such as Scipio and Laelius. The Greek historian Polybius, the philosopher Panaetius, and the Latin poets Terence and Pacuvius (to both of whom Laelius alludes in the dialogue), as well as the satirist Lucilius, are all known with reasonable certainty to have benefited from Scipio's patronage at various times. This was a period when an amateur's interest in Greek learning, philosophy and science, and in literature, was beginning to be respectable for well-born Romans. Cicero did not need to distort reality too much in order to make Laelius talk what was essentially Greek philosophy; the incongruity is much less than in the *Cato Maior* (cf. my edition, p.21; R.E.Jones, *AJP* 60 [1939] 307-325, esp. 315-8). On Cicero's view of the period in general, see also M. Rambaud, *Cicéron et l'histoire romaine* (Paris 1952) 102–8.

The other two characters in the *Laelius*, C.Fannius M.f. and Q.Mucius Scaevola, are much less clearly delineated. They are there largely as a foil to the authoritative figure of Laelius; they had previously been employed as minor characters in the *De Republica*. Fannius and Scaevola were Laelius's sons-in-law, and in real life they were apparently somewhat at odds with each other, one bone of contention being the fact that Scaevola, who was the younger of the two, had married Laelius's elder daughter, in consequence of which, by the favour of Laelius, he gained earlier admission to the augurate.

The historical information on Fannius is rather confused, because of the existence of another Fannius (C.Fannius C.f.): the two are not always clearly distinguished in the sources, and Cicero himself was uncertain about some points concerning them. However, it seems that the Fannius of the dialogue became consul in 122 BC; as consul, he was apparently expected to favour Gaius Gracchus, but in the event opposed him. At an uncertain date, but probably later than his consulship, Fannius wrote a history of his own times, on which Cicero seems to have drawn for at least one item in the *Laelius* (§73), and possibly for others. As a young soldier, Fannius had served under Scipio at the siege of Carthage, and together with Tiberius Gracchus was one of

the first to scale the city walls. At the time of the dialogue, Fannius would have bee.
in his middle thirties (cf. *Rep.* 1.18). See further commentary on §3.

The Scaevola of the dialogue is Q. Mucius Scaevola the Augur, who, at the end of his
life, was Cicero's first legal mentor. He forms, as it were, a living connection between
Laelius's generation and Cicero himself. Cicero imagines the substance of the dialogue
as having been narrated to him by Scaevola, in the same way as P.Rutilius Rufus was
imagined to be the medium of transmission for the conversation of the *De Republica*.

6. The structure of the dialogue   The broad plan of the dialogue is simple
enough; it may be laid out as follows:

> §§1-5: Cicero's prologue.
> §§6-16: Introductory conversation.
> §§17-24: First main speech of Laelius.
> §25: Conversational interlude.
> §§26-32: Second speech of Laelius.
> §32: Conversational interlude.
> §§33-104: Third speech of Laelius.

The introductory conversation concerns the death of Scipio and Laelius's reactions to
it. This leads on to the topic of friendship: Fannius and Scaevola ask Laelius to give
them his views on this subject at length. The first main speech of Laelius is a
generalised encomium of friendship. The second is an examination of the question
how friendship comes into being; the third, continuing from the second, forms the
remainder of the dialogue. It is this speech which presents problems of analysis, but
they are not by any means insuperable.

The apparent difficulties arise from a number of mistakes of interpretation. The first
and greatest mistake is to think that Fannius's words in §16 (... *disputaris de amicitia
quid sentias, qualem existimes, quae praecepta des*) are meant as a formal *divisio* or
announcement of headings under which the subject is to be treated.   This will not
work, for three reasons.

First, as pointed out by K.Neuhausen, *divisiones* are typically produced by a speaker
on his own behalf. In this passage, however, Fannius is requesting Laelius to speak.
We do not naturally expect him to specify the headings under which Laelius is to treat
the subject; and Laelius himself makes no reference to such a division of the subject at
any point.

Secondly, the alleged *divisio* does not itself logically constitute a division of the subject
(this point is made by F.H.Sandbach, *CR* 18 [1968] 310). The phrase *quid sentias*
means only "what you think [about friendship]", not "what you think it is" (which
would be necessary to make a contrast with *qualem existimes*); *quid sentias* embraces
both *qualem existimes* and *quae praecepta des*. Some have seen a resemblance between

Cicero's *quid sentias, qualem existimes, quae praecepta des* and the Aristotelian division τί, ποῖον, πῶς χρηστέον in the *Eudemian Ethics* (1234b); but the two passages simply do not mean the same (Aristotle's τί ἐστι plainly means "what it is"), and Aristotle's division comprises no fewer than seven headings, among which the three quoted do not even follow each other in immediate succession. Some scholars have further alleged that *quid sentirem* in §24 corresponds to *quid sentias* of §16, and serves to mark off the first section specified in the alleged *divisio*: as if the rest of the dialogue were *not* presented as an expression of Laelius's opinion! It has even been said, on the basis of the word *sentire*, that this section constitutes a *sententia* in something like the technical senatorial sense - a very strange idea. The true and obvious interpretation of §24 is that Laelius claims to have said all he has to say: it is only after persuasion that he continues. This surely excludes the possibility that his words are meant to mark off what is only the first of three sections.

Thirdly, such a division (either the threefold one, as in the normal misinterpretation, or the twofold one *qualem existimes - quae praecepta des*) cannot really be made to fit the dialogue, though there have been several different attempts to make it do so; the diversity should in itself provide cause for doubt about the method. There is no really clear boundary between discussion of the nature of friendship, and formulation of precepts to apply to it. The two types of discussion are interspersed throughout, as is natural. Certainly, there is more abstract discussion in some sections, and more practical precepts in others, particularly in the later sections of the dialogue; but that is not the principle on which the material is arranged. Even the most abstract and philosophical sections contain practical examples and advice.

The other mistake that commentators often make is to take the parenthesis *iam enim ... delabitur* in §76 to mark a major division of the dialogue. It is certainly true that Cicero began from discussion of perfect friendship right at the start, and that the latter part of the treatise, being as already said more practical in emphasis, contains more about the imperfect or ordinary types of friendship. But again, discussion of the two types is interspersed throughout the dialogue. In §33, Cicero talks of the manifold misfortunes that threaten friendships and break them apart: here, long before §76, he is already talking about ordinary friendships, and he continues to do so throughout the political section §§36-44. On the other hand, only eight sections after the alleged division of §76, Cicero is back on the topic of the ideal friendship and its advantages (§84). That should be sufficient to show that the theory of a division at §76 does not work.

How, then, are we to arrive at a true analysis of §§33-104, the third main speech of Laelius? The first thing to be noticed is that Cicero introduces summaries at two points, §§44 and 61. They are rather disconcerting summaries, since both of them introduce new material that has not been discussed at all in the previous section. In the case of the former, a topic is raised which is eventually to be discussed more fully towards the end of the dialogue; but in §61 the new material is simply left in mid-air. Despite this, however, the tone of both these sections is clearly that of winding up an argument. Along with these two passages we must also include §§55-6 *sed haec hactenus: constituendi autem sunt,* etc., which clearly marks a transition from one part of the subject to the next.

The summary in §44 quite clearly concludes the first major section of this speech, which was introduced in §36 by the question *quatenus amor in amicitia progredi debeat.* The question is there framed very generally, but the topic under consideration is the specific one of the conflict between friendship and loyalty to one's country. That, therefore, is one clear and self-contained section. Then, in §45, Cicero introduces the "strange doctrines" of those who are thought wise in Greece. At this point he actually enumerates two doctrines: one is that people should not become closely involved in friendships; the other, that friendship should be sought for the sake of utility (another version of the question of origins). These two ideas are refuted in turn, and the refutation extends to §55 *sed haec hactenus.* Then three further Greek doctrines are introduced, which are supposed to constitute "definitions of the scope of friendship". (It should be noted that the reading *diligendi* instead of *deligendi* here has caused considerable obscuration of the structure: see Appendix.) These three are again refuted in order. But Cicero's own attempt at the definition does not immediately follow, for a fourth erroneous thesis has first to be dealt with (§§59-60). Then comes §61, which gives the positive thesis *his igitur finibus utendum arbitror ...,* and winds up this section.

Laelius is then made to allude to Scipio's opinions, as he had already done in introducing this whole speech (§33 above). This marks a change from more abstract and philosophical discussion to more practical advice. The first point made concerns the negligence of most people concerning friendship. This topic is reverted to in §86; it seems reasonable to take this as being an instance of ring composition, framing the passage from §62 to §86. Leaving aside for a moment the detailed organisation of that section, one may observe that the second allusion to negligence is followed by a generalised encomium of friendship, which has the air of a subordinate peroration (ending with the general maxim *natura solitarium nihil amat,* §88). Then comes a fairly clearly self-contained section on the place of advice and criticism in friendship, and the question of distinguishing the true friend from the flatterer: this is naturally placed separately, since flatterers are not properly to be described as friends at all. That continues until §100, and is immediately followed by the peroration of the whole dialogue, which reverts to the themes of the opening conversation.

Finally, the detailed structure of §§62-86 needs to be elucidated. It consists of a number of fairly short, co-ordinated sections. §§62-66 deal with the qualities desirable in a friend; §§66-8 with the question of new friends versus old; §§69-73 with friendships between persons of unequal status; §74 says that friendships can only be properly judged when the parties have reached maturity (it is possible that a passage has been lost from the middle of this paragraph: see Appendix); §75 warns against excessive concern for friends and the desire to monopolise their company; §§76-8 discuss the breaking of friendships; then the precept to be careful in choosing friends is repeated from §§62-3, to recur again at §85; while the intervening section, §§79-84, attacks those who seek friendship for their own profit and not for itself, those who expect from their friends what they cannot give in return, and those who separate friendship from moral virtue. This last-mentioned section presumably finds its natural place here, because it is negative in tone: according to rhetorical precept, refutation of the opponent should normally come after the positive arguments.

It will be seen, then, that there is a rough alternation between philosophical and practical sections. The transitions from the former to the latter are announced, and any potential contradiction between them is alleviated, by the presentation of the more practical material as the opinion of Scipio, not of Laelius himself. The main divisions of the speech are marked off from each other either explicitly or by the familiar ancient (and not only ancient) rhetorical technique of ring composition. Prominent places near the beginning and the end of Laelius's third speech are occupied by discussions of Roman politics; while generalised praise of friendship occurs in Laelius's first speech, at sections 86-88 in the third speech, and at the end of the whole dialogue.

Thus analysed, the arrangement of material, though informal, appears reasonably logical and coherent.

The bibliography on this question of structure is large, and most of it, to speak frankly, makes unprofitable reading. The mistaken interpretation of §16 occurs already in M.Beumlerus, *Analysis logica M.T.Ciceronis Laelii sive de Amicitia dialogi* (Spirae Nemetum 1583), and in most later work on the subject, with the honourable exceptions of Seyffert-Müller's commentary, P.Scheuerpflug, *Quaestiones Laelianae* (Jena 1914) 15 (reviewed by A.Lörcher, *Bursian* 200 (1924) 75-87), and K.A.Neuhausen's recent edition. On §76, the correct view is taken by A.Gercke in A.Gercke-E.Norden, *Einleitung in die Altertumswissenschaft* (Leipzig 1910) I, 75, followed by M.Hoppe, *De M. Tulli Ciceronis Laelii fontibus* (Breslau 1912) 19-29; also apparently by E.Weissenborn, *Gedankengang und Gliederung von Ciceros Laelius* (Progr. Mühlhausen 1882) as reported by P. Schwenke, *Bursian* 35, 104ff. (I have not seen Weissenborn's dissertation itself). There is a roughly correct analysis of the dialogue in R.Combès's Budé edition. Otherwise, the prevalent mistakes referred to above recur frequently, sometimes in combination with speculations about sources (the supposed threefold division taken to reflect Aristotle or, as the case may be, Panaetius – this latter idea based on an unjustified comparison with *Fin.* 4.23); not to mention those who chastise Cicero for obscurity and carelessness in arrangement, and explain these alleged defects by supposing that the dialogue as we have it is a hastily reworked second edition. In addition to those works already cited, one may refer to A.Gernhard, *Opuscula* (Leipzig 1836) 322-39; K.Büchner, author of the double-recension theory, *MH* 9 (1952) 88-106 = *Studien zur römischen Literatur* II (Wiesbaden 1962) 173ff. and 198-9; M.Schäfer, *Gymnasium* 62 (1955) 334-53 (for Panaetius); F.A.Steinmetz, *Die Freundschaftslehre des Panaitios nach einer Analyse von Ciceros "Laelius de amicitia"*, Palingenesia 3 (Wiesbaden 1967), following Schäfer; M. Bellincioni, *Struttura e pensiero del Lelio ciceroniano*, Antichità classica e cristiana 9 (Brescia 1970) (for Aristotle); R. Philippson, *RE* VIIa (1939) 1165; W. Ricken, *Gymnasium* 62 (1955) 360-74, following Büchner; Bringmann, *Untersuchungen* 216-228; H.L.F.Drijepondt, *Acta Classica* 6 (1963) 64-80; K.L.Singh in P. MacKendrick, *The Philosophical Books of Cicero* (London 1989) 214ff.

7. Style and literary characteristics   The most striking literary feature of the dialogue is the characterisation of Laelius himself. One may suspect that Cicero has (consciously or not) put a great deal of himself into the portrait; but nevertheless, he took pains to ensure realism in the background.

In the first place, the dialogue is firmly anchored historically. The death of Scipio (129 BC) forms the starting-point of the conversation, and his career is summarised by Laelius. Political events in the preceding few years receive particular attention in two prominently placed passages of Laelius's exposition: §§36ff., on the Gracchan crisis, and §§96-7, where the contrast between a demagogue and a true statesman is used as a parallel for the friend/flatterer distinction (on this aspect of the structure, see above, §6). In each case Laelius is represented as outspoken in his opposition to the activities of the seditious tribunes.

The Laelius of the dialogue is self-consciously Roman, despite the Greek origin of much of the material in his exposition. He is modest about his philosophical attainments, disclaiming the ability to discourse impromptu on a set subject as the Greeks did (§17; cf. notes on sections §§24-6). He is occasionally disdainful of the subtleties of Greek philosophy (cf. §45); he regards some of the doctrines of the Stoics as impractical (§§18-24 and 48), and those of the Epicureans as thoroughly misguided (see on sections 13, 32, 52, 56; cf. also 45, 79 and 82). The philosophical schools are never mentioned by name: this makes a striking contrast with Cicero's more technical treatises. There would have been no incongruity in making Laelius talk of Stoics or Epicureans, as far as concerns the historical Laelius's presumed acquaintance with Greek philosophy. But the attitude of Laelius in the dialogue resembles Cicero's own in his public speeches (for example, in the *Pro Murena* and *In Pisonem*): he avoids name-dropping and technicality, because it does not do for a Roman gentleman to show himself too deeply acquainted with philosophy. The Greek habits of chopping logic, and of defending paradoxes for their own sake, must be resisted. The point of view throughout is that of Roman common sense and moral earnestness. It should be noted also in this connection that, in contrast with the more technical philosophical works, and, even more, with the letters to Atticus, the Greek language is rigorously excluded from the dialogue. Greek technical terms or neologisms, when absolutely necessary, are represented by Cicero's home-made Latin equivalents (*redamare* = ἀντιφιλεῖν §45; *consentiens* = συμπαθής §65; *convenientia rerum* = ὁμολογία §100).

Not only is explicit Hellenism kept to a minimum: there is also positive assertion of Roman qualities. Near the beginning of the conversation, Laelius praises the wisdom of Cato the Elder in the highest terms, comparing him favourably with Socrates, traditionally the wisest of the Greeks. A Roman criterion of practical virtue or goodness is set up in opposition to the confessedly almost unattainable Stoic ideal of wisdom, and supported by some of the standard Ciceronian examples of old Roman virtue and temperance. Laelius is made to appear proud of the attempts made by himself and Scipio to assert the traditional constitutionalist position, and to maintain the authority of the Senate and of Roman religion.

Roman background is particularly evident not only in the examples taken from Roman history, but also in the recurring allusions to Roman legal terminology and ideas. Cicero's Laelius often has the air of a Roman jurisconsult, "responding" on moral questions about friendship as he would actually have done on questions of civil law or augural procedure. (It is to be remembered that Cicero himself was well trained in the law.) The observant reader may from time to time see legal overtones in the language used: see notes on sections 1, 16, 19, 38, 40, 43, 44, 55.

Cicero's Laelius makes fairly frequent reference to the Latin poetry of his time, in conformity with the tradition of Laelius's literary interests and his association in particular with Terence. Terence himself is quoted explicitly twice (§§89 and 93), and there seem to be a few other verbal allusions, mostly to the first scene of the *Andria* in which there is some general discussion of the topic of friendship (see on §§69, 71, 74 and 87). Reference to comedy was no doubt virtually inevitable in the section on flattery, since the flatterer or parasite is such a standard character in Greek New Comedy and its Roman equivalent (in addition to Terence, Caecilius Statius is quoted in §99). Pacuvius's play on Orestes is quoted with approval (§24), and Ennius also is quoted on two occasions (§§22 and 64). General allusions to mythology (§§70 and 75) doubtless recall primarily the treatments of the myths by Roman tragedians, rather than their Greek originals.

To turn to more properly stylistic matters, one should at least enquire whether Cicero attempts a stylistic characterisation of Laelius; the question is very difficult to answer in the absence of any substantial records of Laelius's own speeches, which were in circulation and admired in Cicero's time. Some have seen in §14 a reminiscence of the funeral oration which Laelius wrote for Scipio, though this is in fact rather doubtful. Otherwise one can point to a few slightly old-fashioned Latin usages, which are on the whole not to be found in Cicero's speeches and letters. It does appear that Cicero cultivated a style with a certain number of old-fashioned touches, not only here, but also in the other dialogues with a second-century setting, the *Cato Maior* and the *De Republica*. (For possibly old-fashioned usages in the *Laelius*, see on §§19 and 47 and Appendix on §§41 and 63; cf. my edition of *Cato Maior*, p. 22; on the *De Republica*, E.Bréguet in *Hommages J.Bayet*, Coll. Latomus 70 (1964) 122-31).

Apart from this, the main stylistic features of the *Laelius* are all easily paralleled in Cicero's other philosophical works. There is informality and urbanity in the conversational sections, while Laelius's speeches ascend to rhetorical heights in such passages as the encomium of friendship in §23. There is extensive use of examples from history to illustrate the points being made; proverbs or proverbial expressions occur frequently, and there is an abundant variety of images, sometimes complex and extended. As in other works of Cicero, symmetrical sentence-structures and rhythmical clausulae are cultivated (cf. I.Blum, *De compositione numerosa dialogi Ciceronis de amicitia* [Innsbruck 1913]). However, given that this is a dialogue, not a speech, and that it was written towards the end of his life, one should not expect to find the elaborate periodic structures characteristic of the speeches of the earlier part of his career.

8. Philosophical content   It should already be sufficiently clear that the *Laelius* is far from being a dry or technical philosophical treatise. Nevertheless, the ideas contained in the *Laelius*, when not derived from Cicero's own personal experience or from Roman history, are inevitably those of Greek philosophy. Cicero's Laelius (like Scipio in the *De Republica*) claims to speak as a plain Roman, not a professional philosopher; but even plain Romans took their intellectual background from the Greeks. Because of the diffidence about naming Greek sources, it is rather difficult to unravel the various philosophical strands represented in the dialogue. Nor is it always possible to identify points of contact with Greek writings, since much of the Greek material that might have been relevant has been lost. However, it is worth while to attempt to distinguish some of the purely philosophical ingredients in Cicero's presentation.

In general, the reader should be reminded, Cicero was a follower of the Academy; but this did not imply adherence to a strict body of doctrine, since the Academics (as Cicero often tells us in the philosophical works) believed in examining every question on its merits. In moral philosophy, there was a large family resemblance between the views of the Stoics, the Peripatetics and the Academy of Cicero's time; a professed Academic such as Cicero might take what he wanted from the moral doctrines of the Stoa or the Peripatos without any breach of loyalty to his own school. The one point on which Cicero never wavered was his opposition to the Epicureans: he regarded their philosophical hedonism as subverting the foundations of morality, and never ceased to attack it as such.   At best, according to him, the Epicureans were inconsistent; at worst, a danger to public morals.

Cicero was clearly attracted by the idealism of Stoic morality, but he did not always accept its more extreme manifestations. In the *Laelius* itself, Cicero makes Laelius argue at some length against the Stoic concept of the wise man, and against the doctrine of ἀπάθεια (impassivity). On the other hand, some passages fairly closely reproduce Stoic teachings which Cicero expounded as such elsewhere, in the third book of the *De Finibus* and later in the *De Officiis*. The theory of the natural community of all mankind, which was prominent in Stoicism, clearly appealed strongly to Cicero. The view of friendship which Cicero adopts in the *Laelius*, according to which friendship originates in Nature, and is based on a complete community of thought and action between virtuous men, does not seem to be fully prefigured in any surviving early Stoic source, but the elements of it are found scattered in the Stoic tradition. Some have thought that Cicero deliberately gave Laelius's discourse a Stoic accent because Laelius was known to have studied Stoic philosophy with Panaetius; but this is not a necessary conclusion, since the ideas expressed are so similar to those found in other passages of Cicero. Indeed, some scholars (see below for bibliography) have argued for Panaetius as a major source of the ideas in the *Laelius*; but this is based on a deduction from the similarities between the *Laelius* and the *De Officiis*, together with the unfounded and implausible assumption that everything in the *De Officiis* - even material already to be found in earlier works of Cicero - came from Panaetius. There is no more reason to attribute Cicero's Stoicising doctrines to Panaetius than to any other individual Stoic.

Cicero will also have owed something, perhaps a great deal, to the Peripatetic tradition. As a starting point, we have the opinion of Aulus Gellius that Cicero "seemed to have read" Theophrastus. Although the work of Theophrastus is not available, we can at least make a comparison between Cicero's work and the treatment of the subject by Theophrastus's predecessor Aristotle. The difference between Cicero and Aristotle is more one of emphasis and approach than of fundamental doctrine. Cicero places great emphasis on the ideal, and treats the imperfect form of friendship, found in everyday life, as something basically different. Aristotle classifies friendship similarly, but does not stress the separation of the types; one has the impression that Aristotle thought the better and worse types of friendship could shade into each other. In general Aristotle's approach is more consistently empirical; and one imagines that his successors would have treated the subject likewise. Cicero himself alternates between a more idealistic point of view, which recalls Stoic approaches to ethics, and sections of a more empirical nature, which may reflect Peripatetic models as well as Roman historical experience.

There are many individual passages of the *Laelius* which present parallels with Aristotle; the mere number of these is less significant than one might initially be tempted to think, since one has to bear in mind also the degree of closeness of each parallel, and the probability that many of these moralistic ideas were current more widely than among the members of one particular philosophical school. The only ones that can really help to prove Peripatetic influence are those where there is a close verbal similarity, or those whose content can be shown to be peculiar to Aristotle and the Peripatetics. The closest parallel of all is in §78, on the need to respect former friendships, where the wording is very similar to Aristotle (*NE* 9.1165b 31-6): this alone would probably be sufficient to show some connection, though not necessarily a direct one. The notion of the friend as *alter ego* is found particularly in the Peripatetics, but by Cicero's time it probably had virtually proverbial status. Otherwise it is mostly a question of common themes and issues, or arguments that seem to have a Peripatetic "flavour" without being definitely attributable to a Peripatetic source. One may instance particularly the argument from the parallel with family affection and with the behaviour of animals (§§27 and 81), the argument that solitary life is intolerable for human beings (§§22, 52-5, and 88), the rarity of true friends (§62, found also in Aristotle and Theophrastus), and the problems about new friends versus old (§67) and unequal friendships (§68), both of which receive much attention in Aristotle. Both Cicero and Aristotle refer to the proverbial saying that two people must eat many measures of salt together in order to be reckoned as true friends. The existence of these parallels makes it clear that Cicero was influenced by the Peripatetic school, although it is not possible in general to make a more specific attribution to particular philosophers or particular works. On the particular question of Theophrastus, see above, §2; on the influence of Aristotle's *Rhetoric*, see ibid. and note on §65.

As for the Epicureans, Cicero attacks their doctrines with great force. He had already discussed Epicurean views on friendship in the *De Finibus*, and some of the material from that discussion recurs in the *Laelius*. The main point of Laelius's attack is the utilitarian theory of the origin of friendship. Laelius also rejects a theory of reciprocity in friendship which was apparently held by the Epicureans (cf. on §56); and, in customary Ciceronian fashion, he expresses disagreement with the Epicurean denial of the immortality of the soul (§13).

Nevertheless, it is possible to take the search for anti-Epicurean polemic in the *Laelius* rather too far. The Epicureans attempted to explain friendship in terms of utility, and Cicero was no doubt right to point out against them that true friendship should be disinterested. However, the fact remained, as indeed it still does remain, that a large number of people who have never heard of Epicurus do actually seek utility in their friendships. In sections 79 and 82 in particular, it is surely these whom Cicero is attacking, not any group of philosophers. And even when he is fairly clearly attacking the Epicureans themselves, he does not explicitly name them. This is partly because of the general reluctance to display familiarity with Greek philosophy, which has already been pointed out (Introd. §7); but there is a further possible reason, which seems to have escaped notice perhaps because of its very simplicity. Cicero dedicated the *Laelius* to Atticus, who had Epicurean sympathies at least, even if he did not consistently profess adherence to the school. Atticus would have known all about Cicero's anti-Epicurean ideas, and clearly the two men never allowed philosophical disagreement to affect their friendship; but it would not have been appropriate for Cicero, even by the slightest implication, to associate Atticus with the objects of his attack in the *Laelius* – "persons who overflow with self-indulgence", who "have no real knowledge" of friendship "either in theory or in practice" (§52). To omit the name of the Epicurean school from these passages would make it less easy for any such tactless implication to obtrude itself.

Thus the philosophical content of the *Laelius* appears as a characteristically Ciceronian mixture, with elements of Stoic idealism incorporated alongside the more practical observations of the Peripatetics. That the mixture is in fact Cicero's, and is not to be attributed to some lost intermediate source, need not be doubted. Nor is the philosophy of the *Laelius* a mere patchwork of incompatible elements from diverse sources. It is true that Cicero has to resort to the device of making Laelius attribute certain views to Scipio, in order to accommodate the change of viewpoint from the idealistic to the practical; but the differing viewpoints do not involve any real contradiction. What strikes the reader (or at least the present editor) most about the *Laelius* is its exemplification of Cicero's often-proclaimed independence of judgement: what matters to Cicero in the case of any philosophical idea about friendship is not whether it is Stoic or Peripatetic, but whether it will stand up to analysis and examination on its own merits.

In the case of this dialogue, as elsewhere in Cicero's philosophy, the source question has been a favourite with scholars. Most of those who have attacked this question argue roughly as I have done above, for a mixture of Stoic and Peripatetic influence, though there may be disagreement over the exact proportions or over the origin of particular doctrines and ideas: the material of these discussions is more appropriately treated in the commentary than here. The earliest dissertation on this subject known to me (though I have not been able to consult it) is R.F.Braxator, *Quid in conscribendo Ciceronis Laelio valuerint Aristotelis Ethicorum Nicomacheorum de amicitia libri* (Halle 1871); thereafter one may refer to G.Heylbut (cited above, p. 3); A.Thiaucourt, *Essai sur les oeuvres philosophiques de Cicéron et leurs sources grecques* (Paris 1885) 188-99, G. Bohnenblust, *Beiträge zum Topos* περὶ φιλίας (Diss. Bern, Berlin 1905), reviewed by M. Pohlenz, *BPW* (1906), 1392; A.Gercke, cited above, §6; M.Hoppe, cited ibid., and the review by M.Pohlenz, *BPW* (1913), 1351; P. Scheuerpflug, *Quaestiones Laelianae* (Jena 1914); R. Philippson, *RE* VIIa, 1166; H.Hommel, "Cicero und der Peripatos", *Gymnasium* 62 (1955) 319-23. The Panaetius theory referred to above was apparently first mooted by A.Bonhöffer, *Die Ethik des Stoikers Epiktet* (Stuttgart 1894) 121 Anm. 94; this was referred to with some approval by Bohnenblust, and rejected by Pohlenz in his review of the latter. It appears that Pohlenz later changed his mind, for he admits the possible truth of the theory in *Antikes Führertum* (1938) 38-9 n.1: this injudicious resurrection was followed by Schäfer and (at considerable length) by Steinmetz, both cited above, §6; cf. F.Wehrli, *MH* 24 (1967) 245; Bringmann, *Untersuchungen* 206ff.; Steinmetz has been most recently followed by Fortenbaugh, *Quellen zur Ethik Theophrasts* 111-3 in the view that material from Theophrastus reached Cicero through Panaetius, although there is (as far as the present editor can see) not the slightest evidence for such a belief.

9. *Amicitia* and Roman politics   It is to be presumed that Cicero meant his ideal of true personal friendship to be attainable in real life, given that the persons concerned were of a sufficiently high moral character, and were compatible in their views and interests. It is reasonably clear that he thought it had been realised in the friendship of Scipio and Laelius, or in his own friendship with Atticus. On the other hand, he makes it clear that what is referred to as friendship usually belongs to the inferior category of *vulgares amicitiae*, and that instances of the ideal are difficult to find, particularly in the highly competitive atmosphere of Roman public life. Though a full treatment of the subject is not in place here, something needs to be said of the relationship between Cicero's *amicitia* and the reality of Roman politics.

During the last century or so there have been great advances in the understanding of Roman political life. It is by now well enough known that, since there was no such thing as a political party at Rome, a Roman politician had to make his way as an individual in competition with other individuals. Politics in the Roman Republic was much less like modern parliamentary democracy than like the competition for power and prestige that goes on *within* modern political parties, or in overtly non-political organisations. An individual could base his career on any of a number of factors: the status and prestige of a noble family, the possession of wealth, the acquisition of military glory, the ability to sway the Senate, the courts or the popular assembly as an orator, or the patronage of geographical or sectional interests within the Roman sphere of influence. But one of the most important factors was the question of his relations with other members of the governing class. In the course of a political career, a Roman would inevitably build up a network of connections of varying degrees of closeness. With some of his contemporaries he would exchange favours, agreeing to further their interests in the hope that they would do the same in return (the Roman sense of honour on such points was both strong and finely tuned). With some, quite apart from political considerations, he might contract genuine personal friendships. On the other hand, to favour one person might easily involve offending another, and a political disagreement could give rise to personal enmity.

None of this is peculiarly Roman, but the Romans were on the whole more open about these things than our society encourages people to be. It is also probably true to say that the Romans were more prone than we are to mix personal and political considerations. In English politics there is a tradition (not, of course, invariably observed) that political disagreement should not be allowed to affect personal friendships; but the Romans expected their friends to support them in public, and a failure of political support could be taken as a personal insult. Friends do seem to have been expected, on the whole, to agree, to support each other, and to share political aims; the definition of friendship as *consensio* (agreement) is not confined to philosophical contexts. It seems also that the Roman virtue of *constantia* (reliability and consistency) embraced consistency in both friendships and enmities.

It appears to have been conventional for any form of political combination, or promise of support, to be accompanied by strong protestations of personal friendship, whether these were sincere or not. Nobody who reads Cicero's letters can fail to be struck by this, and the modern reader can easily be puzzled or repelled by the way Cicero professes warm personal feelings for those whom he privately distrusts or despises. (The question should perhaps be raised whether Cicero is entirely typical; one suspects that he may have taken these things rather further than some Roman politicians. But his letters stand as evidence for what was possible in a Roman political setting.) Cicero's relations with some of his contemporary politicians could well exemplify his category of *vulgares amicitiae*; still more, those with the vast number of acquaintances and hangers-on that thronged any great Roman statesman's house (cf. Cic. *Att.* 1.18.1). The difference, in real life, between those professed friendships and his true personal friendship with Atticus, was presumably no less than the difference between the "ideal" and "ordinary" types of friendship described in the *Laelius*. Doubtless, however, he would have said that it is one thing to flatter insincerely, with no real friendly intentions, and entirely another to make a profession of friendship in pursuit of a political alliance, and attempt to keep to it even if one's private feelings might not be particularly friendly towards the person concerned. A modern politician or businessman, given that we allow for differences of social convention, might well say the same.

The Latin word *amicitia* has come to be used by historians virtually as a technical term for any alliance between Roman aristocrats, even the most temporary or insincere. This should be resisted, since it is unjustified in Latin usage, and unnecessarily confusing. *Amicitia* may have slightly different connotations from the English word "friendship", but nobody who reads the *Laelius* - or indeed any other Latin literature - can doubt that its primary meaning is essentially the same. It refers properly to a personal relationship involving genuine feelings of goodwill and affection on both sides. It is not in any sense a technical political term. It occurs often in political contexts, precisely because of the convention just outlined, that political alliances were *claimed* to be instances of personal friendship, and that political opposition tended to turn into personal enmity. The claim of friendship could not work as a guarantee of good faith if the actual meaning of the word *amicitia* (or its cognates) had been irrevocably cheapened. Cynical modern historians do not always properly convey the complexity of motives and reactions that lie behind the events that they analyse: the actions and thoughts of politicians are not always conditioned by the single-minded pursuit of pure political advantage. R.Syme's statement (*The Roman Revolution* [Oxford 1939] 12) that "*amicitia* was a weapon of politics, not a sentiment based on congeniality" is, like some other sayings of that great historian, no more than an epigrammatic half-truth.

In view of all this, it may be seen more clearly that the *Laelius* is a practical and realistic analysis of friendship as Cicero knew it. It is not to be dismissed as a piece of impractical philosophising based on Greek models, with no real relevance to the society in which Cicero lived. It is what it claims to be: a treatise written largely from a common-sense Roman point of view, but with a background of Greek philosophy, embodying both an ideal of true personal friendship (which was sometimes actually attained) and a set of principles to be applied in dealing with the less perfect type of relationship that was often claimed as "friendship" in ordinary life, including political life. A study of Cicero's principles and examples can increase our understanding of Roman politics, provided that we do not bring mistaken preconceptions to the task of interpreting them.

Those interested in this topic should not omit to read P.A.Brunt, *PCPS* NS 11 (1965) 1-20, reprinted in R.Seager, *The Crisis of the Roman Republic* (Cambridge 1969) and in Brunt's own *Fall of the Roman Republic* (1988). The *Commentariolum Petitionis* attributed to Q. Cicero (16-40) contains useful evidence on political *amicitia*. A standard work on the vocabulary of *amicitia* and related concepts is Hellegouarc'h, *Vocabulaire*, esp. pp. 41ff. However, the schematic treatment inevitable in a work of this sort leads to the impression that "political" usage of words was more clearly demarcated from normal usage than it actually was. Cf. also A.Michel, *Rhétorique et philosophie chez Cicéron* 608ff.; J.P.V.D.Balsdon, in T.A.Dorey ed., *Cicero* (London 1965), 189-90; B.Rawson, *The Politics of Friendship: Pompey and Cicero* (Sydney 1978); L.R.Taylor, *Party Politics in the Age of Caesar* (Berkeley 1949) 7-9, 23, 35; M. Gelzer, *The Roman Nobility* (transl. R.Seager, Oxford 1975), 101-110 (a chapter headed "Political friendship", which is in fact largely about political patronage - a slightly different thing); and for the contrary sentiment to *amicitia*, D.Epstein, *Personal Enmity in Roman Politics 218-43 BC* (London 1987).

10. Later writing on friendship, and the influence of the *Laelius* The topic of friendship continued to be treated by philosophical writers after Cicero. Seneca's *Letters* include two on the subject (*Ep.* 3 and 9; cf. U. Knoche, *Arctos* NS 1 [1954] 83-96; W.Brinckmann, *Der Begriff der Freundschaft in Senecas Briefen* [Diss. Cologne 1963]); he also wrote a treatise, now lost, entitled *Quomodo amicitia continenda sit* ("How to maintain friendship"). Seneca's *De Beneficiis* should also be mentioned, as a work on a related subject (the moral questions raised by the conferment or exchange of favours). Valerius Maximus included some examples of friendship in his collection of "memorable sayings and deeds"; the section *De amicitia* (4.7) is prefaced by some general remarks on friendship that seem to be more or less a rehash of parts of the *Laelius*, and his first example is a paraphrase of the anecdote of Blossius of Cumae from *Lael.* 37. Plutarch wrote treatises "On having many friends" and "How to distinguish the friend from the flatterer". Epictetus *Diss.* 2.22 is concerned with friendship, and takes a cynical view of the ability of imperfect human beings to maintain it. Lucian's *Toxaris* contains an enumeration of examples of faithful friendship. Later Greek authors who wrote on the topic include Maximus of Tyre, Libanius and Themistius.

Apart from the passages of Valerius Maximus just mentioned, it is difficult to see direct influence from the *Laelius* on most of the above authors: they should be seen as belonging to a common tradition. The *Laelius* became much more influential in its own right in the Middle Ages, when it was one of the most often read of Cicero's works; among medieval works that allude to it one may mention the treatises on friendship written by Aelred of Rievaulx (Migne, *PL* 195, 676) and Peter of Blois (ibid. 207, 875), while the *Liber Decem Capitulorum* of Marbod of Rennes contains verse adaptations of parts of the *Cato Maior* and *Laelius*. The *Laelius* was much read and admired in the Renaissance. It is interesting finally to compare with it Montaigne's essay *De l'amitié*, which was clearly influenced by Cicero, but draws principally on Montaigne's own experience.

11. Text and manuscripts The number of extant manuscripts of the *Laelius* is in the region of four or five hundred; most of these are Renaissance copies of little or no use for the constitution of the text. The text in this edition is based largely on the twelve earliest manuscripts, dating from the ninth, tenth and eleventh centuries. These manuscripts are as follows:

P Formerly Parisinus Didotianus; now at Kraków, Jagiellonian Library, Berol. lat. Q. 404, fols. 1r-32r, ninth century.

A Vatican Library, Vat. lat. 5207, fols. 61v-64v, containing *Lael.* 1-28 only, ninth century.

K Vatican Library, Reg. lat. 1762, containing the excerpts of Hadoard from Cicero's philosophical works, including the *Laelius*; ninth century.

M Munich, Bayerische Staatsbibliothek, Clm 15514, fols. 78r-88r, containing *Lael.* 44-104, ninth or tenth century.

O Oxford, Bodleian Library, D'Orville 77, fols. 21-34, tenth century.

L Florence, Laurentian Library, 50,45, fols. 89r-97v, tenth century.

R Paris, Bibliothèque Nationale, lat. 5752-II, fols. 61v-70r, eleventh century.

Q Paris, lat. 544-II, fols. 74r-92r, eleventh century.

G Wolfenbüttel, Gudianus lat. 335, fols. 1r-30v, eleventh century.

V Vienna, lat. 275, fols. 68r-91r, eleventh century.

H London, British Library, Harley 2682, fols. 57r-64r, eleventh century.

Z Graz, Universitätsbibliothek 1703/92 (fragments), tenth century.

To the above may be added two good manuscripts of the twelfth century:

S Munich, Clm 15964 (Salisburgensis), fols. 28r-52v
B Munich, Clm 4611 (Benedictoburanus), fols. 195v-201r.

For readings of the manuscripts listed above, I have relied partly on my own collations, and partly on those already published in editions or in periodical literature.

A reasonably clear *stemma* (see Fig. 2) can be constructed to show the relationships of these earlier manuscripts; it is impossible, however, to fit the later manuscripts (from the twelfth century onwards) into the *stemma*. The constant activity of copying and cross-correction (or "contamination") meant that the branches of the tradition could not stay distinct. Generally these later MSS import many new errors of their own, and present a much worse text than that of the earlier MSS, but in a few places they provide good readings not to be found earlier: these may be due either to inspired conjecture or to the use of earlier copies now lost (it is not possible to tell which).

Some more detailed information and bibliography on the manuscripts may be found in my article in *T. & T.*: the reader should bear in mind, however, that certain statements in that article are already out of date. In particular it should be noted that I there recorded the earliest complete manuscript, P, as missing: it has now happily been rediscovered. In due course I hope to publish a further article bringing information on the manuscripts up to date. Among articles on textual points should be mentioned especially P. Fedeli, "Sul testo del *De Amicitia* di Cicerone", *RhM* 115 (1972) 156-73; see also J.N.Madvig, *Opuscula Academica* II (Copenhagen 1887) 279-87 (a reprint of the preface to his edition), and K.Meissner, "Zu Ciceros Laelius", *N. Jb. Klass. Phil.* 135-6 (1887), 545-57. There are numerous other articles on the text in older scholarly periodicals; most of them have no claim to be cited here, since they consist largely of speculative emendation based on inadequate manuscript evidence. Articles dealing with particular passages are cited in the commentary and appendix.

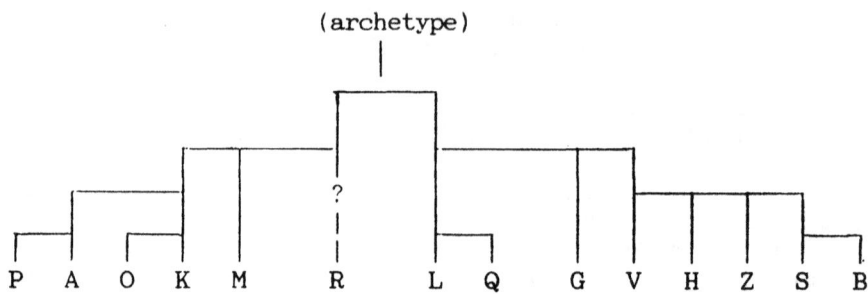

Fig. 2 Simplified stemma, showing the relationship of the earlier manuscripts of the Laelius

LAELIUS, ON FRIENDSHIP
LAELIVS DE AMICITIA

MARCI TVLLI CICERONIS
LAELIVS DE AMICITIA

Note: Asterisks in the text refer to discussion of textual points in the Appendix.

[I.1] Quintus Mucius augur multa narrare de Gaio Laelio socero suo memoriter et iucunde solebat, nec dubitare illum in omni sermone appellare sapientem. Ego autem a patre ita eram deductus ad Scaevolam sumpta virili toga, ut quoad possem et liceret, a senis latere numquam discederem. Itaque multa ab eo prudenter disputata, multa etiam breviter et commode dicta memoriae mandabam, fierique studebam eius prudentia doctior. Quo mortuo me ad pontificem Scaevolam contuli, quem unum nostrae civitatis et ingenio et iustitia praestantissimum audeo dicere. [2] Sed de hoc alias; nunc redeo ad augurem. Cum saepe multa, tum memini domi in hemicyclio sedentem, ut solebat, cum et ego essem una et pauci admodum familiares, in eum sermonem illum incidere, qui tum fere multis erat in ore. Meministi enim profecto, Attice, et eo magis quod Publio Sulpicio utebare multum, cum is tribunus plebis capitali odio a Quinto Pompeio qui tum erat consul dissideret, quocum coniunctissime et amantissime vixerat, quanta esset hominum vel admiratio vel querela. [3] Itaque tum Scaevola, cum in eam ipsam mentionem incidisset, exposuit nobis sermonem Laeli de amicitia, habitum ab illo secum et cum altero genero Gaio Fannio Marci filio, paucis diebus post mortem Africani. Eius disputationis sententias memoriae mandavi, quas hoc libro exposui arbitratu meo; quasi enim ipsos induxi loquentes, ne "inquam" et "inquit" saepius interponeretur, atque ut tamquam a praesentibus coram haberi sermo videretur. [4] Cum enim saepe mecum ageres, ut de amicitia scriberem aliquid, digna mihi res cum omnium cognitione tum nostra familiaritate visa est; itaque feci non invitus, ut prodessem multis rogatu tuo. Sed ut in Catone Maiore, qui est scriptus ad te de senectute, Catonem induxi senem disputantem, quia nulla videbatur aptior persona quae de illa aetate loqueretur quam eius qui et diutissime senex fuerit, et in ipsa senectute praeter ceteros floruisset; sic cum accepissemus a patribus maxime memorabilem Gai Laeli et Publi Scipionis familiaritatem fuisse, idonea mihi Laeli persona visa est quae de amicitia ea ipsa dissereret quae disputata ab eo meminisset Scaevola. Genus autem hoc sermonum positum in hominum veterum auctoritate et eorum illustrium, plus nescioquo pacto videtur habere gravitatis; itaque ipse mea legens sic afficior interdum, ut Catonem, non me loqui existimem. [5] Sed ut tum ad senem senex de senectute, sic hoc libro ad amicum amicissimus scripsi de amicitia; tum est Cato locutus quo erat nemo fere senior

LAELIUS, ON FRIENDSHIP

[I:1] Quintus Mucius [Scaevola], the Augur, used to talk a great deal about his father-in-law, Gaius Laelius. His anecdotes about him were always told pleasantly and with accurate recollection; and in conversation about him in general, he did not hesitate to apply to him the epithet "wise". Now I myself, when I came of age, was taken by my father to Scaevola, with the intention that so far as I was able and permitted, I should never leave the old man's side. In this way I used to commit to memory many learned arguments of his, together with many concise and apposite sayings, and I did my best to take advantage of his learning for my own education. When he died, I moved on to Scaevola the Pontifex, a man whom I would not hesitate to call the most eminent in Rome for both acumen and fairness of judgement. [2] But of him I shall speak another time: now I return to the Augur. Among many other things, I remember in particular one occasion, when he was sitting at home in his semicircular portico, as he often did, with myself present and just a small number of friends, and his conversation turned to the topic which was common talk around that time. You remember of course, Atticus, particularly since you were often in the company of Publius Sulpicius, how amazed or indeed shocked everyone was, when he, as tribune of the people, opposed Quintus Pompeius (who was consul at the time) with deadly enmity - a man with whom he had lived on the closest and friendliest of terms. [3] So it was that Scaevola then happened to mention the subject, and repeated for us the discussion on friendship which Laelius had had with him and with his other son-in-law, Gaius Fannius son of Marcus, a few days after the death of Scipio Africanus. I committed to memory the substance of the discussion, and I have set it out in this book after my own fashion: I have, as it were, brought the characters on stage to speak in person, avoiding the frequent insertion of "I said" or "he said", and giving the impression of a conversation between persons actually present. [4] You have suggested a number of times that I should write something on friendship, and it seemed to me that this was a matter deserving of public interest as well as appropriate in view of our own close association. So I was not at all reluctant to do something of benefit to many at your request. But just as, in the Cato Maior which I wrote for you on old age, I brought in Cato in his old age to lead the discussion, since it seemed that there could be no more suitable character to talk about that age of life than he, who had both lived to be very old and had flourished in old age itself more than other men; so, bearing in mind the tradition of the memorable friendship between Laelius and Scipio, it seemed to me that Laelius was an appropriate character to talk about friendship, in those very terms which Scaevola remembered from the conversation with him. This type of dialogue, grounded in the authority of eminent men of past generations, seems somehow to carry more weight; and indeed, I sometimes get the feeling, when I read my own work, that it is Cato who is speaking, not myself. [5] Anyhow, just as I wrote then as one old man to another on the subject of old age, so in this book I have written to a friend in the friendliest spirit on the subject of friendship.

temporibus illis, nemo prudentior; nunc Laelius et sapiens (sic enim est habitus) et amicitiae gloria excellens de amicitia loquetur. Tu velim a me animum parumper avertas, Laelium loqui ipsum putes. Gaius Fannius et Quintus Mucius ad socerum veniunt post mortem Africani; ab his sermo oritur, respondet Laelius, cuius tota disputatio est de amicitia; quam legens te ipse cognosces.

[II.6] FANNIVS: Sunt ista, Laeli; nec enim melior vir fuit Africano quisquam nec clarior. Sed existimare debes omnium oculos in te esse coniectos*: unum te sapientem et appellant et existimant. Tribuebatur hoc modo M. Catoni, scimus L. Acilium apud patres nostros appellatum esse sapientem, sed uterque alio quodam modo: Acilius quia prudens esse in iure civili putabatur, Cato quia multarum rerum usum habebat. Multa eius et in senatu et in foro vel provisa prudenter vel acta constanter vel responsa acute ferebantur; propterea quasi cognomen iam habebat in senectute sapientis. [7] Te autem alio quodam modo, non solum natura et moribus, verum etiam studio et doctrina esse sapientem: nec sicut vulgus, sed ut eruditi solent appellare sapientem, qualem in reliqua Graecia neminem (nam qui Septem appellantur, eos qui ista subtilius quaerunt in numero sapientium non habent), Athenis unum accepimus, et eum quidem etiam Apollinis oraculo sapientissimum iudicatum: hanc esse in te sapientiam existimant, ut omnia tua in te posita esse ducas, humanosque casus virtute inferiores putes. Itaque ex me quaerunt, credo ex hoc item Scaevola, quonam pacto mortem Africani feras; eoque magis, quod proximis Nonis, cum in hortos D. Bruti auguris commentandi causa, ut adsolet, venissemus, tu non adfuisti, qui diligentissime semper illum diem et illud munus solitus esses obire.

[8] SCAEVOLA: Quaerunt quidem, Gai Laeli, multi, ut est a Fannio dictum. Sed ego id respondeo quod animum adverti, te dolorem quem acceperis cum summi viri tum amicissimi morte, ferre moderate; nec potuisse non commoveri, nec fuisse id humanitatis tuae. Quod autem Nonis in collegio nostro non adfuisses, valetudinem respondeo causae, non maestitiam fuisse.

LAELIVS: Recte tu quidem, Scaevola, et vere. Nec enim ab isto officio, quod semper usurpavi cum valerem, abduci incommodo meo debui, nec ullo casu arbitror hoc constanti homini posse contingere, ut ulla intermissio fiat officii. [9] Tu autem, Fanni, quod mihi tantum tribui dicis quantum ego nec agnosco nec postulo, facis amice, sed ut mihi videris, non recte iudicas de Catone. Aut enim nemo, quod quidem magis credo, aut si quisquam, ille sapiens fuit. Quomodo, ut alia omittam, mortem fili tulit! Memineram Paulum, videram Galum; sed hi in pueris, Cato in perfecto et spectato viro.

Then the speaker was Cato, the oldest and wisest figure of those times; now Laelius, a wise man (for so he was held to be) and pre-eminent on account of his own glorious friendship, will speak about friendship. I should like you to forget me for a little time, and imagine that Laelius himself is speaking. Gaius Fannius and Quintus Mucius come to see their father-in-law after the death of Africanus; they start the conversation, and Laelius replies. To him belongs the whole of the exposition on friendship; and as you read it, you may recognise a portrait of yourself.

[II:6] FANNIUS: That is true, Laelius. There has never been a better or a more illustrious man than Africanus. But you must realise that all eyes are fixed on you: it is you alone whom they call wise, and really consider to be so. That distinction used lately to be given to Marcus Cato, and we know that Lucius Acilius, in our fathers' time, was called wise; but for different reasons in the two cases, Acilius because he was thought learned in civil law, Cato because of his great practical experience. Many instances of prudent policy or firmness in action or sharpness in debate were recorded of him both in the Senate and in the courts, and for that reason in his old age he was accorded, virtually as a surname, the epithet "The Wise". [7] With you, however, it is different again: not just in character and natural gifts, but also in learning and intellectual interests; and not as ordinary people use the word, but as learned men habitually do; the sort of wise man who, according to tradition, was to be found nowhere in the rest of Greece – for the so-called Seven Sages are not included among the wise by those who take a subtler view of these things – but in one instance at Athens; and he, indeed, was judged by the oracle of Apollo to be the wisest of all men. They attribute to you the wisdom that makes you regard as within your own responsibility everything that concerns you, and believe that good qualities of character may overcome all the chances of human life. It is for this reason that they ask me, and I am sure Scaevola here as well, how you are coping with the death of Africanus; and especially since on the Nones of this month, when we arrived in the gardens of Decimus Brutus the augur for our regular practice, you were not there, though you had always been most careful in your attendance at that function.

[8] SCAEVOLA: Yes, many people do ask me, Gaius Laelius, as Fannius has said; but I have always replied what I myself have observed, that you bear your grief at the death of a great man and friend in a controlled way; that you could not fail to be distressed, nor would that be in keeping with your humane character; as for your absence from our college on the Nones, I say that the reason was ill health, not grief.

LAELIUS: You are quite right to say that, Scaevola; what you say is true. Certainly I could not allow my misfortune to take me away from that duty, which I have always performed when in good health; indeed, I do not think that any such circumstances justify a man of reliable character in dropping his obligations. [9] As for you, Fannius, when you say that such a compliment is paid to me, as I neither accept nor ask for, you talk like a friend; but it seems to me that you are not right in your opinion of Cato. Either nobody has ever been wise - which I am more inclined to believe – or, if anybody has been, that man was Cato. To leave other things on one side, how well he bore the death of his son! I remember Paulus, I saw Galus myself; but their sons were boys,

[10] Quamobrem cave Catoni anteponas ne istum quidem ipsum quem Apollo, ut ais, sapientissimum iudicavit: huius enim facta, illius dicta laudantur. De me autem (ut iam cum utroque vestrum loquar) sic habetote.

[III] Ego si Scipionis desiderio me moveri negem, quam id recte faciam viderint sapientes, sed certe mentiar. Moveor enim tali amico orbatus qualis, ut arbitror, nemo umquam erit; ut confirmare possum, nemo certe fuit. Sed non egeo medicina: me ipse consolor, et maxime illo solacio, quod eo errore careo quo amicorum decessu plerique angi solent. Nihil mali accidisse Scipioni puto: mihi accidit, si quid accidit. Suis autem incommodis graviter angi non amicum, sed se ipsum amantis est. [11] Cum illo vero quis neget actum esse praeclare? Nisi enim, quod ille minime putabat, immortalitatem optare vellet, quid non adeptus est quod homini fas esset optare? Qui summam spem civium, quam de eo iam puero habuerant, continuo adulescens incredibili virtute superavit; qui consulatum petivit numquam, factus consul est bis, primum ante tempus, iterum sibi suo tempore, rei publicae paene sero; qui duabus urbibus eversis, inimicissimis huic imperio, non modo praesentia verum etiam futura bella delevit. Quid dicam de moribus facillimis, de pietate in matrem, liberalitate in sorores, bonitate in suos, iustitia in omnes? Nota sunt vobis; quam autem civitati carus fuerit, maerore funeris indicatum* est. Quid igitur hunc paucorum annorum accessio iuvare potuisset? Senectus enim quamvis non sit gravis, ut memini Catonem anno antequam est mortuus mecum et cum Scipione disserere, tamen aufert eam viriditatem in qua etiamnunc erat Scipio. [12] Quamobrem vita quidem talis fuit vel fortuna vel gloria, ut nihil posset accedere; moriendi autem sensum celeritas abstulit. Quo de genere mortis difficile dictu est; quid homines suspicentur videtis; hoc vere tamen licet dicere, Publio Scipioni, ex multis diebus quos in vita celeberrimos laetissimosque viderit, illum diem clarissimum fuisse, cum senatu dimisso domum reductus ad vesperum est a patribus conscriptis, populo Romano, sociis et Latinis, pridie quam excessit e vita, ut ex tam alto dignitatis gradu ad superos videatur deos potius quam ad inferos pervenisse.

[IV.13] Neque enim assentior eis qui haec nuper disserere coeperunt, cum corporibus simul animos interire atque omnia morte deleri. Plus apud me antiquorum auctoritas valet: vel nostrorum maiorum qui mortuis tam religiosa iura tribuerunt, quod non fecissent profecto si nihil ad eos pertinere arbitrarentur; vel eorum qui in hac terra fuerunt, Magnamque Graeciam (quae nunc quidem deleta est, tum florebat) institutis et praeceptis suis erudiverunt; vel eius qui Apollinis oraculo sapientissimus est iudicatus,

Cato's was a full-grown man who had already proved himself. [10] Take care, therefore, that you rank Cato no lower even than that man whom you mentioned, whom Apollo, as you say, judged the wisest of men; Cato is praised for his actions, the other only for his sayings. As for myself - I talk now to both of you – I shall tell you what I think.

[III] If I were to deny that I am affected by grief at the loss of Scipio, the philosophers may judge how right I would be to do so; but certainly I should not be telling the truth. I am indeed affected, since I have been deprived of a friend such as I suppose there will never be again; I can be quite sure that there has never been one like him before. However, I am not lacking in remedies. I act as my own comforter, and I console myself particularly with the knowledge that I am free of the misconception which troubles many people at the death of their friends. I do not believe that anything bad has happened to Scipio; if any bad thing has happened, it has happened to me. But to be gravely troubled by one's own misfortunes argues love for oneself, not for one's friend. [11] As for him, who can deny that he has been dealt with in the best way possible? For, unless he desired to live for ever – which certainly he never thought that he would – what did he fail to achieve that any man could rightly desire? At the very beginning, when he was a young man, he showed incredible qualities of character, surpassing the highest hopes that his fellow-citizens had held for him when he was still a boy; he never stood for the consulate, but was made consul twice, the first time before the legal age, the second at the proper time for him, but for the Republic almost too late; and in destroying two cities that were most hostile to the Roman power, he put an end not only to present wars, but also to any that might happen in the future. What should I say of his charm of manner, his dutiful affection for his mother, his generosity to his sisters, his kindness to the members of his household, and his fairness towards all men? All this is well known to you; and the mourning at his funeral showed how dear he was to the citizen body. What, therefore, could this man have gained from the addition of a few more years? For though old age may not be a burden (as I remember Cato arguing in conversation with me and Scipio, the year before he died), nevertheless it takes away that freshness that Scipio still had. [12] All in all, then, his life was such that nothing could be added to it either in good fortune or in glory; and the quickness of his death removed the sense of dying. Of a death like this one it is difficult to speak with confidence; you see what people suspect; this, however, may be said for certain, that out of all the many days in Publius Scipio's life that were full of rejoicing and public honour for him, the best of all was the day before he died, when, after the Senate had risen, he was escorted home in the evening by the senators, the people of Rome, the allies and the Latins; so that it seemed that from such a high degree of eminence he could only have gone to join the gods above, rather than to the spirits of the underworld.

[IV:13] I do not, indeed, agree with those who, not so long ago, began to argue that the soul dies together with the body, and that everything is destroyed by death. The authority of the ancients influences me more: either our own ancestors, who paid such reverent honours to the dead, which they would surely not have done if they thought the dead could be affected by nothing; or those who settled in this country, and educated with their principles and teachings the people of Magna Graecia (which has now ceased to exist, but flourished at that time); or the man who was judged wisest by the oracle of

qui non tum hoc tum illud, ut in plerisque, sed idem semper, animos hominum esse divinos, eisque cum ex corpore excessissent, reditum in caelum patere, optimoque et iustissimo cuique expeditissimum. [14] Quod idem Scipioni videbatur; qui quidem quasi praesagiret, perpaucis ante mortem diebus, cum et Philus et Manilius adessent et alii plures, tuque etiam, Scaevola, mecum venisses, triduum disseruit de re publica, cuius disputationis fuit extremum fere de immortalitate animorum, quae se in quiete per visum ex Africano audisse dicebat. Id si ita est, ut optimi cuiusque animus in morte facillime evolet tamquam e custodia vinclisque corporis, cui censemus cursum ad deos faciliorem fuisse quam Scipioni? Quocirca maerere hoc eius eventu vereor ne invidi magis quam amici sit. Sin autem illa veriora, ut idem interitus sit animorum et corporum, nec ullus sensus maneat, ut nihil boni est in morte, sic certe nihil mali. Sensu enim amisso fit idem quasi natus non esset omnino; quem tamen esse natum et nos gaudemus, et haec civitas dum erit laetabitur.

[15] Quamobrem cum illo quidem, ut supra dixi, actum optime est, mecum incommodius; quem fuerat aequius, ut prius introieram, sic prius exire de vita. Sed tamen recordatione nostrae amicitiae sic fruor ut beate vixisse videar, quia cum Scipione vixerim; quocum mihi coniuncta cura de publica re et de privata fuit, quocum et domus fuit et militia communis, et id in quo est omnis vis amicitiae, voluntatum studiorum sententiarum summa consensio. Itaque non tam ista me sapientiae, quam modo Fannius commemoravit, fama delectat, falsa praesertim, quam quod amicitiae nostrae memoriam spero sempiternam fore; idque eo mihi magis est cordi, quod ex omnibus saeculis vix tria aut quattuor nominantur paria amicorum; quo in genere sperare videor Scipionis et Laeli amicitiam notam posteritati fore.

[16] FANNIVS: Istuc quidem, Laeli, ita necesse est. Sed quoniam amicitiae mentionem fecisti et sumus otiosi, pergratum mihi feceris, spero item Scaevolae, si quemadmodum soles de ceteris rebus quae ex te quaeruntur, sic de amicitia disputaris quid sentias, qualem existimes, quae praecepta des.

SCAEVOLA: Mihi vero erit gratum, atque id ipsum cum tecum agere conarer, Fannius antevortit. Quamobrem utrique nostrum gratum admodum feceris.

[V.17] LAELIVS: Ego vero non gravarer, si mihi ipse confiderem; nam et praeclara res est, et sumus, ut dixit Fannius, otiosi. Sed quis ego sum, aut quae est in me facultas? Doctorum est ista consuetudo eaque Graecorum, ut eis ponatur de quo disputent quamvis

Apollo, who did not, as he did in many matters, say sometimes one thing and sometimes another, but always held to the same opinion, that the souls of men are divine, and that when they leave the body, the return to heaven awaits them; and the better and more upright the man, the quicker and easier the journey. [14] This also was Scipio's opinion: indeed, it was as if he had a premonition of it, a few days before his death; for, when Philus and Manilius and a number of others were with him, and you too, Scaevola, had come with me, he discussed political philosophy with us for three days, and the last part of his discussion concerned the immortality of the soul – things which he said he had heard in a dream from the elder Africanus. So then, if it is true that the better a man is, the more easily his soul flies away, as it were, from the prison and bondage of the body, who can we think could have had an easier path to heaven than Scipio? For this reason, I fear that it may be simply selfish, and not befitting a friend, to be sad at what has happened to him. But if that other opinion is nearer the truth, that the soul and the body suffer the same death and no feeling remains behind, then, just as there is nothing good in death, so equally there is certainly nothing bad in it. For if sensation is lost, one becomes the same as if one had never been born at all; but the fact that this man was born is a cause of joy to us, and will always bring gladness to this nation as long as it exists.

[15] As far as he is concerned, then, as I said before, matters have turned out in the best way possible. It is I who have been less fortunate; it would have been fairer for me, who entered this life before he did, also to leave it first. However, that aside, I have the memory of our friendship to enjoy; and this makes me feel that my life has been happy, because I have shared it with Scipio. I used to consult him on both public and private matters; I was associated with him both at home and on service abroad; and I had with him that in which the true power of friendship consists – the greatest possible community of interests, wishes and opinions. Hence it is not so much that reputation for wisdom, which Fannius just mentioned, that pleases me, particularly if it is not truly justified, as the hope that the memory of our friendship may be preserved for ever; and this gives me all the more pleasure, inasmuch as in the whole course of history hardly three or four pairs of friends are remembered by name; and I believe there is hope that the friendship of Scipio and Laelius will be known to posterity among these.

[16] FANNIUS. That is surely bound to happen, Laelius; but since you have mentioned the subject of friendship and we are at leisure, it would be most agreeable for me, and I expect for Scaevola as well, if you would give us your opinion on friendship, in the way you usually do when asked about a particular subject: tell us what you think about it, what sort of thing you think it is, and what advice you give in regard to it.

SCAEVOLA. I would certainly appreciate that; in fact I was just about to make the same suggestion when Fannius anticipated me. You may be assured that you will be doing a great favour to both of us.

[V:17] LAELIUS. I should not mind if I were confident in myself; for it is an excellent subject, and as Fannius said, we are at leisure. But who am I, or what ability do I have? It is a habit of learned men, and of Greeks, to ask for a subject to be proposed for

subito; magnum opus est egetque exercitatione non parva. Quamobrem quae disputari de amicitia possunt, ab eis censeo petatis qui ista profitentur: ego vos hortari tantum possum ut amicitiam omnibus rebus humanis anteponatis; nihil est enim tam naturae aptum, tam conveniens ad res vel secundas vel adversas.

[18] Sed hoc primum sentio, nisi in bonis amicitiam esse non posse. Neque id ad vivum reseco, ut illi qui haec subtilius disserunt, fortasse vere, sed ad communem utilitatem parum: negant enim quemquam esse virum bonum nisi sapientem. Sit ita sane; sed eam sapientiam interpretantur, quam adhuc mortalis nemo est consecutus; nos autem ea quae sunt in usu vitaque communi, non ea quae finguntur aut optantur spectare debemus. Numquam ego dicam C. Fabricium, M'. Curium, Ti. Coruncanium, quos sapientes nostri maiores iudicabant, ad istorum normam fuisse sapientes. Quare sibi habeant sapientiae nomen et invidiosum et obscurum: concedant ut viri boni fuerint. Ne id quidem facient; negabunt id nisi sapienti posse concedi. [19] Agamus igitur pingui, ut aiunt, Minerva: qui ita se gerunt, ita vivunt, ut eorum probetur fides integritas aequitas* liberalitas, nec sit in eis ulla cupiditas libido audacia, sintque* magna constantia, ut ei fuerunt modo quos nominavi, hos viros bonos, ut habiti sunt, sic etiam appellandos putemus, quia sequantur quantum homines possunt naturam optimam bene vivendi ducem.

Sic enim mihi perspicere videor, ita natos esse nos, ut inter omnes esset societas quaedam, maior autem ut quisque proxime accederet; itaque cives potiores quam peregrini, propinqui quam alieni; cum his enim amicitiam natura ipsa peperit. Sed ea non satis habet firmitatis; namque hoc praestat amicitia propinquitati, quod ex propinquitate benevolentia tolli potest, ex amicitia non potest; sublata enim benevolentia amicitiae nomen tollitur, propinquitatis manet. [20] Quanta autem vis amicitiae sit, ex hoc intellegi maxime potest, quod ex infinita societate generis humani, quam conciliavit ipsa natura, ita contracta res est et adducta in angustum, ut omnis caritas aut inter duos aut inter paucos iungeretur.

[VI] Est enim amicitia nihil aliud nisi omnium divinarum humanarumque rerum cum benevolentia et caritate consensio; qua quidem haud scio an excepta sapientia nihil melius homini sit a dis immortalibus datum. Divitias alii praeponunt, bonam alii valetudinem, alii potentiam, alii honores, multi etiam voluptates: beluarum hoc quidem extremum; illa autem superiora caduca et incerta, posita non tam in consiliis nostris quam in fortunae temeritate. Qui autem in virtute summum bonum ponunt, praeclare illi quidem, sed haec ipsa virtus amicitiam et gignit et continet, nec sine virtute amicitia esse ullo pacto potest. [21] Iam virtutem ex consuetudine vitae sermonisque nostri

discussion at short notice; it is a difficult task and requires not a little training. As for philosophical discussion of friendship, therefore, I think you should ask those who profess this skill. All that I can do is to exhort you to rank friendship above all other things in human life. There is nothing so natural, nothing so beneficial either in favourable or in unfavourable circumstances.

[18] But first, let me say that in my opinion friendship cannot exist except in good men. Of course I do not wish to prune that definition back to the very limit, as they do who discuss these matters more subtly – perhaps rightly, but not very usefully for ordinary purposes. They say that nobody is a good man who is not wise. That may well be true, but their definition of wisdom is such that no human being has ever yet attained it. But we should pay attention to those things which are available in our own experience and in ordinary life, not things that are merely imagined or wished for. I would never say that Gaius Fabricius, Manius Curius or Tiberius Coruncanius, whom our ancestors judged to be wise men, were wise by the standards of the philosophers. Let them therefore keep for their own use the name of wisdom, invidious and obscure as it is, provided that they grant that those were good men. Yet they will not even do that; for they say that nobody but a wise man is entitled to be called good. [19] Let us, therefore, deal with the question in rough common-sense terms. Those who behave and live in such a way that people praise their honesty, integrity, fairness and generosity, and have in them nothing of greed, intemperance or shamelessness, being also endowed with great strength of character, as were those men whom I have just named: – let us consider them to deserve the name of good men, as they have hitherto been held to be, in that they follow, as far as human beings can, the best guide for living well, that is Nature.

It seems clear to me that we are born into the world with a certain natural bond of association between all of us, but a greater one according as we are placed nearer to each other: fellow-countrymen are closer than foreigners, and relatives closer than strangers. With these, nature itself has created a bond of friendship, but not with sufficient stability; for friendship itself is greater than family connections, in that the latter can exist without goodwill, but not the former. If goodwill is taken away the name of friendship disappears, but that of family relationship still remains. [20] However, the best way to realise the power of friendship is to understand this, that out of the infinitely large association of the human race, which nature itself has brought together, friendship is something so concentrated and brought down into a narrow space, that every instance of real affection exists either between two people, or among a small number.

[VI] For friendship is in fact nothing other than a community of views on all matters human and divine, together with goodwill and affection; and I am not sure that the gods have given men any better gift than this, leaving aside wisdom. Some put wealth before it, some prefer good health, some political power, some public honours; many even prefer pleasure. This last is fit only for animals, but the others too are uncertain and unstable, depending not so much on our own intentions as on the blind chances of fortune. As for those who regard virtue as the highest good, that is very fine; but virtue itself both produces and maintains friendship, nor can friendship exist by any means without virtue. [21] Let us now understand the word virtue in accordance with our

interpretemur, nec eam, ut quidam docti, verborum magnificentia metiamur, virosque bonos eos qui habentur numeremus: Paulos, Catones, Galos, Scipiones, Philos. His communis vita contenta est, eos autem omittamus qui omnino nusquam reperiuntur.

[22] Tales igitur inter viros amicitia tantas opportunitates habet quantas vix queo dicere. Principio qui potest esse vita vitalis, ut ait Ennius, quae non in amici mutua benevolentia conquiescit? Quid dulcius quam habere quicum omnia audeas sic loqui ut tecum? Qui esset tantus fructus in prosperis rebus nisi haberes qui illis aeque ac tu ipse gauderet? Adversas vero ferre difficile esset sine eo qui illas gravius etiam quam tu ferret. Denique* ceterae res quae expetuntur opportunae sunt singulae rebus fere singulis: divitiae ut utare, opes ut colare, honores ut laudere, voluptates ut gaudeas, valetudo ut dolore careas et muneribus fungare corporis. Amicitia res plurimas continet, quoquo te verteris praesto est, nullo loco excluditur, numquam intempestiva, numquam molesta est. Itaque non aqua, non igni, ut aiunt, locis pluribus utimur quam amicitia (neque ego nunc de vulgari aut de mediocri, quae tamen ipsa et delectat et prodest, sed de vera et perfecta loquor, qualis eorum qui pauci nominantur fuit); nam et secundas res splendidiores facit amicitia, et adversas partiens communicansque leviores.

[VII:23] Cumque plurimas et maximas commoditates amicitia continet, tum illa nimirum praestat omnibus, quod bona spe praelucet in posterum, nec debilitari animos aut cadere patitur. Verum enim amicum qui intuetur, tamquam exemplar aliquod intuetur sui. Quocirca et absentes adsunt, et egentes abundant, et imbecilli valent, et quod difficilius dictu est, mortui vivunt: tantus eos honos, memoria, desiderium prosequitur amicorum, ex quo illorum beata mors videtur, horum vita laudabilis. Quodsi exemeris ex rerum natura benevolentiae iunctionem, nec domus ulla nec urbs stare poterit, nec* agri quidem cultus permanebit. Id si minus intellegitur, quanta vis amicitiae concordiaeque sit ex dissensionibus atque discordiis percipi potest. Quae enim domus tam stabilis, quae tam firma civitas est, quae non odiis et discidiis funditus possit everti? Ex quo quantum boni sit in amicitia iudicari potest. [24] Agrigentinum quidem doctum quendam virum carminibus Graecis vaticinatum ferunt, quae in rerum natura totoque mundo constarent quaeque moverentur, ea contrahere amicitiam, dissipare discordiam.

Atque hoc quidem omnes mortales et intellegunt et re probant. Itaque si quando aliquod officium exstitit amici in periculis aut adeundis aut communicandis, quis est qui id non maximis efferat laudibus? Qui clamores tota cavea nuper in hospitis et amici mei Marci Pacuvi nova fabula! cum ignorante rege uter Orestes esset, Pylades Orestem se esse

normal experience of life and of the usage of words, and let us not, like some philosophers, take our measure of it from the grandiloquence of the words we use to define it. Let us count as good men those who are commonly thought to be so: men like Paulus, Cato, Galus, Scipio or Philus. With these, ordinary life is content; let us dismiss from consideration those who are altogether nowhere to be found.

[22] Among such men, then, friendship has such great advantages that I can hardly enumerate them all. First of all, how can one have what Ennius calls a "lively life" without the reassurance which the mutual goodwill of friends can provide? What is more pleasant than to have someone with whom you can safely talk about anything whatever, just as with yourself? And how could there be as much enjoyment in good fortune as there is, if you did not have someone whose pleasure in it is equal to your own? As for adversity, truly it would be difficult to endure without that person who takes your misfortune even harder than you do yourself. And after all, the other things that are desired are as a rule advantageous each one for a particular purpose: wealth for its uses, power for the honour it brings, political appointments for the increase of one's fame, pleasures for the enjoyment of them, health for a life free from pain and for the ability to engage in physical activities. But friendship contains in itself many of these things. It is at hand wherever you turn; it is nowhere excluded, never inopportune, never a nuisance. So in fact, as they say, we use fire and water no less often than we make use of friendship (I speak now not of the common or incomplete sort, which nevertheless is still both pleasurable and profitable, but about the true and perfect friendship that is found among the few who are remembered for it); for friendship both enhances the splendour of good fortune, and by sharing and dividing troubles makes them easier to bear.

[VII:23] Given, moreover, that friendship contains very many great advantages, the greatest of all is surely this, that it lights a beacon of hope for the future, nor does it allow the human spirit to weaken or to stumble. For he who looks at a true friend, sees as it were a reflection of himself. Thus those who are absent are made present, the needy are made rich, and the weak strong; and, a harder saying still, the dead still live: so lively is the memory that follows after them among their friends, so great the respect, so keen the longing; and through this the dead even seem to be happy in death, while those who mourn gain honour while yet alive. But if the bond of goodwill be removed from the world, no house or city will be able to stand, nor even will the tilling of the land continue. If this is not yet understood, one may perceive the power of friendship and concord from that of discord and dissension. What house is so well established, what state is so strong that it may not be entirely torn to pieces by hatred and division? From this it may be judged how great is the good in friendship. [24] They say that a wise man of Agrigentum declared in Greek verses the doctrine that all things which exist and move in nature and in the whole universe, are brought together by friendship, and dispersed by discord.

This, indeed, all men understand and endorse in fact; thus, if circumstances call for some action on a friend's part either in facing or in sharing danger, there is nobody who would not praise that action in the highest terms. What applause there was from the whole theatre recently during the new play by my friend Marcus Pacuvius! The king did not

diceret ut pro illo necaretur, Orestes autem ita ut erat, Orestem se esse perseveraret. Stantes plaudebant in re ficta: quid arbitramur in vera facturos fuisse? Facile indicabat ipsa natura vim suam, cum homines quod facere ipsi non possent, id recte fieri in altero iudicarent.

Hactenus mihi videor de amicitia quid sentirem potuisse dicere: si qua praeterea sunt (credo autem esse multa) ab eis, si videbitur, qui ista disputant quaeritote.

[25] FANNIVS: Nos autem a te potius; quamquam etiam ab istis saepe quaesivi et audivi, non invitus equidem; sed aliud quoddam filum orationis tuae.

SCAEVOLA: Tum magis id diceres, Fanni, si nuper in hortis Scipionis, cum est de republica disputatum, adfuisses: qualis tum patronus iustitiae fuit contra accuratam orationem Phili!

FANNIVS: Facile id quidem fuit, iustitiam iustissimo viro defendere.

SCAEVOLA: Quid amicitiam? nonne facile ei qui ob eam summa fide constantia iustitiaque servatam maximam gloriam ceperit?

[VIII:26] LAELIVS: Vim hoc quidem est adferre! Quid enim refert qua me ratione cogatis? cogitis certe; studiis enim generorum, praesertim in re bona, cum difficile est, tum ne aequum quidem obsistere.

Saepissime igitur mihi de amicitia cogitanti maxime illud considerandum videri solet, utrum propter imbecillitatem atque inopiam desiderata sit amicitia, ut dandis recipiendisque meritis, quod quis minus per se ipse posset, id acciperet ab alio vicissimque redderet, an esset hoc quidem proprium amicitiae, sed antiquior et pulchrior et magis a natura ipsa profecta alia causa. Amor enim, ex quo amicitia nominata est, princeps est ad benevolentiam coniungendam; nam utilitates quidem etiam ab eis percipiuntur saepe qui simulatione amicitiae coluntur et observantur temporis causa; in amicitia autem nihil fictum est, nihil simulatum, et quidquid est, id est verum et voluntarium. [27] Quapropter a natura mihi videtur potius quam ab indigentia orta amicitia, applicatione magis animi cum quodam sensu amandi quam cogitatione quantum illa res utilitatis esset habitura.

Quod quidem quale sit etiam in bestiis quibusdam animadverti potest, quae ex se natos ita amant ad quoddam tempus et ab eis ita amantur, ut facile earum sensus appareat;

know which of the two men was Orestes: Pylades said he was Orestes, so that he should be killed in his place; but the real Orestes insisted that he himself was Orestes. The audience stood up to applaud this imagined incident: what are we to think they would have done in a real case of this sort? On this occasion the power of nature asserted itself easily, when people judged another's action to be right, though they could not have done it themselves.

Well, I think that is as much as I can say of my opinions on friendship. As for anything else there may be to say (and I am sure there is a great deal) I suggest that you enquire of those who lecture on those subjects, if you are so minded.

[25] FANNIUS: But we would rather enquire of you. I have, indeed, myself often put questions to those to whom you refer, and listened to their answers; not that they have disappointed me, but the texture of your argument is somehow different.

SCAEVOLA: You would say that all the more, Fannius, if you had been present in Scipio's gardens during that recent conversation on politics: what a staunch defender of justice he was then, against the carefully argued speech of Philus!

FANNIUS: Well, that was easy enough, for the most just of men to defend justice.

SCAEVOLA: What of friendship, then? Is that not also easy for a man who has gained the greatest glory for maintaining it with exceptional good faith, constancy and fairness?

[VIII:26] LAELIUS. This is what I call the application of force! I see that you are determined to compel me, by whatever means. It is difficult to resist the enthusiasm of my sons-in-law, especially on such a noble subject; nor indeed would it be right to do so.

Well then: I have often had occasion to think about friendship, and it has always seemed to me that a point that deserves most serious thought is this: whether friendship is something that we need because of our own weakness and insufficiency, whereby, in a mutual exchange of favours, each man receives from another what he could not achieve for himself, and vice-versa; or whether, though this might indeed be a characteristic of friendship, its cause is something else, more fundamental and nobler, with its source in nature herself. For the first thing to bring people together in a relationship of goodwill is love (*amor*), from which friendship (*amicitia*) derives its name. There are, indeed, practical advantages to be enjoyed also by those whose society is cultivated by others and who receive favours, under the pretence of friendship, for temporary expediency; but in friendship itself, pretence and deception have no place; whatever is done, must be done freely and truthfully. [27] For this reason it seems to me that friendship originates in nature, rather than in need: more because of an attachment of the mind, accompanied by a sense of affection, than because of a calculation of the amount of advantage that the association will bring.

What sort of thing this is, can be observed even in certain of the animals, which love their offspring for a certain length of time, and are loved by them, in such a way that

quod in homine multo est evidentius, primum ex ea caritate quae est inter natos et parentes, quae dirimi nisi detestabili scelere non potest, deinde cum similis sensus exstitit amoris, si aliquem nacti sumus cuius cum moribus et natura congruamus, quod in eo quasi lumen aliquod probitatis et virtutis perspicere videamur. [28] Nihil est enim virtute amabilius, nihil quod magis alliciat ad diligendum, quippe cum propter virtutem et probitatem etiam eos quos numquam vidimus quodam modo diligamus. Quis est qui C. Fabrici, M'. Curi non cum caritate aliqua benevola memoriam usurpet, quos numquam viderit? Quis autem est qui Tarquinium Superbum, qui Sp. Cassium, Sp. Maelium non oderit? Cum duobus ducibus de imperio in Italia est decertatum, Pyrrho et Hannibale: ab altero propter probitatem eius non nimis alienos animos habemus, alterum propter crudelitatem semper haec civitas oderit. [IX:29] Quodsi tanta vis probitatis est ut eam vel in eis quos numquam vidimus, vel quod maius est in hoste etiam diligamus, quid mirum est si animi hominum moveantur, cum eorum quibuscum usu coniuncti esse possunt, virtutem et bonitatem perspicere videantur?

Quamquam confirmatur amor et beneficio accepto et studio perspecto et consuetudine adiuncta; quibus rebus ad illum primum motum animi et amoris adhibitis, admirabilis quaedam exardescit benevolentiae magnitudo. Quam si qui putant ab imbecillitate proficisci, ut sit per quem adsequatur quod quisque desideret, humilem sane relinquunt et minime generosum, ut ita dicam, ortum amicitiae, quam ex inopia atque indigentia natam volunt. Quod si ita esset, ut quisque minimum esse in se arbitraretur, ita ad amicitiam esset aptissimus; quod longe secus est; [30] ut enim quisque sibi plurimum confidit, et ut quisque maxime·virtute et sapientia sic munitus est ut nullo egeat, suaque omnia in se ipso posita iudicet, ita in amicitiis expetendis colendisque maxime excellit. Quid enim? Africanus indigens mei? Minime hercule, ac ne ego quidem illius; sed ego admiratione quadam virtutis eius, ille vicissim opinione fortasse nonnulla quam de meis moribus habebat, me dilexit; auxit benevolentiam consuetudo; sed quamquam utilitates multae et magnae consecutae sunt, non sunt tamen ab earum spe causae diligendi profectae. [31] Ut enim benefici liberalesque sumus non ut exigamus gratiam (neque enim beneficium feneramur, sed natura propensi ad liberalitatem sumus), sic amicitiam non spe mercedis adducti, sed quod omnis eius fructus in ipso amore inest, expetendam putamus.

[32]   Ab his, qui pecudum ritu ad voluptatem omnia referunt, longe dissentiunt; nec mirum; nihil enim altum, nihil magnificum ac divinum suspicere possunt, qui suas omnes cogitationes abiecerunt in rem tam humilem tamque contemptam.   Quamobrem

their feelings are easily seen. This appears much more clearly in mankind; first in the affection that exists between parents and children, which cannot, except by some abominable crime, be broken apart; secondly, in cases when we find a person with whom we have an affinity in character and personality, and a similar feeling of love arises, because we seem to see in him as it were a gleam of virtue and good character. [28] For excellence of character excites affection more than anything else, and attracts others to love its possessor. In fact, on account of virtue and good character, we may even in a certain sense love those we have never seen. Who does not recall Gaius Fabricius or Manius Curius with a certain affection and goodwill, even though he has never seen them? Yet who does not hate Tarquinius Superbus, Spurius Cassius, Spurius Maelius? We have fought for supremacy in Italy against two leaders, Pyrrhus and Hannibal. Because of the former's good character, we are not too hostile to his memory; but the other will always be hated by our people for his cruelty. [IX:29] If, then, the force of good character is such that we love it even in those we have never seen, or for that matter even in an enemy, what wonder if the minds of men are affected in this way when they observe virtue and goodness in those with whom they are able to be associated in everyday life?

Yet the strengthening of love does indeed come from the receiving of kindnesses, from the observation of the other's interest, and from the building up of familiarity. When these things are added to that first stirring of the mind and of the affections, a truly amazing intensity of goodwill blazes forth. If any think that this derives from weakness, and from the necessity for each to acquire from the other what he himself lacks, certainly they leave friendship with a mean origin and, so to speak, with no aristocratic lineage, since they wish us to believe it born of Need and Insufficiency. If this were so, those fittest for friendship would be those with least confidence in themselves; but the facts are quite otherwise. [30] In fact an individual excels most in the acquisition and preservation of friendships according as he is fortified with good qualities and wisdom in himself and stands least in need of another, regarding everything that concerns him as within his own control. Do you think that Africanus was in need of me? Of course not, and neither was I in need of him; but I grew to love him because of admiration for his excellent qualities, and he, in return, perhaps because of some opinion he had formed of my character, loved me. Goodwill was increased by familiarity; but though many great advantages followed, it was not from the hope of these that the cause of affection initially arose. [31] For as we practise kindness and generosity not for the purpose of exacting a reward (for we do not invest our kindness at a rate of interest; it is by nature that we are disposed to generosity), so friendship is desirable for us not because we are attracted by the thought of recompense, but because the affection contains its own fruits within itself.

[32] Very different from this is the opinion of those who, in swinish manner, refer everything to pleasure. That is not surprising, since they have thrown away all their thoughts on something so lowly and despised, and cannot look up towards anything high and noble and divine. Let us therefore leave them out of this argument, and let us

hos quidem ab hoc sermone removeamus, ipsi autem intellegamus natura gigni sensum diligendi et benevolentiae caritatem, facta significatione piobitatis. Quam qui appetiverunt, applicant se et propius admovent, ut et usu eius quem diligere coeperunt fruantur et moribus, sintque pares in amore et aequales, propensioresque ad bene merendum quam ad reposcendum, atque haec inter eos sit honesta certatio. Sic et utilitates ex amicitia maximae capientur, et erit ortus a natura quam ab imbecillitate gravior et verior. Nam si utilitas amicitias conglutinaret, eadem commutata dissolveret; sed quia natura mutari non potest, idcirco verae amicitiae sempiternae sunt. Ortum quidem amicitiae videtis, nisi quid ad haec forte vultis.

FANNIVS: Tu vero perge, Laeli; pro hoc enim, qui minor est natu, meo iure respondeo.

[33] SCAEVOLA: Recte tu quidem; quamobrem audiamus.

[X] LAELIVS: Audite vero, optimi viri, ea quae saepissime inter me et Scipionem de amicitia disserebantur. Quamquam ille quidem nihil difficilius esse dicebat quam amicitiam usque ad extremum vitae diem permanere; nam vel ut non idem expediret incidere saepe, vel ut de re publica non idem sentiretur; mutari etiam mores hominum saepe dicebat, alias adversis rebus, alias aetate ingravescente. Atque earum rerum exemplum ex similitudine capiebat ineuntis aetatis, quod summi puerorum amores saepe una cum praetexta toga ponerentur. [34] Sin autem ad adulescentiam perduxissent*, dirimi tamen interdum contentione, vel uxoriae condicionis vel commodi alicuius quod idem adipisci uterque non posset. Quodsi qui longius in amicitia provecti essent, tamen saepe labefactari si in honoris contentionem incidissent; pestem enim nullam maiorem esse amicitiis quam in plerisque pecuniae cupiditatem, in optimis quibusque honoris certamen et gloriae, ex quo inimicitias maximas saepe inter amicissimos exstitisse. [35] Magna etiam discidia et plerumque iusta nasci, cum aliquid ab amicis quod rectum non esset postularetur, ut aut libidinis ministri aut adiutores essent ad iniuriam; quod qui recusarent, quamvis honeste id facerent, ius tamen amicitiae deserere arguerentur ab eis quibus obsequi nollent. Illos autem, qui quidvis ab amico auderent postulare, postulatione ipsa profiteri omnia se amici causa esse facturos; eorum querela non inveteratas modo* familiaritates exstingui solere, sed odia etiam gigni sempiterna. Haec ita multa quasi fata impendere amicitiis, ut omnia subterfugere non modo sapientiae sed etiam felicitatis diceret sibi videri.

[XI:36] Quamobrem id primum videamus, si placet, quatenus amor in amicitia progredi debeat. Numne si Coriolanus habuit amicos, ferre contra patriam arma illi cum

ourselves understand that the sense of loving, and that affection that consists in goodwill, come into being by nature, when an indication of good character has been given; and once one has been attracted by this, one attaches oneself to it and moves closer, so as to enjoy the society and the way of life of the person one has begun to love; with the result that the affection becomes equal and reciprocal, each partner being more disposed to do favours than to ask for them in return, and each competing honourably with the other in this matter. Thus the greatest advantages will be obtained from friendship, but at the same time it will also be true that it has its origin in nature – a truer and nobler beginning – and not in weakness. If it were simple expediency that cemented friendships together, a change in what is expedient would dissolve them; but since nature itself cannot be changed, true friendships are for that reason everlasting. You see, then, the origin of friendship – unless perhaps you have something to add to this.

FANNIUS. No, please go on, Laelius. (I think I can reply on behalf of Scaevola, who is younger than I am).

[33] SCAEVOLA. Yes, that's fine. Let us go on listening.

[X] LAELIUS. Listen then, my good friends, to some things concerning friendship that Scipio and I used very often to discuss. Yet now that I think of it, he used to say that nothing was more difficult than for friendship to continue until the last day of one's life; for it often happened that people's interests or their political opinions grew to differ; and he often said that men's characters changed with adverse fortune or with advancing age. As an illustration of this he used to make the comparison with the beginning of one's career, when the greatest of friendships among boys are often laid aside together with the toga praetexta. [34] If they carry them on into early manhood, they are sometimes torn apart by competition, whether over a marriage arrangement or some other desirable aim which they cannot both achieve. If any continue still further in their friendship, its foundations are often shaken if they come into competition for public office; for there is no greater plague affecting friendships than, in most people, the desire for money, but in the top ranks of society the race for public honour and glory, on account of which the greatest enmities may arise between those who were the best of friends. [35] Also, he would say, great divisions would arise, often with justification, when people were asked by their friends to do something that was not right, to help them in illicit pleasures or to assist them in doing wrong to another. Those who refuse to do such a thing, however honourably they may be acting, nevertheless are accused of deserting the duties of friendship by those with whose wishes they were unwilling to conform. As for those who have no scruples about asking anything whatever from their friends, they proclaim in the very act of asking that they themselves would do anything for the sake of a friend. Their accusations not only may put an end to old friendships, but also may cause lasting hatred. All these various kinds of fate, as it were, hang over friendships, in such a way that to escape them all requires, as he used to say, not only prudence but also good luck.

[XI:36]   Therefore let us first examine, if you will, the question of how far love for a friend ought to be taken. Do we think that, if Coriolanus had any friends, they ought to have taken up arms with him against their country? Should Vecellinus or Maelius have

Coriolano debuerunt? Num Vecellinum amici, regnum appetentem, num Maelium debuerunt iuvare? [37] Tiberium quidem Gracchum rem publicam vexantem a Q.Tuberone aequalibusque amicis derelictum videbamus; at C. Blossius Cumanus, hospes familiae vestrae, Scaevola, cum ad me (quod aderam Laenati et Rupilio consulibus in consilio) deprecatum venisset, hanc ut sibi ignoscerem causam adferebat, quod tanti Tiberium Gracchum fecisset ut quidquid ille vellet sibi faciendum putaret. Tum ego: "Etiamne si te in Capitolium faces ferre vellet?" "Numquam," inquit, "voluisset id quidem; sed si voluisset, paruissem." Videtis quam nefaria vox! Et hercule ita fecit, vel plus etiam quam dixit; non enim paruit ille Tiberii Gracchi temeritati, sed praefuit, nec se comitem illius furoris sed ducem praebuit. Itaque hac amentia, quaestione nova perterritus, in Asiam profugit, ad hostes se contulit, poenas rei publicae graves iustasque persolvit. Nulla est igitur excusatio peccati si amici causa peccaveris; nam cum conciliatrix amicitiae virtutis opinio fuerit, difficile est amicitiam manere si a virtute defeceris.

[38] Quodsi rectum statuerimus vel concedere amicis quidquid velint, vel impetrare ab eis quidquid velimus, perfecta quidem sapientia si simus*, nihil habeat res viti. Sed loquimur de eis amicis qui ante oculos sunt, quos videmus aut de quibus memoria accepimus, quos novit vita communis; ex hoc numero nobis exempla sumenda sunt, et eorum quidem maxime qui ad sapientiam proxime accedunt. [39] Videmus Papum Aemilium Luscino familiarem fuisse (sic a patribus accepimus), bis una consules, collegas in censura; tum et cum eis et inter se coniunctissimos fuisse Manium Curium, Tiberium Coruncanium memoriae proditum est. Igitur ne suspicari quidem possumus quemquam horum ab amico quidpiam contendisse quod contra fidem, contra ius iurandum, contra rem publicam esset. Nam hoc quidem in talibus viris quid attinet dicere, si contendisset impetraturum non fuisse, cum illi sanctissimi viri fuerint, aeque autem nefas sit tale aliquid et facere rogatum et rogare? At vero Tiberium Gracchum sequebantur C. Carbo, C. Cato et minime tum quidem Gaius frater, nunc idem acerrimus. [XII:40] Haec igitur lex in amicitia sanciatur, ut neque rogemus res turpes, nec faciamus rogati. Turpis enim excusatio est et minime accipienda, cum in ceteris peccatis, tum si quis contra rem publicam se amici causa fecisse fateatur.

Etenim eo loco, Fanni et Scaevola, locati sumus, ut nos longe prospicere oporteat futuros casus rei publicae. Deflexit iam aliquantum de spatio curriculoque consuetudo maiorum. [41] Tiberius Gracchus regnum occupare conatus est, vel regnavit is quidem paucos menses: numquid simile populus Romanus audierat aut viderat? Hunc etiam post mortem secuti amici et propinqui quid in Publio Nasica* effecerint, sine lacrimis non queo dicere. Nam Carbonem, quoquo modo potuimus*, propter recentem poenam

been helped by their friends, when aiming at tyranny? [37] Indeed, when Tiberius Gracchus was stirring up political turmoil, we saw him deserted by Quintus Tubero and his friends of the same age; yet Gaius Blossius of Cumae, a guest of your family, Scaevola, when he came to me to plead on his own behalf (since I was then assisting the consuls Laenas and Rupilius in an advisory capacity), brought forward this as a reason why I should pardon him, that he had such respect for Tiberius Gracchus that he would consider himself bound to carry out whatever Gracchus wanted. "Even," I said, "if he wanted you to set the Capitol on fire?" "He would never have wanted that," he answered, "but if he had, I would have complied." You can see what a pernicious thing to say that was; and, in fact, he put it into practice, or even did more than he said: he did not simply follow the rash designs of Tiberius Gracchus, but was the author of them; he made it clear that he was not just a companion in Gracchus's madness, but took the lead in it. In this state of folly, frightened by the new tribunal that was set up, he fled to Asia and delivered himself to the enemies of Rome; and in due course suffered the dire and just retribution that the Republic demanded. Thus it is no excuse for wrongdoing if one does wrong for the sake of a friend, for, since the belief in each other's good character was the agent that brought the friends together in the first place, it is difficult for friendship to remain if one leaves the path of goodness.

[38] Yet there would be nothing wrong in laying down that it is right either to grant our friends whatever they wish, or to obtain whatever we desire from them, supposing that we were equipped with perfect wisdom. However, we are speaking of those friends who are before our eyes, whom we can see or have heard of in history, those with whom ordinary life is acquainted; from their number we must take our examples, and in particular those of them who come nearest to wisdom. [39] We see that Aemilius Papus was a friend of Fabricius Luscinus (so we have heard from our fathers): they were consuls together twice, and colleagues in the censorship; and the tradition is that Manius Curius and Tiberius Coruncanius were at that time very closely associated both with them and with each other. We cannot, then, suspect that any of these asked their friends to do anything which went against their duty, against their oath of office, or against the public interest. In connection with such men, it is hardly relevant to say that if they had asked it would not have been granted; they were men of the highest virtue, and it would be equally wicked either to do such a thing when asked, or to ask another to do it. Yet, on the other hand, Gaius Carbo and Gaius Cato followed Tiberius Gracchus; his brother Gaius did not, indeed, follow him then, but is now doing so most determinedly. [XII:40] Therefore let us enact this law concerning friendship, that we should not ask disgraceful things, nor do them if asked. It is a bad and unacceptable excuse for any sort of wrongdoing, but particularly if a man says that he has acted against the interests of the state for the sake of his friend.

Indeed, Fannius and Scaevola, our position is such that it is our duty to look far ahead towards the future state of the Republic. Already the old ways of doing things have veered to some extent off the straight course. [41] Tiberius Gracchus tried to establish a tyranny; indeed one may say that he acted as a tyrant for a few months. Had the people of Rome seen or heard anything like it before? As for what his friends and relatives, following him after his death, did to Publius Nasica, I cannot speak of it without tears. We kept Carbo in check as best we could, since the fate of Tiberius Gracchus was still

Ti. Gracchi sustinuimus; de Gai Gracchi autem tribunatu quid exspectem, non libet augurari. Serpit diem e die res quae proclivis ad perniciem, cum semel coepit, labitur. Videtis in tabella iam ante quanta sit facta labes, primo Gabinia lege, biennio post Cassia. Videre iam videor populum a senatu disiunctum, multitudinis arbitrio res maximas agi; plures enim discent quemadmodum haec fiant, quam quemadmodum his resistatur.

[42] Quorsum haec? Quia sine sociis nemo quidquam tale conatur. Praecipiendum est igitur bonis, ut si in eiusmodi amicitias ignari casu aliquo inciderint, ne existiment ita se alligatos ut ab amicis in magna aliqua re* peccantibus non discedant; improbis autem poena statuenda est, nec vero minor eis qui secuti erunt alterum quam eis qui ipsi fuerint impietatis duces. Quis clarior in Graecia Themistocle, quis potentior? qui cum imperator bello Persico servitute Graeciam liberavisset, propterque invidiam in exsilium expulsus esset, ingratae patriae iniuriam non tulit quam ferre debuit: fecit idem quod viginti annis ante apud nos fecerat Coriolanus. His adiutor contra patriam inventus est nemo; itaque mortem sibi uterque conscivit. [43] Quare talis improborum consensio non modo excusatione amicitiae tegenda non est, sed potius supplicio omni vindicanda est, ut ne quis concessum putet amicum vel bellum patriae inferentem sequi; quod quidem, ut res ire coepit, haud scio an aliquando futurum sit; mihi autem non minori curae est qualis res publica post mortem meam futura, quam qualis hodie sit.

[XIII:44] Haec igitur prima lex amicitiae sanciatur, ut ab amicis honesta petamus, amicorum causa honesta faciamus; ne exspectemus quidem dum rogemur; studium semper adsit, cunctatio absit; consilium vero* dare audeamus libere; plurimum in amicitia amicorum bene suadentium valeat auctoritas; eaque et adhibeatur ad monendum, non modo aperte sed etiam acriter, si res postulabit, et adhibitae pareatur.

[45] Nam quibusdam, quos audio sapientes habitos in Graecia, placuisse opinor mirabilia quaedam (sed nihil est quod illi non persequantur argutiis): partim fugiendas esse nimias amicitias, ne necesse sit unum sollicitum esse pro pluribus; satis superque esse sibi suarum cuique rerum, alienis nimis implicari molestum esse; commodissimum esse quam laxissimas habenas habere amicitiae, quas vel adducas cum velis, vel remittas; caput enim esse ad beate vivendum securitatem, qua frui non possit animus si tamquam parturiat unus pro pluribus. [46] Alios autem dicere aiunt, multo etiam inhumanius (quem locum breviter paulo ante perstrinxi), praesidi adiumentique

fresh in the mind; but I do not like to prophesy what I expect from Gaius Gracchus's tribunate. This evil creeps onwards from day to day; and once such a thing has begun, it slides steadily downhill towards disaster. You see what damage has been done even before in the matter of the ballot, first by Gabinius's law, then two years later by that of Cassius. Already I seem to see the people and Senate divided from each other, and the greatest decisions taken according to the will of the mob; for more will learn how these things can be done than how they may be resisted.

[42] Why all this? Because nobody tries to do anything of this sort without accomplices. For good men, therefore, we must lay down this rule, that if by some chance they fall unknowingly into a friendship of this sort, they must not think themselves bound by it to such an extent that they should not part company with their friends when the latter do wrong in some great matter; while for bad men a penalty must be laid down, no less for those who follow another than for those who are themselves the leaders in evil deeds. Who in Greece was more famous or powerful than Themistocles? After he had been supreme commander in the Persian war, and had liberated Greece from the threat of slavery, he was driven out into exile because of the jealousy he had aroused. He did not, as he should have done, put up with the wrong done to him by his ungrateful homeland; he did the same thing as Coriolanus had done here twenty years earlier. Yet neither of these found any helper in fighting against their country; so both in the end committed suicide. [43] Therefore not only should we not use the excuse of friendship to protect this sort of conspiracy of bad men, but it should be punished with all possible severity, so as to prevent anyone from thinking that he can follow even a friend who is waging war on his country – which I am not sure will not happen one of these days, given the way things have started to go. For I am no less concerned with the state of the Republic after I am dead, than with the way it is today.

[XIII:44] So then, let this first law of friendship be enacted: that we should ask only honourable things of our friends, and do honourable things for their sake; indeed, we should not wait until we are asked, but should always show keenness, never hesitation. We should have the confidence to give advice freely; in friendship the influence of those friends who give good advice should be paramount, and it should be applied where advice is necessary, not only openly but even forcefully, if circumstances demand; and when applied, it should be heeded.

[45] Now some who are, as I hear, considered in Greece to be wise men, have held, I believe, some very strange doctrines on this subject; but then there is no subject on which they do not exercise their subtleties. Some of them think that excessively close friendships are to be avoided, lest it be necessary for one person to be troubled on account of others; that everyone has enough and to spare of his own affairs, and it is troublesome to be involved too much in those of other men; that it is best to keep the reins of friendship as loose as possible, so that you can draw them in when you wish, or slacken them again; for they say that the chief requirement for a happy life is freedom from care, which one cannot enjoy if (as it were) one's mind is in labour on behalf of many. [46] Others are reported to say, in a way even less consistent with human nature – I touched briefly on this subject earlier – that friendships should be sought for the sake

causa, non benevolentiae neque caritatis, amicitias esse expetendas; itaque ut quisque minimum firmitatis haberet minimumque virium, ita amicitias appetere maxime; ex eo fieri ut mulierculae magis amicitiarum praesidia quaerant quam viri, et inopes quam opulenti, et calamitosi quam ei qui putentur beati.

[47] O praeclaram sapientiam! Solem enim e mundo tollere videntur qui amicitiam e vita tollunt, qua nihil a dis immortalibus melius habemus, nihil iucundius. Quae est enim ista securitas? Specie quidem blanda; sed reapse multis locis repudianda. Neque enim est consentaneum ullam honestam rem actionemve, ne sollicitus sis, aut non suscipere aut susceptam deponere; quodsi curam fugimus, virtus fugienda est, quae necesse est cum aliqua cura res sibi contrarias aspernetur atque oderit, ut bonitas malitiam, temperantia libidinem, ignaviam fortitudo; itaque videas rebus iniustis iustos maxime dolere, imbellibus fortes, flagitiosis modestos; ergo hoc proprium est animi bene constituti, et laetari bonis rebus et dolere contrariis. [48] Quamobrem si cadit in sapientem animi dolor (qui profecto cadit, nisi ex eius animo exstirpatam humanitatem arbitramur), quae causa est cur amicitiam funditus tollamus e vita, ne aliquas propter eam suscipiamus molestias? Quid enim interest, motu animi sublato, non dico inter pecudem et hominem, sed inter hominem et truncum aut saxum aut quidvis generis eiusdem? Neque enim sunt isti audiendi, qui virtutem duram et quasi ferream esse quandam volunt; quae quidem est cum multis in rebus, tum in amicitia, tenera atque tractabilis, ut et bonis amici quasi diffundatur, et incommodis contrahatur. Quamobrem angor iste qui pro amico saepe capiendus est, non tantum valet ut tollat e vita amicitiam, non plus quam ut virtutes quia nonnullas curas et molestias adferunt repudientur.

[XIV] Cum autem contrahat amicitiam, ut supra dixi, si qua* significatio virtutis eluceat, ad quam se similis animus applicet et adiungat, id cum contigit, amor exoriatur necesse est. [49] Quid enim tam absurdum quam delectari multis inanibus rebus, ut honore, ut gloria, ut aedificio, ut vestitu cultuque corporis, animo autem virtute praedito, eo qui vel amare vel (ut ita dicam) redamare possit, non admodum delectari? Nihil est enim remuneratione benevolentiae, nihil vicissitudine studiorum officiorumque iucundius. [50] Quid si illud etiam addimus, quod recte addi potest, nihil esse quod ad se rem ullam tam illiciat et tam trahat quam ad amicitiam similitudo? Concedetur profecto verum esse, ut bonos boni diligant adsciscantque sibi quasi propinquitate coniunctos atque natura; nihil est enim appetentius similium sui nec rapacius quam natura. Quamobrem hoc quidem, Fanni et Scaevola, constet, ut opinor: bonis inter bonos quasi

of protection and help, but not because of goodwill and affection; therefore, whoever has the least strength and stability ought to seek friendships most of all. From this it would follow that the protection that comes from friendship should be looked for more by women than by men, by the poor more than the wealthy, and by those in disastrous circumstances more than by those who are thought happy.

[47] Wonderful wisdom indeed! It is as though they were to tear the sun out of the sky, these people who deprive human life of friendship, than which we have no better or pleasanter gift from the gods. For what is that freedom from care that they talk of? In appearance, indeed, it is attractive, but in truth it is in many instances to be rejected. It is not reasonable to refuse to undertake any honourable task or activity, or to lay it aside once undertaken, in order to avoid trouble. If we are to run away from anxiety, we must run away from virtue, which naturally feels a certain sense of anxiety when it meets things contrary to itself, and finds them hateful and repulsive; as good nature is repelled by ill nature, self-control by excess, courage by cowardice; similarly one may see that just men are most distressed by instances of injustice, brave men by cowardly behaviour, decently-behaved men by indecency. It is the property of a well-constituted mind to be glad at good things, and to be distressed by the opposite. [48] Therefore, if distress of mind is permissible in a wise man at all (which it surely is, unless we think that human qualities have been altogether uprooted from his mind), what reason is there why we should totally remove friendship from life merely to avoid having to go to some trouble because of it? If you take away the mind's capacity to feel emotion, what difference is there, I do not say between an animal and a man, but between a man and a tree-trunk or a rock or anything else of that kind? We must not listen to those who wish virtue to be something hard and, as it were, ironclad; in fact, in many matters, but particularly in friendship, it is tender and malleable, so as to spread itself (as it were) on account of a friend's good fortune, and to contract when he is unfortunate. Therefore the fact that one often has to be anxious on behalf of a friend has no more power to remove friendship from life, than it has to make us abandon such virtuous actions as bring with them certain cares and anxieties.

[XIV] Further, given that, as I said before, it is the appearance of some sign of good character in a person that draws friendship together, shining out, as it were, and inviting another similar person to join with him and attach himself to him, it is inevitable that, when that happens, a feeling of affection should arise. [49] But what can be so absurd as to take pleasure in all sorts of empty things, like honour and glory, buildings or fine clothes or bodily ornaments, and yet not to take the highest pleasure of all in a mind endowed with good character – the one thing which is capable of loving or (if I may use the word) reciprocating love? There is surely nothing more pleasant than to receive a return for one's kindness, or to exchange support and assistance with another. [50] Suppose that we grant in addition what can quite rightly be granted, that nothing has such a power to attract and draw things to itself, as likeness does in drawing people together into friendship: then, surely, it will be conceded to be true that good men love good men and are attracted to one another, being linked as if by a natural bond or a family relationship; for there is no stronger desire or tendency than that of human nature to seize upon things like itself. Therefore, Fannius and Scaevola, let us agree on this:

necessariam benevolentiam, qui est amicitiae fons a natura constitutus. Sed eadem bonitas etiam ad multitudines pertinet; non enim est inhumana virtus neque immanis* neque superba, quae etiam populos universos tueri eisque optime consulere soleat, quod non faceret profecto si a caritate vulgi abhorreret.

[51] Atque etiam mihi quidem videntur qui utilitatum causa fingunt amicitias, amabilissimum nodum amicitiae tollere. Non enim tam utilitas parta per amicum, quam amici amor ipse delectat; tumque illud fit quod ab amico est profectum iucundum, si cum studio est profectum; tantumque abest ut amicitiae propter indigentiam colantur, ut ei qui opibus et copiis, maximeque virtute (in qua plurimum est praesidi), minime alterius indigeant, liberalissimi sint et beneficentissimi. Atqui* haud sciam an ne opus sit quidem nihil umquam omnino deesse amicis; ubi enim studia nostra viguissent, si numquam consilio, numquam opera nostra nec domi nec militiae Scipio eguisset? Non igitur utilitatem amicitia, sed utilitas amicitiam secuta est.

[XV:52] Non ergo erunt homines deliciis diffluentes audiendi, si quando de amicitia, quam nec usu nec ratione habent cognitam, disputabunt. Nam quis est, pro deorum fidem atque hominum, qui velit, ut neque diligat quemquam nec ipse ab ullo diligatur, circumfluere omnibus copiis atque in omnium rerum abundantia vivere? Haec enim est tyrannorum vita nimirum, in qua nulla fides, nulla caritas, nulla stabilis benevolentiae potest esse fiducia: omnia semper suspecta atque sollicita, nullus locus amicitiae; [53] quis enim aut eum diligit quem metuat, aut eum a quo se metui putet? Coluntur tamen simulatione dumtaxat ad tempus; quodsi forte, ut fit plerumque, ceciderunt, tum intellegitur quam fuerint inopes amicorum; quod Tarquinium dixisse ferunt exsulantem, tum se intellexisse quos fidos amicos habuisset, quos infidos, cum iam neutris gratiam referre posset; [54] quamquam miror, illa superbia et importunitate, si quemquam amicum habere potuit; atque ut huius quem dixi mores veros amicos parare non potuerunt, sic multorum opes praepotentium excludunt amicitias fideles. Non enim solum ipsa Fortuna caeca est, sed eos etiam plerumque efficit caecos quos complexa est; itaque efferuntur fere fastidio et contumacia, nec quidquam insipiente fortunato intolerabilius fieri potest. Atque hoc quidem videre licet, eos qui antea commodis fuerint moribus, imperio potestate prosperis rebus immutari, sperni ab eis veteres amicitias indulgeri novis. [55] Quid autem stultius quam cum plurimum copiis facultatibus opibus possint, cetera parare quae parantur pecunia – equos, famulos, vestem egregiam, vasa pretiosa – amicos non parare, optimam et pulcherrimam vitae, ut ita dicam, supellectilem? Etenim cetera cum parant, cui parent nesciunt, nec cuius causa laborent;

that as far as good men are concerned, goodwill between one and another is more or less inevitable, and that this is the origin of friendship as determined by nature. Yet this same goodness extends also to groups of people collectively; for virtue is not inhuman or savage or arrogant, being accustomed as it is to watch over whole peoples and to provide as well as possible for them. It would certainly not do this if the affection of the multitude were abhorrent to it.

[51] Again, it seems to me that those who pretend that friendships exist for the sake of utility remove the pleasantest bond of friendship. It is not so much the advantage gained through a friend, as the love of the friend itself that delights one. What comes from a friend becomes pleasant precisely when it is done with goodwill. And so far from friendships being cultivated because of need, it is those who have least need of the wealth and resources of others, and especially of their virtue (in which the greatest protection lies), who are the kindest and most generous. And yet perhaps it is not an advantage either if friends never lack anything at all. For how could our kindness have had a chance to flourish if Scipio had never wanted my advice or my help either at home or abroad? The friendship did not follow from the pursuit of utility, but utility certainly followed from friendship.

[XV:52] We must not, then, listen to persons who overflow with self-indulgence when they argue about friendship, of which they have no real knowledge either in theory or in experience. For who, in the name of all the gods, would wish to be surrounded by every sort of wealth and live in an abundance of everything he could desire, on condition that he should not love anyone or be himself loved by anyone? This is, indeed, the life that tyrants live, in which there can be no good faith, no affection, no certain confidence of another's goodwill; in which there is constant suspicion and vexation, and no place for friendship; [53] for who loves a person whom he fears, or a person by whom he thinks he is feared? Of course, tyrants have pretended friends who pay them attentions for a time, for expediency's sake; but if they should happen to fall from power, as often happens, then it is realised how short of friends they were. They say that Tarquin, when he was in exile, said that he only then realised which of his friends were loyal and which were not, now that he could no longer reward either as they deserved; [54] though I am surprised that he, with his arrogance and lack of consideration for others, could have had any friends at all. Indeed, often the wealth and influence of powerful men excludes the possibility of faithful friendships, in the same way that Tarquin's mode of life could not attract real friends. For not only is Fortune herself blind, but she also often makes blind those of whom she takes hold, with the result that they tend to be carried away by pride and arrogance. There can be nothing more intolerable than a man who is stupid and successful at the same time. And we see too that men who were previously of a reasonable nature are changed by power and influence and good fortune; they cast away their old friendships and favour new ones. [55] But what is more foolish than for men who have the wealth, the influence and the opportunity to achieve as much as they want, to obtain those other things that money can buy – horses, slaves, fine clothing, valuable tableware – and not to obtain friends, which are (so to speak) the best and finest sort of furniture for life? Indeed, when they procure the other things, they do not know for whom they are getting them, or for whose benefit they are taking all that trouble, for all

eius enim est istorum quidque qui vicit viribus; amicitiarum sua cuique permanet stabilis et certa possessio, ut etiamsi illa maneant quae sunt quasi dona fortunae, tamen vita inculta et deserta ab amicis non possit esse iucunda.

Sed haec hactenus; [XVI:56] constituendi autem sunt qui sint in amicitia fines et quasi termini deligendi.* De quibus tres video sententias ferri, quarum nullam probo: unam ut eodem modo erga amicum adfecti simus quo erga nosmet ipsos; alteram ut nostra in amicos benevolentia illorum erga nos benevolentiae pariter aequaliterque respondeat; tertiam ut quanti quisque se ipse facit, tanti fiat ab amicis. [57] Harum trium sententiarum nulli prorsus assentior. Nec enim illa prima vera est, ut quemadmodum in se quisque sit, sic in amicum sit animatus: quam multa enim, quae nostra causa numquam faceremus, facimus causa amicorum – precari ab indigno, supplicare, tum acerbius in aliquem invehi insectarique vehementius; quae in nostris rebus non satis honeste, in amicorum fiunt honestissime. Multaeque res sunt in quibus de suis commodis viri boni multa detrahunt detrahique patiantur, ut eis amici potius quam ipsi fruantur.

[58] Altera sententia est quae definit amicitiam paribus officiis ac voluntatibus. Hoc quidem est nimis exigue et exiliter ad calculos vocare amicitiam, ut par sit ratio acceptorum et datorum. Divitior mihi et affluentior videtur esse vera amicitia, nec observare restricte ne plus reddat quam acceperit; neque enim verendum est ne quid excidat, aut ne quid in terram defluat, aut ne plus aequo quid in amicitiam congeratur.

[59] Tertius vero ille finis deterrimus, ut quanti quisque se ipse faciat, tanti fiat ab amicis. Saepe enim in quibusdam aut animus abiectior est, aut spes amplificandae fortunae fractior. Non est igitur amici talem esse in eum qualis ille in se est, sed potius eniti et efficere ut amici iacentem animum excitet, inducatque spem cogitationemque meliorem.

Alius igitur finis verae amicitiae constituendus est, si prius quid maxime reprehendere Scipio solitus sit edixero. Negabat ullam vocem inimiciorem amicitiae potuisse reperiri, quam eius qui dixisset ita amare oportere, ut si aliquando esset osurus; nec vero se adduci posse ut hoc, quemadmodum putaretur, a Biante esse dictum crederet, qui sapiens habitus esset unus e Septem: impuri cuiusdam aut ambitiosi aut omnia ad suam potentiam revocantis esse sententiam. Quonam enim modo quisquam amicus esse poterit eius cui se putabit inimicum esse posse? Quin etiam necesse erit cupere et optare

those things belong in the end to whoever can lay his hands on them by force; but each man has a permanent, stable and undisputed possession of those friendships which he has. Even if those other things, which are more or less gifts of fortune, were to remain with one, nevertheless a life devoid of friends and deserted by them could not be enjoyable.

But that is enough on that point. [XVI:56] It remains to decide on a definition of the scope of friendship, and, as it were, on the boundaries we are to choose for it. On this subject I see that three opinions are current, none of which I approve of: first, that we should have the same attitude towards a friend as we have towards ourselves; second, that our goodwill towards our friends should correspond equally and fairly to theirs towards us; third, that a man should be valued by his friends at precisely the value he puts upon himself. [57] I do not agree at all with any of these three views. The first, that each man should have the same attitude towards his friend as he has towards himself, is certainly not right: look at all the things we do for friends, that we should never do on our own account, such as begging and beseeching for favour from someone unworthy of such deference, or attacking and inveighing against a person more strongly than we otherwise would. It would be undignified to do either of these things for one's own sake, but it is perfectly honourable to do so on behalf of a friend. And there are many occasions when a good man diminishes his own advantage, or allows it to be diminished, in order that his friends rather than he himself should have the benefit.

[58] The second view is the one that defines friendship in terms of equality of favours and of goodwill. Surely this constitutes calling friendship to account in too mean and narrow a fashion, making sure that the debit and credit sides balance equally. True friendship seems to me to be richer and more generous than this; it should not worry too precisely whether it has paid out more than it has received; for there is no need to fear that something may escape notice or fall to the ground, or that one may tie up in a friendship more of one's assets than one should.

[59] But the third definition is surely the worst of the three, the idea that a man should be valued by his friends as he values himself. For it often happens that some people's self-confidence is low, or that their hopes of improving their lot have been dashed. In such a case it would not be a friend's duty to take the same view of a person as he takes of himself, but rather to make every effort to revive his low spirits, and induce in him greater confidence and a better frame of mind.

We must therefore decide on a different definition of real friendship; but first let me make known to you what Scipio used to object to most of all. He used to say that no saying more unfriendly to friendship could have been invented, than that of whoever said that one ought to love as if one were some day going to hate. Nor, he said, could he be brought to believe that this was said, as was alleged, by Bias, who was thought to be a wise man, one of the Seven: it must be the opinion of some corrupt character, or an ambitious politician, or one who looked at everything from the point of view of his own power. How can anyone be a friend to a person, when he thinks he may one day be his enemy? Indeed, in that case it is inevitable that one would desire and hope that the friend

ut quam saepissime peccet amicus, quo plures det sibi tamquam ansas ad reprehendendum; rursum autem recte factis commodisque amicorum necesse erit angi, dolere, invidere. [60] Quare hoc quidem praeceptum, cuiuscumque est, ad tollendam amicitiam valet. Illud potius praecipiendum fuit, ut eam diligentiam adhiberemus in amicitiis comparandis, ut ne quando amare inciperemus eum quem aliquando odisse possemus. Quin etiam si minus felices in deligendo* fuissemus, ferendum id Scipio potius quam inimicitiarum tempus cogitandum putabat.

[XVII:61] His igitur finibus utendum arbitror, ut cum emendati mores amicorum sint, tum sit inter eos omnium rerum, consiliorum, voluntatum sine ulla exceptione communitas; ut etiam si qua fortuna acciderit ut minus iustae amicorum voluntates adiuvandae sint, in quibus eorum aut caput agatur aut fama, declinandum de via sit, modo ne summa turpitudo sequatur. Est enim quatenus amicitiae dari venia possit. Nec vero neglegenda est fama, nec mediocre telum ad res gerendas existimare oportet benevolentiam civium; quam blanditiis et assentando colligere turpe est: virtus, quam sequitur caritas, minime repudianda est.

[62] Sed - saepe enim redeo ad Scipionem, cuius omnis sermo erat de amicitia – querebatur quod omnibus in rebus homines diligentiores essent: capras et oves quot quisque haberet dicere posse, amicos quot haberet non posse dicere; et in illis quidem parandis adhibere curam, in amicis eligendis neglegentes esse, nec habere quasi signa quaedam et notas, quibus eos qui ad amicitias essent idonei iudicarent.

Sunt igitur firmi et stabiles et constantes eligendi, cuius generis est magna penuria. Et iudicare difficile est sane nisi expertum; experiendum autem est in ipsa amicitia. Ita praecurrit amicitia iudicium, tollitque experiendi potestatem. [63] Est igitur prudentis sustinere ut currum, sic impetum benevolentiae, quo utamur quasi equis temptatis, sic amicitia aliqua parte periclitatis moribus amicorum.* Quidam saepe in parva pecunia perspiciuntur quam sint leves; quidam autem, quos parva movere non potuit, cognoscuntur in magna. Sin vero erunt aliqui reperti qui pecuniam praeferre amicitiae sordidum existiment, ubi eos inveniemus qui honores, magistratus, imperia, potestates, opes, amicitiae non anteponant, ut cum ex altera parte proposita haec sint, ex altera ius amicitiae, non multo illa malint? Imbecilla enim est natura ad contemnendam potentiam; quam etiamsi neglecta amicitia consecuti sint, obscuratum iri arbitrantur, quia non sine magna causa sit neglecta amicitia. [64] Itaque verae amicitiae difficillime reperiuntur in eis qui in honoribus reque publica versantur; ubi enim istum invenias, qui honorem amici anteponat suo? Quid, haec ut omittam, quam graves, quam difficiles

should do wrong as often as possible, so as to provide all the more handles (as it were) for complaint; conversely, it would be inevitable that one would be worried and hurt and envious when one's friend did something well or had a stroke of good luck. [60] This precept, then, whoever it belongs to, has the effect of destroying friendship. It ought rather to have been laid down that we should employ such care in forming friendships that we should never begin to love a person that we might one day hate. Even if we have been unlucky in our choice of friends, Scipio thought we should endure it, rather than look for the opportunity to start a quarrel.

[XVII:61] This, then, I think, is the definition we must use. Whenever the characters of friends are blameless, they should have a complete community in all things without exception; they should share their thoughts together, and have identical aims in their actions. However, if by some chance it happens that one has to help a friend in some objective that is not quite right, and their life or reputation is at stake, one should depart from the straight course as long as extreme disgrace does not follow. There is a certain extent to which faults can be pardoned on account of friendship. However, one's reputation is certainly not to be neglected. One must not think that the goodwill of the people is of less than prime importance as a weapon for achieving one's objects; and while to court it by flattery and blandishments is a base thing, one must not on any account reject genuine virtue, which is a source of popularity.

[62] But Scipio – for I keep returning to Scipio, who used to talk constantly about friendship – used to complain that men took less care about it than about anything else; everyone could say how many goats and sheep he had, but could not say how many friends he had; and he said that people take care over buying the former, but are careless in the choice of the latter, and do not have (as it were) any sure signs and marks whereby they can tell who is suitable for friendship.

One ought, then, surely to choose those who are strong and stable and reliable; but there is a great shortage of this kind of men. And it is difficult to judge except when one has tried them out; and the trial must be made in friendship itself. So friendship runs on ahead of judgement, and pre-empts the possibility of making the trial. [63] Therefore it is a wise man's duty to hold back the first rush of goodwill, as he would hold in the reins of a chariot, in order that one may test the characters of one's friends, as one tries out a team of horses, before pursuing friendship. Some are often shown to be unreliable with small amounts of money; some, who cannot be corrupted by small sums, are seen for what they are when large ones are in question. Yet supposing that one has found some who think it disgraceful to put money before friendship, where shall we find those who do not attach more importance to public honours, magistracies, commands, power and wealth, so that when these are placed on one side, and the demands of friendship on the other, they do not greatly prefer the former? Human nature is at its weakest when it comes to refusing power; and those who achieve power at the expense of friendship think the fact will go unnoticed, because they had a good reason for their neglect of friendship's duties. [64] Thus true friendships are very difficult to find among those who spend their lives in politics and in positions of power. For where would you find a person who would prefer a friend's success in gaining office to his own? And besides

plerisque videntur calamitatum societates? Ad quas non est facile inventu qui descendant. Quamquam Ennius recte "Amicus certus in re incerta cernitur", tamen haec duo levitatis et infirmitatis plerosque convincunt, aut si in bonis rebus contemnunt, aut in malis deserunt. Qui igitur utraque in re gravem, constantem, stabilem se in amicitia praestiterit, hunc ex maxime raro genere hominum iudicare debemus et paene divino.

[XVIII:65] Firmamentum autem stabilitatis constantiaeque est, eius quam in amicitia quaerimus, fides: nihil est enim stabile quod infidum est. Simplicem praeterea et communem et consentientem, id est qui rebus eisdem moveatur, eligi par est; quae omnia pertinent ad fidelitatem. Neque enim fidum potest esse multiplex ingenium et tortuosum, neque vero qui non eisdem rebus movetur naturaque consentit aut fidus aut stabilis potest esse. Addendum eodem est ut ne criminibus aut inferendis delectetur aut credat oblatis; quae pertinent omnia ad eam quam iamdudum tracto constantiam. Ita fit verum illud quod initio dixi: amicitiam nisi inter bonos esse non posse. Est enim boni viri, quem eundem sapientem licet dicere, haec duo tenere in amicitia: primum ne quid fictum sit neve simulatum (aperte enim vel odisse magis ingenui est quam fronte occultare sententiam); deinde non solum ab aliquo allatas criminationes repellere, sed ne ipsum quidem esse suspiciosum, semper aliquid existimantem ab amico esse violatum. [66] Accedat huc suavitas quaedam oportet sermonum atque morum, haudquaquam mediocre condimentum amicitiae; tristitia autem et in omni re severitas habet illa quidem gravitatem, sed amicitia remissior esse debet et liberior et dulcior et ad omnem comitatem facilitatemque proclivior.

[XIX:67] Exsistit autem hoc loco quaedam quaestio subdifficilis: num quando amici novi digni amicitia veteribus sint anteponendi, ut equis vetulis teneros anteponere solemus. Indigna homine dubitatio: non enim debent esse amicitiarum, sicut aliarum rerum, satietates; veterrima quaeque, ut ea vina quae vetustatem ferunt, esse debent* suavissima, verumque illud est quod dicitur, multos modios salis simul edendos esse ut amicitiae munus expletum sit. [68] Novitates autem, si spem adferunt ut tamquam in herbis non fallacibus fructus appareat, non sunt illae quidem repudiandae, vetustas tamen loco suo conservanda; maxima est enim vis vetustatis et consuetudinis. Quin in ipso equo cuius modo feci mentionem, si nulla res impediat, nemo est quin eo quo consuevit libentius utatur quam intractato et novo. Nec vero in hoc*, quod est animal, sed in eis etiam quae sunt inanima consuetudo valet, cum locis ipsis delectemur, montuosis etiam et silvestribus, in quibus diutius commorati sumus.

[69] Sed maximum est in amicitia parem esse inferiori. Saepe enim excellentiae quaedam sunt, qualis erat Scipionis in nostro (ut ita dicam) grege. Numquam se ille

that, consider how unpleasant and intolerable most people find association with the unsuccessful: it is not easy to find those who would lower themselves to it. Though Ennius was right to say "Sure friends in unsure times are surely seen", still most people stand convicted of unreliability and inconstancy by one or other of these two things, when they neglect friends in their success, or desert them when they fail. So anyone who has shown himself to be reliable and stable and constant in friendship in both of these situations, should be judged to belong to a rare and almost divine breed of men.

[XVIII:65] The foundation of that stability and reliability that we look for in friendship, is good faith; nothing is stable which is unfaithful. Besides this, it is reasonable to choose someone of straightforward character, sociable, and sympathetic (that is to say, one who is affected by things in the same way as oneself), and all these things tend towards faithfulness. A many-sided and devious personality cannot be faithful; nor is it possible for a person who is not affected similarly to oneself, and has no natural sympathy for one, to be a faithful or reliable friend. To this we must add that a friend should not be eager to make accusations, or believe them when they are put forward; all this tends towards the reliability that I have been discussing all along. So it comes about that what I said at the beginning is true, that friendship cannot exist except in good men. For it requires a good man (whom we may also call a wise man) to keep hold of these two aspects of friendship: first that there should be no pretence or deceit (for even open hatred is more befitting a free man than to hide one's feelings under a false exterior), and second that he should not only repel accusations brought by any person, but neither should he himself be suspicious and always thinking that his friend has committed some offence. [66] There should also be a certain pleasantness of manner and conversation, not by any means an unimportant seasoning for friendship. For sternness and severity in all matters do indeed carry dignity with them, but friendship should be rather more relaxed and generous and pleasant, and more inclined to be easy-going and agreeable.

[XIX:67] Here there arises a slightly difficult question: whether there are occasions when one should prefer new friends, worthy of friendship, to old ones, in the same way as we usually prefer young horses to those that are jaded. But a civilised human being should be above such doubts. One should not get tired of friendships as one does of other things. As with wines that improve with age, the oldest should be the most pleasant; and it is a true saying that, to fulfil the requirements of friendship, one must eat many bags of salt together. [68] Novelty is not to be rejected, if like a healthy green cornfield it brings hope of a good harvest to come; but old friendship must be preserved in its rightful place, for the force of habit and long acquaintance is great. Even with horses, to revert to the comparison I just made, there is nobody who would not use one he is accustomed to in preference to a new and unbroken one, unless there is some special reason not to. Not only in the case of the horse, which is a living creature, but even in regard to inanimate things, the force of habit prevails; we take pleasure in places where we have stayed a long time, even mountainous and wild ones.

[69] It is very important in friendship to treat inferiors as equals. Often it happens that one person stands out over others, as Scipio did in what I may call our flock. He never

Philo, numquam Rupilio, numquam Mummio anteposuit, numquam inferioris ordinis amicis; Quintum vero Maximum fratrem, egregium virum omnino, sibi nequaquam parem, quod is anteibat aetate, tamquam superiorem colebat; suosque omnes per se ipsos* esse ampliores volebat. [70] Quod faciendum imitandumque est omnibus, ut si quam praestantiam virtutis ingeni fortunae consecuti sint, impertiant ea suis communicentque cum proximis; ut si parentibus nati sint humilibus, si propinquos habeant imbecilliore vel animo vel fortuna, eorum augeant opes eisque honori sint et dignitati; ut in fabulis, qui aliquamdiu propter ignorationem stirpis et generis in famulatu fuerint, cum cogniti sunt et aut deorum aut regum filii inventi, retinent tamen caritatem in pastores quos patres multos annos esse duxerunt. Quod est multo profecto magis in veris patribus certisque faciendum; fructus enim ingeni et virtutis omnisque praestantiae tum maximus capitur, cum in proximum quemque confertur. [XX:71] Ut igitur ei qui sunt in amicitiae coniunctionisque necessitudine superiores exaequare se cum inferioribus debent, sic inferiores non dolere se a suis aut ingenio aut fortuna aut dignitate superari. Quorum plerique aut queruntur semper aliquid aut etiam exprobrant, eoque magis si habere se putant quod officiose et amice et cum labore aliquo suo factum queant dicere: odiosum sane genus hominum, officia exprobrantium, quae meminisse debet is in quem collata sunt, non commemorare qui contulit. [72] Quamobrem ut ei qui superiores sunt submittere se debent in amicitia, sic quodammodo inferiores extollere. Sunt enim quidam qui molestas amicitias faciunt cum ipsi se contemni putant; quod non fere contingit nisi eis qui etiam contemnendos se arbitrantur; qui hac opinione non modo verbis sed etiam opere* levandi sunt. [73] Tantum autem cuique tribuendum; primum quantum ipse efficere possis, deinde etiam quantum ille, quem diligas atque adiuves, sustinere. Non enim tu possis, quamvis excellas, omnes tuos ad honores amplissimos perducere; ut Scipio P. Rupilium potuit consulem efficere, fratrem eius Lucium non potuit. Quodsi etiam possis quidvis deferre ad alterum, videndum est tamen quid ille possit sustinere.

[74] Omnino amicitiae corroboratis iam confirmatisque et ingeniis et aetatibus iudicandae sunt; nec si qui ineunte aetate venandi aut pilae studiosi fuerunt, eos habere necessarios* quos tum eodem studio praeditos dilexerunt. Isto enim modo nutrices et paedagogi iure vetustatis plurimum benevolentiae postulabunt; qui neglegendi quidem non sunt, sed alio quodam modo est* <.......> Aliter amicitiae stabiles permanere non possunt; dispares enim mores disparia studia sequuntur, quorum dissimilitudo dissociat amicitias;nec ob aliam causam ullam boni improbis, improbi bonis amici esse non possunt, nisi quod tanta est inter eos quanta maxima potest esse morum studiorumque distantia.

put himself before Philus or Rupilius or Mummius, or his friends of lower rank; and as for Quintus Maximus his brother, who was doubtless a fine character, but in no way equal to Scipio, he used to respect him as a superior, because he was older. His intention was that all his associates should have higher status in their own right. [70] This example should be followed by everyone. If a person possesses some outstanding quality, either in character or in intellectual gifts or in wealth, he should share it with his friends and hold it in common with those around him, so that, if he was born of humble parents, or has relatives who are weaker in their abilities or their fortune, he should add to their wealth, and be a cause of honour and dignity for them; just as in mythology, those who have been in slavery for a period because of ignorance of their birth and family, when they are recognised and found to be the sons of gods or kings, nevertheless retain their affection for the shepherds whom they thought for many years to be their fathers. Of course this applies all the more to real and legitimate fathers. The greatest benefit of intelligence or character or any excellence is felt when it is shared with those close to one. [XX:71] Not only should the superior partners in a friendship or association make themselves equal to the inferior; the inferior, also, should not mind being surpassed by their friends in intellect or wealth or rank. Many such people constantly complain, or even reproach their friends, about some matter or other, and all the more so if they can claim to have performed some service or friendly action and to have taken some trouble over it. An annoying breed of men, surely, who turn their services into a reproach. Such things should be remembered with gratitude by the recipient – not always talked about by the person who performed them. [72] Thus, as those who are superior should play down their own dignity in the context of friendship, so the inferior should as it were lift themselves up. There are some who make friendship troublesome by thinking that they themselves are being neglected; but this hardly happens except to those who think they are in a position where they do not deserve attention. They should be cured of this idea not only by argument, but also by helping them in practice. [73] As for the amount of consideration one should show, one should give each person in the first place as much as one can manage oneself, but one should also consider how much the person one is helping can take. However much you excel, you cannot raise all your friends to the highest honours; Scipio could make Publius Rupilius consul, but not his brother Lucius Rupilius. But even if you are able to give another man everything you wish to, you must still consider what he is capable of supporting.

[74] In general one cannot judge friendships until the parties have reached full strength and maturity, both in age and in intellect. If one was keen on hunting or ball-games when young, one does not have to keep as one's friends those whom one liked then because they had the same enthusiasm. On that principle one's nurse or tutor, simply on grounds of age, has the greatest claim of all to one's goodwill. Of course one should not neglect those; but ...... in some other way .... otherwise stable friendships cannot last. Different ways of life entail different interests, and difference of interests pushes friendships apart. Indeed there is no other reason why good men cannot be the friends of bad men, or bad men of good, than that there is the greatest possible difference of interests and way of life between them.

[75] Recte etiam praecipi potest in amicitiis, ne intemperata quaedam benevolentia, quod persaepe fit, impediat magnas utilitates amicorum. Nec enim, ut ad fabulas redeam, Troiam Neoptolemus capere potuisset, si Lycomedem, apud quem erat educatus, multis cum lacrimis iter suum impedientem audire voluisset. Et saepe incidunt magnae res, ut discedendum sit ab amicis; quas qui impedire vult eo quod desiderium non facile ferat, is et infirmus est mollisque natura, et ob eam ipsam causam in amicitia parum iustus. [76] Atque in omni re considerandum est et quid postules ab amico, et quid patiare a te impetrari.

[XXI] Est etiam quaedam calamitas in amicitiis dimittendis nonnumquam necessaria (iam enim a sapientium familiaritatibus ad vulgares amicitias oratio nostra delabitur). Erumpunt saepe vitia amicorum, tum in ipsos amicos, tum in alienos, quorum tamen ad amicos redundet infamia. Tales igitur amicitiae sunt remissione usus eluendae, et ut Catonem dicere audivi, dissuendae magis quam discindendae, nisi quaedam admodum intolerabilis iniuria exarserit, ut neque rectum neque honestum sit nec fieri possit ut non statim alienatio disiunctioque facienda sit. [77] Sin autem aut morum aut studiorum commutatio quaedam, ut fieri solet, facta erit, aut in rei publicae partibus dissensio intercesserit (loquor enim iam, ut paulo ante dixi, non de sapientium, sed de communibus amicitiis), cavendum erit ne non solum amicitiae depositae, sed etiam inimicitiae susceptae videantur. Nihil enim est turpius quam cum eo bellum gerere quocum familiariter vixeris. Ab amicitia Q. Pompei meo nomine se removerat, ut scitis, Scipio; propter dissensionem autem quae erat in re publica, alienatus est a collega nostro Metello; utrumque egit graviter ac moderate* et offensione animi non acerba. [78] Quamobrem primum danda opera est ne qua amicorum discidia fiant; sin tale aliquid evenerit, ut exstinctae potius amicitiae quam oppressae esse videantur. Cavendum vero ne etiam in graves inimicitias convertant se amicitiae, ex quibus iurgia maledicta contumeliae gignuntur. Quae tamen si tolerabiles erunt, ferendae sunt, et hic honos veteri amicitiae tribuendus, ut is in culpa sit qui faciat, non is qui patiatur iniuriam. Omnino omnium horum vitiorum atque incommodorum una cautio est atque una provisio, ut ne nimis cito diligere incipiant, neve non dignos. [79] Digni autem sunt amicitia quibus in ipsis est causa cur diligantur: rarum genus, et quidem omnia praeclara rara, nec quidquam difficilius quam reperire quod sit omni ex parte in suo genere perfectum.

Sed plerique neque in rebus humanis quidquam bonum norunt, nisi quod fructuosum sit, et amicos, tamquam pecudes, eos potissimum diligunt ex quibus sperant se maximum fructum esse capturos. [80] Ita pulcherrima illa et maxime naturali carent amicitia, per se et propter se expetita, nec ipsi sibi exemplo sunt, haec vis amicitiae et

[75] It is also right to warn against the possibility that an excessive concern for one's friends may, as often happens, get in the way of their real interests. To return to mythology, Neoptolemus could never have taken Troy if he had listened to Lycomedes, in whose house he was brought up, when he tried, amid floods of tears, to keep him from going on his journey. Often there are good reasons why one should have to part from one's friends; and anyone who tries to prevent this, on the ground that he will not easily put up with his friend's absence, is weak and soft in nature, and for that very reason not properly able to perform the duties of friendship. [76] And in every instance one must consider both what one is asking of one's friend, and what one is prepared to do for him.

[XXI] Sometimes there is an inevitable loss to be sustained in breaking off friendships (now our discussion is slipping from the companionships of the wise down towards ordinary friendships). Often a person's faults burst out to the surface: sometimes they affect his friends themselves, sometimes people who are unconnected, but the dishonour they cause still flows back to include the friends. Friendships of this sort are to be dissolved by gradually leaving off the habit of association; and, as I have heard Cato say, one should unpick the seam rather than tear it apart; that is, unless some really intolerable and flagrant wrong has been committed, so that it is not right or honourable or even possible to avoid an immediate estrangement and· separation. [77] But if some change of character or interests takes place, as it often does, or if friends are separated by a political disagreement (for I am now talking, as I said just now, not about the friendships of the wise, but about ordinary ones), one will need to be careful to avoid the impression that one has not only ended a friendship, but also started a quarrel. Nothing is more unbecoming than to wage war against someone with whom one has lived on friendly terms. As you know, Scipio broke off his friendship with Quintus Pompeius on my account, and because of a disagreement in politics he was estranged from our colleague Metellus. On both occasions he acted with dignity and restraint, and though he took offence, he did so without acrimony. [78] In the first place, therefore, one should make an effort to prevent separations of friends; but if such a thing does happen, one should make it appear that the friendship has burnt out of its own accord, and has not been suddenly quenched. And one should take care that friendships do not transform themselves into serious quarrels, giving rise to public confrontations, insults and injuries. But supposing that such things happen, they should be tolerated if they can be, and the former friendship should be respected to the extent that the doer of the injury, not the sufferer, should be blamed. But all in all, there is only one provision and precaution against all these faults and misfortunes: one should not start a friendship too quickly, and one should not make friends with those who do not deserve it. [79] By "those who deserve friendship" I mean those who carry in themselves the reason why they should be loved – a rare breed; and indeed all fine things are rare, and nothing is more difficult than to find what is in all respects perfect of its kind.

But many people have no idea of anything good in human life, other than what is profitable, and, just as with cattle, so with friends, they esteem the most those from whom they hope to gain the greatest profit. [80] Accordingly they are deprived of the finest and most natural form of friendship, the sort which is desired in itself and for its c·vn sake; and they do not see the example which they themselves provide of the

qualis et quanta sit. Ipse enim se quisque diligit, non ut aliquam a se ipse mercedem exigat caritatis suae, sed quod per se sibi quisque carus est; quod nisi idem in amicitiam transferetur, verus amicus numquam reperietur; est enim is qui est tamquam alter idem. [81] Quodsi hoc apparet in bestiis, volucribus nantibus agrestibus, cicuribus feris*, primum ut se ipsae diligant (id enim pariter cum omni animante nascitur), deinde ut requirant atque appetant ad quas se applicent eiusdem generis animantes, idque faciunt cum desiderio et cum quadam similitudine amoris humani, quanto id magis in homine fit natura, qui et se ipse diligit, et alterum anquirit cuius animum ita cum suo misceat ut efficiat paene unum ex duobus.

[XXII:82] Sed plerique perverse, ne dicam impudenter, habere talem amicum volunt quales ipsi esse non possunt, quaeque ipsi non tribuunt amicis, haec ab eis desiderant. Par est autem primum ipsum esse virum bonum, tum alterum similem sui quaerere. In talibus, ea quam iamdudum tractamus stabilitas amicitiae confirmari potest, cum homines benevolentia coniuncti primum cupiditatibus eis quibus ceteri serviunt imperabunt, deinde aequitate iustitiaque gaudebunt, omniaque alter pro altero suscipiet, neque quidquam umquam nisi honestum et rectum alter ab altero postulabit; neque solum colent inter se et diligent, sed etiam verebuntur; nam maximum ornamentum amicitiae tollit qui ex ea tollit verecundiam. [83] Itaque in eis perniciosus est error, qui existimant libidinum peccatorumque omnium patere in amicitia licentiam. Virtutum amicitia adiutrix a natura data est, non vitiorum comes; ut quoniam solitaria non posset virtus ad ea quae summa sunt pervenire, coniuncta et consociata cum altera perveniret. Quae si quos inter societas aut est aut fuit aut futura est, eorum est habendus ad summum naturae bonum optimus beatissimusque comitatus; [84] haec est, inquam, societas, in qua omnia insunt quae putant homines expetenda – honestas, gloria, tranquillitas animi atque iucunditas - ut et cum haec adsint, beata vita sit, et sine his esse non possit. Quod cum optimum maximumque sit, si id volumus adipisci, virtuti opera danda est, sine qua nec amicitiam neque ullam rem expetendam consequi possumus. Ea vero neglecta qui se amicos habere arbitrantur, tum se denique errasse sentiunt, cum eos gravis aliquis casus experiri cogit. [85] Quocirca (dicendum est enim saepius) cum iudicaris diligere oportet, non cum dilexeris iudicare. Sed cum multis in rebus neglegentia plectimur, tum maxime in amicis et deligendis et colendis; praeposteris enim utimur consiliis, et acta agimus, quod vetamur vetere proverbio; nam implicati ultro et citro vel usu diuturno vel etiam officiis, repente in medio cursu amicitias, exorta aliqua offensione, dirumpimus.

[XXIII:86] Quo etiam magis vituperanda est rei maxime necessariae tanta incuria: una est enim amicitia in rebus humanis de cuius utilitate omnes uno ore consentiunt;

greatness and quality of this power of friendship. For every person loves himself, not in order to recover some reward of his affection from himself, but because everyone is naturally valued by himself; now unless this same principle is transferred into friendship, one will never find a true friend, who is, as it were, another self. [81] But if this comes out clearly in animals, in birds, beasts and fish, both tame and wild, first that they love themselves (for this instinct is inborn in every living creature), then that they desire and search for animals of the same sort to associate with, and do so with a sense of longing and with something resembling human love, how much more naturally does this happen in man, who both loves himself, and looks for another whose mind he may, so to speak, mingle with his own so as to turn the two into one.

[XXII:82] Yet many people perversely, not to say impudently, wish their friends to be such as they cannot themselves be, and expect from their friends what they do not themselves give in return. But the proper thing is to be a good man oneself first, then to look for another like oneself. Among such men one can ensure that stability of friendship which we have been discussing all along, when persons with a bond of goodwill between them, firstly are in control of those desires to which others are enslaved, and secondly take pleasure in justice and fairness: when each will undertake anything for the sake of the other, but never ask the other for anything except what is right and honourable; and when they not only do each other kindnesses and services, but also have respect for each other; for to remove the feeling of respect from friendship is to remove its greatest ornament. [83] Disastrous indeed is the error of those who think that friendship involves the licence to commit all sorts of wrongdoing and to pursue every chance desire. Friendship was given by nature as a helper in virtue, not an accomplice in crime, so that, because virtue cannot reach the greatest heights in solitude, it should reach them when joined and allied with another. If there are any between whom this alliance exists or has existed or will exist in future, we must believe that theirs is the best and happiest companionship on the road to the highest natural good; [84] it is this alliance, I say, which contains everything that men think desirable – honour, glory, peace of mind and enjoyment: those things which are desirable in such a way that in their presence life is happy, and without them it cannot be so. And, insofar as this is the best and greatest thing of all, if we wish to obtain it, we must cultivate goodness, without which we cannot attain either friendship or anything else desirable. Those who think they have friends while neglecting goodness, realise in the end how wrong they were, when some great misfortune compels them to learn from experience. [85] So (for it must be said again and again) you must judge before making friends, and not make friends before judging them. But we suffer from our own negligence in many matters, and most of all in the way we choose our friends and behave towards them; we plan our lives back to front, and re-open closed cases (which the old proverb [*actum ne agas*] forbids us to do); for when we have become involved in mutual ties either by long-standing association or even by debts of gratitude, as soon as some cause of offence arises, we suddenly break friendships apart in mid-course.

[XXIII:86] Such negligence, in a matter which is of all things the most necessary in human life, is all the more to be deplored. For friendship is the one thing in human

quamquam a multis virtus ipsa contemnitur, et venditatio quaedam atque ostentatio esse dicitur; multi divitias despiciunt, quos parvo contentos tenuis victus cultusque delectat; honores vero, quorum cupiditate quidam inflammantur, quam multi ita contemnunt ut nihil inanius, nihil esse levius existiment! Itemque cetera quae quibusdam admirabilia videntur, permulti sunt qui pro nihilo putent; de amicitia omnes ad unum idem sentiunt, et ei qui ad rem publicam se contulerunt, et ei qui rerum cognitione doctrinaque delectantur, et ei qui suum negotium gerunt otiosi, postremo ei qui se totos tradiderunt voluptatibus: sine amicitia vitam esse nullam, si modo velint aliqua ex parte liberaliter vivere. [87] Serpit enim nescioquo modo per omnium vitas amicitia, nec ullam aetatis degendae rationem patitur esse expertem sui.

Quin etiam si quis asperitate ea est et immanitate naturae, congressus ut hominum fugiat atque oderit, qualem fuisse Athenis Timonem nescioquem accepimus, tamen is pati non possit ut non anquirat aliquem apud quem evomat virus acerbitatis suae. Atque hoc maxime iudicaretur si quid tale posset contingere, ut aliquis nos deus ex hac hominum frequentia tolleret et in solitudine uspiam collocaret, atque ibi suppeditans omnium rerum quas natura desiderat abundantiam et copiam, hominis omnino aspiciendi potestatem eriperet. Quis tam esset ferreus, qui eam vitam ferre posset, cuique non auferret fructum voluptatum omnium solitudo? [88] Verum ergo illud est, quod a Tarentino Archyta, ut opinor, dici solitum nostros senes commemorare audivi, ab aliis senibus auditum: si quis in caelum ascendisset, naturamque mundi et pulchritudinem siderum perspexisset, insuavem illam admirationem ei fore, quae iucundissima fuisset si aliquem cui narraret habuisset. Sic natura solitarium nihil amat, semperque ad aliquod tamquam adminiculum adnititur, quod in amicissimo quoque dulcissimum est.

[XXIV] Sed cum tot signis eadem natura declaret quid velit, anquirat, desideret, tamen obsurdescimus nescioquo modo, nec ea quae ab ea monemur audimus. Est enim varius et multiplex usus amicitiae, multaeque causae suspicionum offensionumque dantur; quas tum evitare, tum elevare, tum ferre sapientis est. Una illa sublevanda* offensio est, ut et utilitas in amicitia et fides retineatur; nam et monendi amici saepe sunt et obiurgandi, et haec accipienda amice cum benevole fiunt; [89] sed nescioquo modo verum est quod in Andria familiaris meus dicit, "Obsequium amicos, veritas odium parit". Molesta veritas, siquidem ex ea nascitur odium, quod est venenum amicitiae; sed obsequium multo molestius, quod peccatis indulgens praecipitem amicum ferri sinit; maxima autem culpa in eo qui et veritatem aspernatur et in fraudem obsequio impellitur. Omni igitur hac in re habenda ratio [et]* diligentia est, primum ut monitio acerbitate, deinde ut obiurgatio

affairs on whose value everyone is unanimously agreed. Virtue itself is despised by many, who say that it is a form of hypocrisy and self-advertisement; many consider wealth of no account, being content with a little, and enjoying a modest style of life; as for honours, for which some are inflamed with desire, see how many there are who think so little of them that nothing is to them more empty or worthless! It is the same with other things that seem wonderful to some people: in each case there are many who consider them worth nothing; but with regard to friendship, all without exception share the same opinion: those who take part in politics, those who take pleasure in science and learning, those who are uninvolved in public life and attend only to their own business, and lastly also those who give themselves up entirely to the pursuit of pleasure. They all think that life is nothing without friendship, if, that is, they wish to live in a civilised fashion to any extent at all. [87] For friendship creeps in some way or other into everybody's life, and does not allow any mode of life to be free of it.

Indeed, even if we suppose that there is someone so harsh and wild by nature that he hates human society and flees from it, as a certain Timon of Athens was said to have been, nevertheless even he could not endure to have nobody to whom he could spew out the poison of his hatred. And this could be most easily discerned if something like this were possible: that some power might take us out of this crowd of men and place us somewhere in solitude, there providing an abundant supply of all things that nature requires, but depriving us of the possibility of seeing any human being at all. Who would be so steely in nature as to be able to endure that life? Would not solitude steal away from him all enjoyment of his pleasures? [88] So that saying appears to be true, which I have heard attributed to Archytas of Tarentum, I think, by our elders, who had heard it themselves from the previous generation: if anyone were to ascend into the heavens, and see the beauty of the stars and the universe as it really was, his amazement at it would cause him no pleasure, though it would be most enjoyable if he had someone to tell about it. Human nature abhors solitude, and always, as it were, leans towards some prop, and the closer the friend, the more pleasant this is.

[XXIV] But, though our nature demonstrates by so many signs what it wants, and what it searches and longs for, still somehow we are deaf to it, and fail to hear the warnings it gives. Our experience of friendship is multifarious and changeable, and often there arise causes of offence and suspicion. A wise man can sometimes avoid these altogether; sometimes he can lessen their impact; sometimes he must put up with them. There is one particular case in which offence must be lessened as far as it can, in order to preserve the advantages of friendship as well as the demands of honesty. Friends often need to be advised and criticised, and these things should be taken in good part when they are done with good intentions. [89] I suppose it is in some way true, what my friend says in *The Woman of Andros*: "The truth makes enemies: complaisance, friends". Certainly, the truth can be a nuisance if it gives rise to dislike, which poisons friendship; but complaisance is much more so, in that it is indulgent towards wrongdoing, and allows a friend to rush away out of control. The greatest fault is in the person who ignores the truth, and is driven into self-deception by his friends' tolerance. In this matter, therefore, one must employ all possible care in making sure firstly that one's advice is given without sharpness, and then that reproof is administered without being insulting. And as

contumelia careat; in obsequio autem (quoniam Terentiano verbo libenter utimur) comitas adsit, assentatio vitiorum adiutrix procul amoveatur, quae non modo amico sed ne libero quidem digna est; aliter enim cum tyranno, aliter cum amico vivitur. [90] Cuius autem aures clausae veritati sunt, ut ab amico verum audire nequeat, huius salus desperanda est. Scitum est enim illud Catonis, ut multa: melius de quibusdam acerbos inimicos mereri quam eos amicos qui dulces videantur; illos verum saepe dicere, hos numquam. Atque illud absurdum, quod ei qui monentur eam molestiam quam debent capere non capiunt, eam capiunt qua debent vacare; peccasse enim se non anguntur, obiurgari moleste ferunt; quod contra oportebat delicto dolere, correctione gaudere.

[XXV:91] Ut igitur et monere et moneri proprium est verae amicitiae, et alterum libere facere, non aspere, alterum patienter accipere, non repugnanter, sic habendum est nullam in amicitiis pestem esse maiorem quam adulationem, blanditiam, assentationem; quamvis enim multis nominibus est hoc vitium notandum, levium hominum atque fallacium, ad voluptatem loquentium omnia, nihil ad veritatem. [92] Cum autem omnium rerum simulatio vitiosa est - tollit enim iudicium veri idque adulterat - tum amicitiae repugnat maxime; delet enim veritatem, sine qua nomen amicitiae valere non potest. Nam cum amicitiae vis sit in eo ut unus quasi animus fiat ex pluribus, qui id fieri poterit si ne in uno quidem quoque unus animus erit idemque semper, sed varius commutabilis multiplex? [93] Quid enim potest esse tam flexibile, tam devium, quam animus eius qui ad alterius non modo sensum ac voluntatem, sed etiam vultum atque nutum convertitur? "Negat quis, nego; ait, aio; postremo imperavi egomet mihi I Omnia assentari," ut ait idem Terentius, sed ille in Gnathonis persona. Quod amici genus adhibere omnino levitatis est; [94] multi autem Gnathonum similes cum sint loco fortuna fama superiores, horum est assentatio molesta cum ad vanitatem accessit auctoritas.

[95] Secerni autem blandus amicus a vero et internosci, tam potest adhibita diligentia quam omnia fucata et simulata a sinceris atque veris. Contio, quae ex imperitissimis constat, tamen iudicare solet quid intersit inter popularem, id est assentatorem et levem civem, et inter constantem severem gravem. [96] Quibus blanditiis C. Papirius nuper influebat in aures contionis, cum ferret legem de tribunis plebis reficiendis! Dissuasimus nos, sed nihil de me; de Scipione dicam libentius; quanta illa, di immortales, fuit gravitas, quanta in oratione maiestas, ut facile ducem populi Romani, non comitem* diceres! Sed adfuistis et est in manibus oratio. Itaque lex popularis suffragiis populi repudiata est. Atque ut ad me redeam, meministis, Q. Maximo fratre Scipionis et L. Mancino consulibus, quam popularis lex de sacerdotiis C. Licini Crassi videbatur; cooptatio enim collegiorum ad populi beneficium transferebatur; atque is

regards complaisance (since we choose to use Terence's word), by all means let us be friendly, but let flattery, the encourager of faults, be banished far away, since it is not even worthy of a free man, let alone a friend; one does not live with a friend as one would with a dictator. [90] If anyone's ears are so closed to the truth that he cannot hear it from a friend, his moral health is to be despaired of. On this point Cato had a witty saying, as so often: he said that bitter enemies do some people better service than friends who appear sweet, since the former often tell the truth, the latter never. It is paradoxical that when people receive criticism, they are not annoyed by the thing that should annoy them, but are annoyed by what should not; they feel no distress at having done wrong, but are annoyed at being reproved, whereas on the contrary they should feel pain at their own error and should be pleased to be corrected.

[XXV:91] Given, then, that it is proper to true friendship both to give and receive advice, the former freely but not harshly, the latter with patience and not unwillingly; in the same way, one must believe that there is no greater plague for friendships than flattery, fawning, obsequiousness – however many names one uses to describe it, it is to be disapproved of as a fault that belongs to unreliable and deceitful men, who say things in order to please, regardless of the truth. [92] Any sort of pretence is wrong; it removes one's capacity to see the truth, and substitutes a counterfeit version of it; but above all it is incompatible with friendship, as it destroys that truthfulness without which the name of friendship cannot mean anything. Since friendship has the effect of (as it were) turning a number of minds into one, how can that happen if even the individual himself does not have a single mind that is always the same, but one that is changeable and inconstant and many-sided? [93] What can be so changeable or devious as the mind of one who alters himself to suit not only another's wishes and opinions, but even his facial expression and his every gesture? – "A man says no, I say no; he says yes, I say yes; in short, I have given myself a standing order to agree with everything", as Terence also says, but in the person of Gnatho. To use him as an example of a friend would be quite frivolous, [94] but there are many people like Gnatho who are superior to him in position, wealth and reputation: it is they whose flattery is annoying, when their worthless talk goes hand in hand with power and influence.

[95] As for distinguishing and recognising the difference between a flatterer and a true friend, one may do it with care to just the same extent as one can distinguish anything false and disguised from what is true and unadulterated. A popular assembly consists of uneducated people, but it usually manages to judge the difference between a demagogue – that is, an unreliable politician who flatters the electorate – and a reliable, serious and consistent statesman. [96] Think of the way Gaius Papirius recently caressed the ears of the Assembly with every flattering trick at his command, when he was proposing a law on re-election to the tribunate. We argued against it, but I shall say nothing of myself; I prefer to talk about Scipio. What dignity and majesty there was in his speech! You could easily tell that he was leading the Roman people, not merely going along with them. But you were both there, and the speech is in circulation. Thus a popular law was defeated by popular vote. To return to myself, you remember how popular Gaius Licinius Crassus's law on priesthoods seemed likely to be (when Q.Maximus, Scipio's brother, and L.Mancinus were consuls): election to the priestly colleges was to be put

primus instituit in forum versus agere cum populo; tamen illius vendibilem orationem religio deorum immortalium, nobis defendentibus, facile vincebat. Atque id actum est praetore me, quinquennio antequam consul sum factus; ita re magis quam summa auctoritate causa illa defensa est. [XXVI:97] Quodsi in scaena, id est in contione, in qua rebus fictis et adumbratis loci plurimum est, tamen verum valet, si modo id patefactum et illustratum est, quid in amicitia fieri oportet, quae tota veritate perpenditur? in qua nisi, ut dicitur, apertum pectus videas tuumque ostendas, nihil fidum, nihil exploratum habeas, ne amare quidem aut amari, cum id quam vere fiat ignores.

Quamquam ista assentatio, quamvis perniciosa sit, nocere tamen nemini potest nisi ei qui eam recipit atque ea delectatur. Ita fit ut is assentatoribus patefaciat aures suas maxime, qui ipse sibi assentetur et se maxime ipse delectet. [98] Omnino est amans sui virtus, optime enim se ipsa novit, quamque amabilis sit intellegit; ego autem non de virtute nunc loquor, sed de virtutis opinione. Virtute enim ipsa non tam multi praediti esse quam videri volunt; hos delectat assentatio, his fictus ad ipsorum voluntatem sermo cum adhibetur, orationem illam vanam testimonium esse laudum suarum putant. Nulla est igitur haec amicitia, cum alter verum audire non vult, alter ad mentiendum paratus est. Nec parasitorum in comoediis assentatio faceta nobis videretur, nisi essent milites gloriosi. "Magnas vero agere gratias Thais mihi?": satis erat respondere "Magnas"; "Ingentes," inquit. Semper auget assentator id quod is cuius ad voluntatem dicitur vult esse magnum. [99] Quamobrem quamquam blanda ista vanitas apud eos valet qui ipsi illam allectant et invitant, tamen etiam graviores constantioresque admonendi sunt ut animadvertant, ne callida assentatione capiantur. Aperte enim adulantem nemo non videt nisi qui admodum est excors; callidus ille et occultus ne se insinuet studiose cavendum est; nec enim facillime agnoscitur, quippe qui etiam adversando saepe assentetur, et litigare se simulans blandiatur atque ad extremum det manus vincique se patiatur, ut is qui illusus sit plus vidisse videatur. Quid autem turpius quam illudi? quod ut ne accidat magis cavendum est. "Ut me hodie ante omnes comicos stultos senes | Versaris atque illuseris lautissime" - [100] haec enim etiam in fabulis stultissima persona est, improvidorum et credulorum senum.

Sed nescioquo pacto ab amicitiis perfectorum hominum, id est sapientium (de hac dico sapientia, quae videtur in hominem cadere posse), ad leves amicitias defluxit oratio; quamobrem ad illa prima redeamus eaque ipsa concludamus aliquando.

in the hands of the people. He was the first to stand facing the Forum when presiding over the popular assembly. Despite this, piety towards the gods (with some help from ourselves) easily won against his cheapjack oratory. That was done when I was praetor, five years before I became consul; so the issue was decided more on its merits than because of any supreme magistrate's influence. [XXVI:97] But if the truth can prevail, provided it is brought into the open and made clear, even on the public stage (that is to say the popular assembly), where there is the greatest scope for pretence and obfuscation, what must be the case in friendship, whose existence depends entirely on truthfulness? There, unless you can (as they say) see into the other's heart, and lay your own open as well, you cannot rely on anything nor know anything for certain, not even concerning the friendly feelings on either side, since you cannot tell how genuine they are.

Yet this flattery of which we are speaking, however harmful it may be, can do no harm to anyone except those who fall for it and take pleasure in it. The person who opens his ears most of all to flatterers is, consequently, the one who flatters himself, and is pleased more with himself than with anything else. [98] Of course, good character has a high opinion of itself; it knows itself better than anyone does, and realises how much it deserves love; I am not, however, talking about good character, but about people's opinion of their own character. Fewer people are endowed with real virtue than wish to seem so; and it is the latter who like to be flattered. When this sort of person is exposed to talk made up to suit himself, he takes this empty verbiage as evidence for his own high reputation. This, indeed, is no friendship at all, when the one does not wish to hear the truth, and the other is all set to tell lies. We would not think the flattery of parasites in comedies funny if it were not for the braggart soldiers. "You say that Thais thanks me very much?" – it would have been enough to reply "Yes, very much"; "Enormously," he says. Whatever the victim thinks is important, the flatterer always magnifies it further. [99] So, although that sort of seductive nonsense only works with those who attract and invite it themselves, still even persons of greater dignity and stronger character must be warned to look out for it, so as not to be caught by the subtle varieties of flattery. One who flatters openly is seen through by anyone except perhaps the most stupid; but one must take constant care not to let the clever and subtle type worm their way in. That type is not always easily recognised, particularly since their attentions often take the form of opposition. They flatter by pretending to argue against one, then at the end give in and confess themselves beaten, so that the victim appears to have been right all along. There is nothing more disgraceful than to be fooled in this way, and all the more care must be taken to avoid it. "The tribe of senile idiots that you see in every play I Are nothing to the proper fool you've made of me today!" [100] This too is the most foolish possible character on stage, that of credulous and heedless old men.

But somehow our discussion has wandered away from the friendships of perfect men, that is, wise men (I talk of that wisdom which is thought accessible for a human being), towards those of no value. Let us, therefore, go back to that first topic, and finally wind up our discussion of it.

[XXVII] Virtus, virtus inquam, Gai Fanni et tu Quinte Muci, et conciliat amicitias et conservat. In ea est enim convenientia rerum, in ea stabilitas, in ea constantia. Quae cum se extulit et ostendit suum lumen, et idem aspexit agnovitque in alio, ad id se admovet vicissimque accipit illud quod in altero est; ex quo exardescit sive amor sive amicitia (utrumque enim ductum* est ab amando); amare autem nihil est aliud nisi eum ipsum diligere quem ames nulla indigentia, nulla utilitate quaesita, quae tamen ipsa efflorescit ex amicitia etiamsi tu eam minus secutus sis. [101] Hac nos adulescentes benevolentia senes illos, L. Paulum, M. Catonem, C. Galum, P. Nasicam, Ti. Gracchum, Scipionis nostri socerum, dileximus; haec etiam magis elucet inter aequales, ut inter me et Scipionem, L. Furium, P. Rupilium, Sp. Mummium. Vicissim autem senes in adulescentium caritate acquiescimus, ut in vestra, ut in Q. Tuberonis; equidem etiam admodum adulescentis P. Rutili, A. Vergini familiaritate delector. Quoniamque ita ratio comparata est vitae naturaeque nostrae, ut alia ex alia* aetas oriatur, maxime quidem optandum est ut cum aequalibus possis, quibuscum tamquam e carceribus emissus sis, cum eisdem ad calcem, ut dicitur, pervenire; [102] sed quoniam res humanae fragiles caducaeque sunt, semper aliqui anquirendi sunt quos diligamus et a quibus diligamur. Caritate enim benevolentiaque sublata omnis est e vita sublata iucunditas.

Mihi quidem Scipio, quamquam est subito ereptus, vivit tamen semperque vivet. Virtutem enim amavi illius viri, quae exstincta non est, nec mihi soli versatur ante oculos, qui illam semper in manibus habui, sed etiam posteris erit clara et insignis. Nemo umquam animo aut spe maiora suscipiet, qui sibi non illius memoriam atque imaginem proponendam putet. [103] Equidem ex omnibus rebus quas mihi aut fortuna aut natura tribuit, nihil habeo quod cum amicitia Scipionis possim comparare; in hac mihi de republica consensus, in hac rerum privatarum consilium, in eadem requies plena oblectationis fuit. Numquam illum ne minima quidem re offendi, quod quidem senserim; nihil audivi ex eo ipse quod nollem. Una domus erat, idem victus isque communis, neque solum militia, sed etiam peregrinationes rusticationesque communes. [104] Nam quid ego de studiis dicam cognoscendi semper aliquid atque discendi, in quibus remoti ab oculis populi omne otiosum tempus contrivimus? Quarum rerum recordatio et memoria si una cum illo occidisset, desiderium coniunctissimi atque amantissimi viri ferre nullo modo possem; sed nec illa exstincta sunt, alunturque potius et augentur cogitatione et memoria mea. Et si illis plane orbatus essem, magnum tamen adfert mihi aetas ipsa solacium; diutius enim iam in hoc desiderio esse non possum; omnia autem brevia tolerabilia esse debent, etiamsi magna sunt.

Haec habui de amicitia quae dicerem; vos autem hortor ut ita virtutem locetis, sine qua amicitia esse non potest, ut ea excepta nihil amicitia praestabilius putetis.

[XXVII] It is goodness, human goodness, I say, Gaius Fannius, and you, Quintus Mucius, which both brings friendships together and preserves them. In it is found all harmony, stability and trust. Whenever it rises up and shows forth its light, and sees and recognises the same thing in another, it moves out towards it and in turn receives what the other has to give. Thence love, or friendship (for both have their origin in loving) blazes forth; and loving is nothing other than showing affection for the object of love for his own sake, not because of any lack in oneself, or the prospect of any advantage; though advantage does indeed flower from friendship even if one was not particularly aiming at it. [101] This was the goodwill and affection that we, as young men, felt for our elders – Lucius Paulus, Marcus Cato, Gaius Galus, Publius Nasica, Tiberius Gracchus the father-in-law of our own Scipio. Even more, it shines out among contemporaries, as between myself and Scipio, Lucius Furius, Publius Rupilius, Spurius Mummius. In turn, as old men, we enjoy the affection of young men like yourselves or Quintus Tubero, and I myself delight in the company of Publius Rutilius and Aulus Verginius, who are still very young. Since the nature of our life is so arranged that one generation must succeed another, one must of course wish most of all to be able, as they say, to reach the finishing-line together with one's contemporaries, with whom one started the race; [102] but since human affairs are fragile and transitory, we must always be looking for people to whom we can give and from whom we can receive affection. For without affection and goodwill, every pleasant quality is removed from human life.

Although Scipio was suddenly snatched away from us, for me he still lives and always will live. It was his fine qualities that I loved, and those are not dead. Not only are they constantly before my own eyes (since I always had them close at hand), but they will always be famous and eminent among future generations. No man of high courage and hope will undertake any great matter, without having Scipio's memory and example before him. [103] As for me, of all the things that nature or fortune has given me, I have nothing else to compare with the friendship of Scipio. It embraced agreement on public matters, consultation on private affairs, and relaxation full of delight. I never offended him in the slightest way, as far as I was aware; I never heard anything from him that I would rather not have heard. We had one house, one common way of life, and shared not only our military service but also our travels and country holidays. [104] What shall I say of the enthusiasm for always investigating and learning something, in which we spent all our leisure time far from the public eye? If the memory and recollection of those things had died together with him, I would in no way be able to bear the loss of such a friendly and loving man; but those things are not dead, and indeed rather grow and increase as I remember and ponder them. And even if I had been completely deprived of them, still my very age brings me great consolation; for it is impossible that I should have to bear this loss for much longer; and any suffering that is short-lived should be tolerable, even if it is great.

That is what I had to say about friendship; as for you, I recommend you to place such a value on goodness, without which friendship cannot exist, that with that one exception you regard nothing as more excellent than friendship.

LAELIUS DE AMICITIA: COMMENTARY

Title: **Laelius, On Friendship** The principal title of the work is *Laelius*, after the chief character of the dialogue; the subtitle, describing the subject of the work, is *de amicitia*. (For the evidence for the title, see Appendix). The double title is exactly parallel to that of the *Cato Maior de senectute* (cf. Introd. §4, and my edition of the *Cato*, pp. 93-4). Similar double titles are found attached to Plato's dialogues (probably later than Plato's own time), e.g. *Lysis, on Friendship*, and there are precedents elsewhere in Greek philosophical literature.

1-5. Prologue This carefully constructed and elegant preface falls into two approximately equal halves. The first (§§1-3) introduces the dialogue by means of an account of how Cicero himself is alleged to have heard about the conversation represented in it; the second (§§4-5) explains Cicero's reasons for writing. The reconciliation of fiction (the discourse of Laelius) and reality (Cicero's writing on friendship) is characteristically urbane. The hypothesis of a double recension of the preface, proposed in the edition of Meissner-Wessner, and developed at length by E.Ruch (alias M.Ruch), *Das Prooemium von Ciceros Laelius de amicitia* (Strasbourg 1943), and id., *Le Préambule dans les oeuvres philosophiques de Cicéron* (Paris 1958) 303ff., is misguided: arguments against it are assembled by H.Heusch, *RhM* 96 (1953) 67-77.

The presentation of a fictional dialogue as having been narrated to the author is a standard device, used by Cicero also in the *De Republica* (see *Rep.* 1.13), with precedents in a number of dialogues of Plato. Cicero was obviously fond of the idea of an oral tradition linking the great men of the past with his own time (see also on §88); the idea is not as implausible as many readers of these dialogues have thought, and examples of authentic recollection over equally long periods of time can easily be collected in the academic or legal professions today, and no doubt elsewhere. N. Horsfall, *CR* 39 (1989) 229, misunderstands my position on this point: it is precisely because such oral tradition was a genuine part of Roman life that it could be used by Cicero to lend plausibility to his dialogues, but this is a quite separate question from that of the truth or otherwise of any particular alleged instance of such tradition in Cicero. In this case, it is of course quite possible that Cicero remembered some sayings of Laelius that had been transmitted to him by Scaevola, and even that some of these concerned friendship; but the substance of the dialogue is Cicero's own. Any contemporary reader would accept this preface as a way of introducing a dialogue of Cicero's own composition, just as such things are commonplace in novels in our own time.

The suggestion by Atticus that Cicero should write on friendship may be genuine enough, although certainly in later times the topic of a request by the dedicatee became an empty literary convention (cf. the anecdote in Pliny, *Ep.* 6.15). The most obvious parallel in Cicero is the prologue to the *Orator*. See T.Janson, *Latin Prose Prefaces* (Stockholm 1964) 21-2, 27, 43f., 116-20.

1. Quintus Mucius [Scaevola] the Augur Q. Mucius Scaevola, c. 170-87 BC; consul 117 BC. His first cousin (P. Mucius Scaevola) was the father of Q. Mucius

Scaevola the Pontifex (consul 95 BC; also mentioned by Cicero here). Both Scaevolae were eminent jurists. Scaevola the Augur was elected to the augural college through the influence of Laelius (Cic. *Brutus* 101), clearly before 129, the dramatic date of this dialogue (§8 "our college" implies that Scaevola is already a member).

Cicero mentions his connections with Scaevola also in *Leg.* 1.13; in *Brutus* 306 the manuscripts read *P(ubli) f(ilius)*, but the Augur (who was son of Quintus, not Publius) must be meant, since the time referred to is 89-88 BC, as in the present passage. Cicero mentions Scaevola with respect in *Brut.* 212, *Phil.* 8.31, and introduces him as a character in *De Oratore* I (cf. *Att.* 4.16.2); see also Plutarch *Cicero* 3.2.

Gaius Laelius See Introd. §5.

the epithet "wise" cf. *Fin.* 2.24 *Laelius ... dictus est sapiens* quoting Lucilius 1235 M.; Cic. ibid. 2.40, 3.16; also *Tusc.* 4.5, *Phil.* 11.17, *Rep.* 3.5, *De Or.* 2.154. Plutarch, *Tiberius Gracchus* 8, offers a cynical explanation of the epithet, viz. that it was due to his political back-tracking as consul in 140 BC; but Cicero's view that Laelius acquired it because of Greek culture and philosophical interests is at least as plausible (cf. §6 below, which further develops the idea). The word *sapiens* can equally well indicate either type of "wisdom". Cf. G.Panico, "Caton et Lélius chez Cicéron: sagesse grecque ou sagesse romaine?", *Mélanges d'études offerts à M.Lebel* (Quebec 1980) 257-66; G.Petrocchi, "I Lelii, gli Scipioni e il mito del "sapiens" in Cicerone", *Ciceroniana* 1.2 (1959) 20-77.

when I came of age lit. "when I had assumed the *toga virilis*", i.e. at the age of 16 (this would have been in 90 BC); on the *toga virilis* cf. §33 below. On this period of Cicero's life see Rawson, *Cicero* 12-17.

taken by my father to Scaevola Cicero's legal "apprenticeship" to Scaevola is commonly taken as typical of Republican Roman practice. There was no institutional instruction in the law at Rome, and a young aspirant would naturally learn by imitation, attaching himself to a prominent practitioner. Cicero says in *Brutus* 306 that Scaevola gave no formal instruction, but allowed his protégés to listen to his legal consultations. The custom bears a slight resemblance to pupillage at the English Bar. In a later period, when education took place largely in the rhetorical schools, Quintilian and Tacitus looked back fondly on this aspect of Republican education (Quint. *Inst.* 10.5.19; 12.11.5, pointing out that Cicero himself took "pupils" in this way; Tacitus, *Dialogus* 34, in which the interlocutor Messalla presents an idealised picture of Republican education, surely drawing heavily on Cicero). In modern works of scholarship, the legal apprenticeship is called *tirocinium fori*, but the phrase, which is unknown in Cicero, is merely a somewhat jocular metaphor (*tirones in foro*, "raw recruits in the courts") deriving from a later period (cf. my note on *Cato Maior* 10). Atticus, to whom this preface is addressed, was also a student of Scaevola's (*Leg.* 1.13) at the same time as Cicero, though he did not pursue a legal career. Cf. K.A.Neuhausen, "Ciceros Vater, der Augur Scävola und der junge Cicero", *WS* 92 (NF 13) (1979) 76-87.

his learning The word used here is *prudentia*, which often means "wisdom" in general, but has also the specific connotation of legal learning (as in our word "jurisprudence"). Similarly, the words used in the next sentence to praise Scaevola the Pontifex, *ingenium* and *iustitia*, while in themselves general terms, should be taken here as having a special reference to legal acumen and fairness of judgement.

2. semicircular portico *Hemicyclium*: no doubt resembling the one at Praeneste (Palestrina) in which the *Fasti Praenestini* were displayed (Suet. *De grammaticis* 17; A.Degrassi, *Inscriptiones Italiae* XIII.2 [Rome 1963] 107-45: not to be confused with the also semicircular temple of Fortuna Primigenia, a much larger building), or the one referred to in Plutarch *Alcibiades* 17; cf. *Thesaurus Linguae Latinae* VI, 2602, 17; Schneider, *RE* VIII, 243. Presumably this construction was a notable feature of Scaevola's house.

Publius Sulpicius The tribune of 88 BC (he is not given a *cognomen* in the sources). His brother Servius Sulpicius was married to Anicia, cousin of Atticus (Nepos, *Atticus* 2). The political troubles in which Sulpicius lost his life apparently discouraged Atticus from pursuing a political career. Sulpicius was a notable orator, and is a minor character in Cicero's *De Oratore* .

when he, as tribune of the people, opposed Quintus Pompeius The consuls of 88, Sulla and Q.Pompeius, decreed a cessation of public business in order to prevent the vote being taken on legislation proposed by Sulpicius. Sulpicius retorted by attacking the consuls with armed force, and in the ensuing violence the son of the consul Pompeius was killed. Both consuls left Rome. Sulpicius then carried his bill appointing Marius to the command against Mithridates (and ousting Sulla from it). Sulla returned with his army, expelled Marius and Sulpicius from the city and had them declared public enemies; soon afterwards Sulpicius was killed. The main sources for these events are Plutarch, *Sulla* 8, *Marius* 34; [Livy] *Periocha* 77; Appian *Bell. Civ.* 1.55; the detailed order and interpretation of events is somewhat disputed. See Broughton, *MRR* II, 41-2; H.Last, *Cambridge Ancient History* IX, 203; E.Badian, *Foreign Clientelae 264-70 BC* (Oxford 1958) 230ff.; A.Lintott, *CQ* 21 (1971) 442ff.; and my article in *Historia* 39 (1990) 446-60.

3. Scaevola then happened to mention the subject Scaevola's narration of the discourse of Laelius on friendship is thus placed in 88 BC, the year before his death. This feature is common to several dialogues of Cicero. The *De Republica* is set in the year of Scipio's death (129), while its conversation was supposed to have been narrated to Cicero by P. Rutilius Rufus in 78, the year before Rutilius himself died. The *De Oratore* is set in 91, the year of Crassus's death, and the *Cato Maior* in 150, a year before the death of Cato (cf. §11 below). Cf. A.Cameron, *CR* 1967, 258; id., *JRS* 56 (1966) 289.

Gaius Fannius son of Marcus Cf. Introd. §5. Cicero twice wrote to Atticus (who often provided him with historical information) on the subject of this Fannius. In *Att.* 12.5b, Cicero asks him whether Fannius the son-in-law of Laelius was the same man as Fannius the historian, while in *Att.* 16.13a.2 (written in November 44, probably soon after the publication of the *Laelius*) he enquires in what year C.Fannius M.f. was tribune of the people, saying that he "seems to remember hearing" that it was in 142 BC. In *Brutus* 99, however, Cicero states that another C.Fannius, son of Gaius, was tribune in 142. Further, in the same passage of the *Brutus*, C.Fannius son of Gaius is credited with the consulship of 122 BC, which the Fasti accord to C.Fannius the son of Marcus (no doubt Laelius's son-in-law). It is generally taken that the son of Marcus was the son-in-law of Laelius, the consul of 122 and the historian; G.V.Sumner, *Orators in Cicero's Brutus* (Toronto 1973) 53ff. further argues that Cicero's information in the *Brutus* on the tribune of 142 is to be preferred to his vague recollection in the letter, and consequently that the tribunate of 142 belonged to the son of Gaius; the son of Marcus may well have been tribune in a later year. The *Laelius* adds no further evidence, since nothing of the career or interests of Fannius (except a vague interest in Greek philosophy, §25) is here mentioned; Cicero could not have mentioned Fannius's history here even if he was by then satisfied that this Fannius was the author, since it was almost certainly written after 129 BC. For an entirely separate problem involving Fannius, see on §§14 and 25.

Scipio Africanus i.e. Aemilianus, the younger Africanus; Cicero often refers to him simply as *Africanus*. Cf. Introd. §5.

brought the characters on stage *induxi*, a theatrical word. This self-conscious statement about the nature of the ensuing dialogue is imitated from Plato (who is, if anything, even more self-conscious about the matter), *Theaetetus* 143b: cf. R. Hirzel, *Der Dialog* (Leipzig 1895) I, 212ff and 544. Both there and here, the purpose is to introduce a change from narrative to direct dramatic presentation of the dialogue. The same point is made by Cicero more briefly in the preface to the *Tusculans* (1.8 *quasi agetur res, non quasi narretur*). Neither passage should be taken to suggest that there was anything unfamiliar in the idea of a dialogue set out in dramatic form; there is no such apology in the other dialogues by Cicero in this form (*Cato Maior, De Legibus, Part. Or.*), although he employed narrative form more often. The distinction is referred to by Diogenes Laertius 3.50 in connection with Plato's dialogues.

4. This type of dialogue Like the *Cato Maior* and the *De Republica*; in the preface to the former, Cicero says that the choice of Cato as speaker gives the exposition more authority than the mythical Tithonus would have had, while in *Q.Fr.* 3.5.1 he says of an early draft of the *De Republica* that the dignity of the characters gave weight to the dialogue. The inspiration for Cicero's use of characters from past generations is often thought, on the basis of the letter just cited and of *Att.* 13.19.4, to have come from the lost dialogues of Heraclides Ponticus; but there are other possible precedents (e.g. Xenophon), and probably Heraclides is referred to in the two letters only as a convenient example. There is nothing (except scholarly conjecture) to link the projected "Heraclidean" work, mentioned in the letters to Atticus in 44, with the *Laelius* or any other surviving work. Cf. my edition of *Cato Maior*, introd. 6-7.

more weight i.e. than an essay written by Cicero in his own person.

that it is Cato who is speaking, not myself An ironically urbane compliment to Cicero's own literary realism; cf. below "imagine that Laelius himself is speaking".

5. as one old man to another Cicero was 62 in 44 BC, Atticus three years older. The parallelism *ad senem senex de senectute - ad amicum amicissimus de amicitia* is much neater and more natural in Latin than any possible translation.

recognise a portrait of yourself Presumably this means that Atticus is to recognise himself as an example of the ideal friend delineated in the dialogue; Cicero will have had Atticus in mind throughout. It can hardly be taken to imply that the characters of Laelius and Atticus are themselves being compared, though a casual reading might suggest that. It is possible that Cicero saw his own friendship with Atticus as resembling that of Scipio with Laelius, but he never says so, here or elsewhere, and to imply it here would be tactless in view of the highly encomiastic terms in which Scipio is presented in the dialogue. See also Introd. §8 fin.

6-16. Introductory conversation

6. That is true, Laelius Unusually, and realistically, Cicero begins in the middle of a conversation that has evidently been going on for some time. For the phrase *sunt ista* (ἔστι ταῦτα) cf. *Acad.* 1.9 and Reid's note.

Marcus Cato Apart from this passage, Cicero calls Cato the Elder "wise" (*sapiens*) in *Div. in Caec.* 66, *Verr.* II 2.5, *Leg.* 2.5, *Off.* 3.16. There is no evidence outside Cicero for *sapiens* as a sobriquet of Cato, though it is to be noticed that the name *Cato* itself was thought to be derived from *catus* "clever". Cf. my note on *Cato Maior* 5.

Lucius Acilius Mentioned as a jurist in *Leg.* 2.59; little else seems to be known of him.

his great practical experience Cf. Plutarch *Cato Maior* 25 (also echoing Cicero *Cato Maior* 46). Cato is the type of Roman native wit and practical wisdom. Cf. G.Panico, cited above on §1; U.Kammer, *Untersuchungen zu Ciceros Bild von Cato Censorius* (Frankfurt 1964).

prudent policy ... sharpness in debate The sentence-structure is notably symmetrical (in the Latin, three co-ordinated groups of neuter plural participle + adverb). *Responsa acute* literally means "acute answers", presumably referring both to sharp repartee (cf. Quintil. *Inst.* 6.3.105) and to percipient replies to consultation (cf. the legal sense of *responsa*): "debate" covers the former but not the latter.

7. With you, however Cicero here rivals Plato's dialogue-writing in a studied looseness of construction that imitates the style of actual conversation. In the Latin the construction is accusative and infinitive, with the main verb unexpressed; something like *existimant* must be understood (but not inserted into the text in the interests of a spurious regularity).

Seven Sages There were many variants on the list of seven wise men, but the most usual version comprised Thales of Miletus (the only one now counted as a philosopher), Pittacus of Mitylene, Bias of Priene, Solon of Athens, Cleobulus of Rhodes, Periander of Corinth, and Chilon of Sparta. Diogenes Laertius 1.40 quotes Dicaearchus to the effect that they were not "wise" (σοφοί) but intelligent and good lawgivers (συνετοὶ καὶ νομοθετικοί); it is no doubt to this opinion that Cicero refers here (cf. F.Egermann, *Sitzungsberichte der Akademie der Wissenschaften in Wien*, Phil.-hist. Klasse, 214,3 (1932) 53-4). Cf. §59 below; *Tusc.* 5.7; *De Rep.* 1.12; Plato, *Protagoras* 343a; Diels-Kranz I[6], 61ff.; B.Radice, "The Sayings of the Seven Sages of Greece", in *The Translator's Art*, ed. W.Radice and B.Reynolds (Harmondsworth 1987), 241-253.

one instance at Athens Socrates, said to be the wisest of men by the oracle given to Chaerephon: Plato, *Apology* 21a; the scholiast on Aristophanes, *Clouds* 144 gives the purported words of the oracle; cf. also Cic. *Cato Maior* 78.

you regard as within your own responsibility everything that concerns you Literally "you think that everything of yours is placed within you"; an expression of the Greek philosophical ideal of self-reliance or self-sufficiency (*autarkeia*); it was not the peculiar property of any of the schools, but was common to the philosophy of Plato (cf. Plato, *Menexenus* 247e and Cic. *Tusc.* 5.36-42, also *Cato Maior* 4), the Stoics and the Epicureans. Cf. also §30 below.

how you are coping with the death of Africanus Bereavement was naturally seen as a test-case for the efficacy of philosophy in overcoming the effects of misfortune; to bear it bravely was also an aspect of traditional Roman virtue, as in the examples below (see on §9).

on the Nones of this month Scipio died in the early part of 129 BC, but some time after the start of the campaigning season; Appian, *Bell. Civ.* 1.19 records that the consul Tuditanus departed for Illyria before Scipio's death. The conversation of the *De Republica* is set during the Feriae Latinae, which marked the beginning of the campaigning season, and were attended by all magistrates; traditionally this festival was held in March, when, until 154 BC, the consuls took office, but at this date it may have been held earlier. The presence of Decimus Brutus as host of the augural meeting has been thought relevant to fixing the date; he too was on campaign in Illyria that year, but it is clear from the Livian Epitome (59) that he only went out to join Tuditanus later in the year, when the latter had already suffered military setbacks. It is most probable that the month in question was April or May, but certainty is impossible (hence "Nones" must be preserved in translation: if the month was April, the date would be the 5th; if May, the 7th). For augural meetings on the Nones, cf. Cic. *Div.* 1.90, showing that such meetings no longer took place at the time of writing in 44 BC.

Decimus Brutus consul 138 BC; cf. previous note; Plutarch *Quaest. Rom.* 34, Cic. *Leg.* 2.54.

regular practice The augural ceremonies, involving observation of the sky, will have required rehearsal out of doors. Cicero was proud of his own position as augur, and is fond of referring to the augural college and its activities; cf. *Cato Maior* 65, *N.D.* 3.5; see C.W.Tucker, "Cicero augur", *CW* 70 (1976) 171ff.

8. Gaius Laelius Scaevola, the younger of the two sons-in-law, uses the more respectful form of address with both the *praenomen* and the *nomen*, whereas Fannius above used the *nomen* alone. Such nuances are characteristic of Cicero's dialogue style; cf. *Cato Maior* 4.

in a controlled way *moderate*: this word usually preserves (in Cicero) something of its original sense, from *moderari* "to control"; it is not precisely equivalent to English "moderately".

humane character Latin *humanitas*; the quality of one who is "humane" or "civilised" may according to the circumstances involve both the capacity to feel emotion and the capacity to control it. To be emotionally unaffected at a friend's death would be *inhumanum*.

reliable character *Constans* is used in Latin as a term of praise in a way that is difficult to render precisely in English, though the qualities it embraces – courage and endurance, firmness and "solidity" of character, reliability – are ones which are or used to be much admired in England.

9. nobody has ever been wise Laelius inclines here towards the Stoic view that the word "wise" should only be applied to instances of perfect wisdom, which, though theoretically attainable, has in fact never been realised in practice. However, he disputes the Stoic doctrine below, §18.

the death of his son Cato's son, called like him M. Porcius Cato, died about 152 BC as praetor designate. Cf. *Cato Maior* 68 and 84; *Tusc.* 3.70; *Fam.* 4.6.1; Plutarch, *Cato Maior* 24; [Livy] *Periocha* 48.

Paulus L. Aemilius Paulus, the victor of Pydna (168 BC) and the father of Scipio Aemilianus. Apart from Scipio Aemilianus and Q. Fabius Maximus Aemilianus (for whom see §§69 and 96), who were both adopted into other families, Paulus had two sons, both of whom died around the time of his triumph in 168, one at the age of 14, the other at 12: see Plutarch, *Aemilius* 35; Livy 45.40-41; Val. Max. 5.10.2; Sen. *Cons. ad Marc.* 13.6; id. *Polyb.* 14.5. Cicero (*Fam.* 4.6), writing to Servius Sulpicius in reply to his consolatory letter on the death of Tullia, cites the examples of Cato, Paulus and Galus, as here, adding also that of Q. Fabius Maximus Cunctator, who is referred to also in *Cato Maior* 12 in terms very similar to those of the present passage.

Galus C. Sulpicius Galus (this spelling is more correct than *Gallus*, cf. *Der Kleine Pauly* s.v. Sulpicius col. 424), a contemporary and friend of Aemilius Paulus, best known for his astronomical studies. It appears that, like Paulus, he lost a son, but this is known only from this passage and *Fam.* 4.6.1. See also below, §§21 and 101.

10. that man whom you mentioned Socrates, §7 above.

I shall tell you what I think *sic habetote*, lit. "have it this way"; the meaning is "this is what you are to believe" (*habeo* = "hold" as in "we hold these truths to be self-evident"). The more formal imperative in -*tote* is usual in this phrase.

remedies The metaphor is explicitly medical (*medicina* in Latin). The image occurs commonly in the context of consolation for grief; cf. e.g. *Tusc.* 3.35 and 54; Fantham, *Imagery* 14-15; R.Kassel, *Untersuchungen zur griechischen und römischen Konsolationsliteratur*, Zetemata 18 (Munich 1958) 20.

act as my own comforter cf. *Cato Maior* 84. Cicero may have had in mind the fact that he himself had written (in 45 BC) a *Consolatio* to himself on the death of his daughter Tullia.

argues love for oneself The same argument is used in *Tusc.* 1.30, 1.111, *Brutus* 4.

11. to live for ever *Immortalitas* is used here literally of an indefinite extension of earthly life, with no reference to life after death. The tone is clearly ironical.

when he was a young man There is a conflict of evidence on the early life of Scipio Aemilianus. Plutarch (*Aemilius* 22) and Livy (44.44.1f.) record that he took part, aged 17, in the battle of Pydna under his father Paulus, caused him considerable concern by pursuing the enemy further than was necessary, and took part in his triumph in November 167. This might form the basis for what Cicero says here. On the other hand, Polybius says that at the age of 18 Scipio had a reputation for inactivity, and that he only corrected this later by devotion to hunting (with Polybius as his companion). One is led to suspect that Plutarch and Livy, and perhaps Cicero here, represent a eulogistic tradition: either a deliberate fiction designed to provide the great man with suitable youthful exploits, or a confusion in popular memory between the younger Scipio and the elder, who was famed for his bravery as a young soldier. Cf. Astin, *Scipio* 14; also Cic. *Rep.* 1.23.

was made consul twice (On the word order *factus consul est bis* see P.Fedeli, *RhM* 1972, 161.) First in 147 BC, when Scipio had been a candidate for the aedileship, not the consulate, at the age of 37 (40 being the normal minimum age for the consulate); this gave him the command against Carthage. The second time was in 134 BC, when Scipio was made consul in order to finish the war against Numantia (in Spain), which had already continued for several years without success. The two cities are Carthage and Numantia. Cf. *Somn. Scip.* 3 (11).

affection for his mother, his generosity to his sisters See Polybius 31.26.6; 31.28.8. On Scipio's generosity cf. also Cic. *Paradoxa* 48.

his funeral   Appian, *Bell. Civ.* 1.19 says that Scipio was not granted the honour of a state funeral, but his death could have been the occasion of considerable public mourning nevertheless. On Scipio's funeral cf. also Valerius Maximus 4.1.12.

how dear he was to the citizen body   In the *First Philippic* (35) Cicero represents this as an aim of the true statesman; cf. below on §§12 and 14 for other points of similarity with this speech; Introd. §3.

What ... a few more years?   A common theme in ancient writings dealing with death and its consolations: it is better to die at the height of one's success than to live longer and face an inevitable decline; or at any rate the addition of more time will make no difference to one's happiness. Socrates argues to this effect in Xenophon's *Apology* (6 and 8) and *Memorabilia* (4.8.1 and 8); the Stoics and Epicureans also used the argument. For a list of passages illustrating this theme, see my notes on *Cato Maior* 69 and 71.

as I remember Cato arguing   Cicero is of course referring here to his own *Cato Maior*, in which Laelius was a subsidiary speaker. Similarly, Laelius is made to recall the conversation of the *De Republica* below, §14; and cf. §25.

it takes away that freshness   ("Freshness" = *viriditas*, lit. "greenness".) Cicero here narrowly escapes contradicting his own arguments on old age as presented in the *Cato Maior*. Scipio had in fact apparently enjoyed excellent health throughout his life (Polybius 31).

12.   nothing could be added to it either in good fortune or in glory   This is similar to Caesar's statement *Satis diu vixi vel naturae vel gloriae* (reported by Cicero in *Pro Marcello* 25) and Cicero's own version of it at the end of *Philippic* I. (A similar idea reappears also in Tacitus, *Agricola* 44.) One is tempted to wonder whether this passage, written as it was in 44 BC during the aftermath of Caesar's death, might not have recalled Caesar to the minds of Roman readers; "the quickness of his death" might allude to Caesar's preference for a quick death as recorded by Plutarch *Caesar* 63.7, and Scipio's passage to heaven may recall Caesar's deification. If so, the allusion could hardly be unintentional: a gesture of reconciliation with Caesar's memory?

removed the sense of dying   This idea occurs also in *Cato Maior* 74 and *Tusc.* 1.82.

you see what people suspect   The puzzle of Scipio's death was never resolved at the time or later. All sources agree that he was found dead in his bed, having been perfectly healthy the previous night. Rumours of poisoning, etc., multiplied. The blame was variously directed towards Scipio's wife Sempronia ([Livy], *Epit.* 59, Appian *Bell.Civ.* 1.19, Schol. Bob. p. 118 Stangl), his sister Cornelia (Appian), Gaius Gracchus (Plutarch *C.Gracchus*, Schol. Bob. ibid.); Fulvius Flaccus (Plutarch), C. Carbo (Cic. *Fam.* 9.21.3, *Q.Fr.* 2.3.3); some talked of suicide (Appian); for additional passages see A.H.J.Greenidge and A.M.Clay, *Sources for Roman History 133–70 B.C.* (ed. 2, Oxford 1960) 21-2. Cicero in *Somnium Scipionis* 4 (12) refers to the "impious hands of [Scipio's] relatives", implying that he thought members of the family were involved. Apparently it was given out officially that the death was natural, if one may go by the transmitted text of the fragment of Laelius's funeral oration preserved in Schol. Bob. ibid., cf. Cic. *Mur.* 75; see E.Badian, *JRS* 46 (1956) 220; at any rate there was no official enquiry into his death (Cic. *Mil.* 16, [Livy] *Periocha* 59, Vell. Pat. 2.46, Plut. *C.Gracchus* 10.4). Cf. Astin, *Scipio* 241; R.Werner, "Die gracchischen Reformen und der Tod des

Scipio Aemilianus", in *Festschrift für F.Altheim* (Berlin 1969) I, 413-40; I.Worthington, *Hermes* 117 (1989) 253ff.

the best of all was the day before he died   This contrasts oddly with Appian's statement (*BC* 1.19) that Scipio was unpopular at the time of his death. Some have connected it with the remark in the *Somnium Scipionis* (4 [12]) that Scipio ought to have been made dictator, but that is surely nothing more than Cicero's imagination of what might have happened if he had lived (cf. ad loc.). The Livian Epitome makes no reference to Scipio's popularity or otherwise.

the allies and the Latins   There were in fact representatives of allied and Latin communities in Rome at the time, and Scipio had been acting on their behalf, attempting to protect them against the effects of Tiberius Gracchus's law (Appian).

13. those who, not so long ago, began to argue   Epicureans are primarily referred to. "Not so long ago" is somewhat dismissive and tendentious; the doctrine that the soul was material and mortal went back at least to Democritus, whose contemporary Socrates is counted in the next sentence among the "ancients"! Cicero perhaps thought that Epicureanism was beginning to become more fashionable at Rome around the dramatic date of the dialogue; he refers to such a fashion (though without precise dating) in *Tusc.* 4.6-7. Cicero attacks philosophers who denied the immortality of the soul also in *Cato Maior* 85 and *Tusc.* 1.18, 1.50, 1.77, 1.79.

The authority of the ancients   Cicero briefly alludes here to the arguments for immortality which he had set out at length in *Tusc.* 1.26ff.; cf. also *Cato Maior* 79.

those who settled in this country   The Pythagoreans, who flourished in the Greek cities of southern Italy (Magna Graecia) in the sixth and fifth centuries BC. Their doctrine of reincarnation is assimilated by Cicero to Platonic views on immortality. Cicero is fond of claiming the Pythagoreans as Italians; see *Cato Maior* 79, *Tusc.* 4.2.

has now ceased to exist   Cicero can only mean that the cities of Magna Graecia were no longer a considerable political force; they did not literally cease to exist, but were only more or less Romanised.

who did not ... say sometimes one thing and sometimes another   Not, perhaps, an entirely fair characterisation of Socrates's method, but rather recalling that of his admirers in the later Academy, who held to no fixed view but attempted to argue equally on both sides of any question. More accurate is *Tusc.* 1.99 *suum illud nihil ut adfirmet* ([Socrates's] characteristic habit of affirming nothing). The opinions on immortality attributed here to Socrates are of course those expressed by the Socrates of the Platonic dialogues; Cicero does not raise the question whether they are authentically Socratic.

the souls of men are divine   See on *Somnium Scipionis* 5 (13) and 18 (26).

14. when Philus and Manilius ... for three days   Cicero refers to his own *De Republica*, and in particular to its ending, the *Somnium Scipionis*. For L.Furius Philus cf. on §21 below. For Manius Manilius, cf. *Somn. Scip.* 1 (9).

you too, Scaevola, had come with me   Here and in §25 below, it is specifically said that only Scaevola, not Fannius, was present at the conversation of the *De Republica*. This is very odd indeed, since in that work (1.18) Fannius is explicitly mentioned as being there together with Scaevola. Some have maintained that Fannius must have been present only for the first day's discussion in the *De Rep.*; this would indeed explain how he came to miss the speech of Laelius on justice (§25 below), but would not account for Cicero's phrasing in both of these passages, which distinctly implies that Fannius was not present for any of the conversation. Some have tried to link this with the confusion over the two Fannii (§3 above) but there is no future in that line of explanation; Fannius is specified as the son-in-law of Laelius in both the *Laelius* and the *De Republica*. The only really possible explanation is that Cicero had a lapse of memory, which is not impossible considering that the *De Republica* was written some years before, and had been through several drafts; Cicero might well not have bothered to check the point.

the prison and bondage of the body A common image throughout Platonism. Cf. *Somn. Scip.* 6 (14) – 7 (15) and note; also my notes on *Cato Maior* 77 and 81.

selfish *invidi*, literally "envious", "jealous" or "grudging", i.e. wanting Scipio's company for oneself to the detriment of his own happiness.

But if that other opinion ... Cicero states the problem of the afterlife in the form of a dilemma, as in Plato, *Apology* 40c; [Plato], *Axiochus* 365d; Xenophon, *Cyropaedia* 8.7.21; Cicero uses the argument often elsewhere, *Cato Maior* 66, 74, 81, 85; *Tusc.* 1.25-6, 1.82, 1.117-8; *Fam.* 5.16.4; *Sest.* 47; it is also a favourite argument with Seneca.

no feeling remains behind cf. *Tusc.* 1.87ff.; Lucretius 3.830ff.

will always bring gladness to this nation Compare the epitaph of Cn. Scipio Hispanus (*CIL* I².2, no.15), ... *Maiorum optenui laudem, ut sibei me esse creatum / laetentur*. Some have supposed that there is a connection with the fragment of Laelius's funeral oration for Scipio (Schol. Bob. p. 118 Stangl, = Malcovati, *Oratorum Romanorum Fragmenta* p. 121), which reads ... *neque tanta dis immortalibus gratia haberi potest quanta habenda est, quod is cum illo animo atque ingenio hac e civitate potissimum natus est*. The similarity is less striking than has been thought; here the idea is simply that the Romans will always be glad that Scipio was born; there the point is that Romans should thank the gods that Scipio was born as a Roman rather than a member of another nation. Whatever may be the truth about this passage, there is no evidence whatsoever for further use of the funeral oration by Cicero. The idea recurs in *Philippic* 1.35 *ita guberna rem publicam ut natum esse te cives tui gaudeant.*

15. as I said before §11 init.

entered this life before he did Laelius was a few years older than Scipio; cf. Introd. §5.

at home and on service abroad Cicero's *et domus fuit et militia communis* literally means that Scipio and Laelius had "both home and military service in common"; one would naturally take this to mean simply that they were associated both when in Rome and when abroad, were it not for the more explicit statement in §103 *una domus erat, idem victus isque communis*, which apparently must mean that the two men literally shared a household. On military service, Scipio and Laelius could well have lived together as *contubernales*, but the implication of sharing a house in Rome is more surprising. Horace, *Sat.* 2.1.71-4 envisages Scipio and Laelius as relaxing together (with Lucilius) when waiting for dinner, which certainly implies *victus communis* if not permanent house-sharing; the scholiast Pseudo-Acro on that passage reports an anecdote that Laelius once came upon Lucilius chasing Scipio round the table with a rolled-up napkin, and such an occurrence would certainly be easier to envisage if Laelius lived in Scipio's house.

community of interests Foreshadows the more formal definition of friendship at §20.

reputation for wisdom See on §§5 and 6.

three or four pairs of friends The three mythological examples, Theseus and Pirithous, Orestes and Pylades, Achilles and Patroclus, plus no doubt Damon and Phintias, whose story is told in Cic. *Off.* 3.45, cf. *Tusc.* 5.63, Val. Max. 4.7.ext.1, Diod. Sic. 6.243, Iamblichus *Vit. Pyth.* 234. Plutarch, περὶ πολυφιλίας 2 adds Epaminondas and Pelopidas to these four (doubtless from Boeotian patriotism). Cf. *Fin.* 1.65 *fictae veterum fabulae declarant, in quibus ... tria vix amicorum paria reperiuntur, ut ad Orestem pervenias profectus a Theseo*; ibid. 2.79, 5.63. Valerius Maximus lists other notable pairs of Roman friends, but they are mostly later than the dramatic date of this dialogue; compare also Lucian, *Toxaris* for development of the same theme; Ovid, *Pont.* 2.3.41.

will be known to posterity Cicero's hindsight makes this an inevitable expectation.

16. we are at leisure Leisure is a necessary condition for a philosophic dialogue, and is regularly mentioned in those of Cicero: cf. e.g. *Fin.* 1.14; Becker, *Technik und Szenerie* 12-13.

it would be most agreeable Cicero in a number of instances in the dialogues represents a younger speaker as respectfully asking an older one for his opinion; cf. *De Rep.* 1.34, *Cato Maior* 6; Becker, *Technik und Szenerie* 16-17.

what you think about it, what sort of thing you think it is, and what advice you give in regard to it For discussion of this passage and its function in the dialogue, see Introd. §6.

17-24. First main speech of Laelius

17. what ability do I have? Cf. the modesty of Cicero himself in *Leg.* 1.58, and that of Crassus in *De Or.* 1.99. Its ultimate literary antecedent is presumably the εἰρωνεία of the Platonic Socrates. Laelius himself would have been thought "learned" by Roman standards.

to ask for a subject to be proposed Greek philosophers would regularly ask for questions (ζητήματα) to be proposed from the audience; to lecture on such questions impromptu was no doubt a form of display, akin to that of sophists and rhetoricians. Cicero refers to the practice in *Fin.* 2.1-2 (tracing it back to Gorgias and the Sophists); in *De Or.* 1.102, Crassus makes the same point as Laelius here, but with much more asperity. Note also *Fam.* 9.26 to Paetus, who, in response to a philosopher's request for questions, asked where his dinner was to come from.

above all other things in human life The comparison of friendship with other things normally counted as good, such as health, wealth or political power, is expanded on in §20 below. The phrase *rebus humanis* would naturally be taken to exclude moral and spiritual qualities, which Cicero (following the Academy, Peripatos and Stoa) would place on a higher level. Aristotle, *NE* 1169b10 says that friendship appears to be the greatest of external goods; cf. also Epicurus, *Kyriai Doxai* 27.

nothing so natural Lit. "so much in accordance with nature". "In accordance with nature", *secundum naturam*, κατὰ φύσιν: the philosophical cliché, common to all the schools.

either in favourable or in unfavourable circumstances cf. §22 below.

18. friendship cannot exist except in good men Because only good men are capable of the unselfish affection and fair dealing that friendship demands. This idea appears to originate with Socrates; it appears in Plato *Lysis* 214c-d (although it is attacked by Socrates himself in the following section of that dialogue) and in Xenophon, *Memorabilia* 2.6.16-20. Aristotle quotes the view in *EE* 7.1235a; in *NE* 8, 1157a 16 he says that true and perfect friendship is only to be found in the good, though he admits the existence of inferior forms of friendship, as does Cicero later. The view seems, naturally enough, to have appealed most of all to the Stoics: it occurs in the summary of Stoic doctrine in Diogenes Laertius (7.124) and, with "wise" substituted for "good", in that of Stobaeus (*Ecl.* II p. 108 W.-H. = *SVF* III p. 161); cf. Sen. *Ep.* 81.12 *solus sapiens amicus est*. Epictetus *Diss.* 2.22 concerns the difficulty of maintaining friendship among ordinary, non-"wise" people. Here Cicero follows this tradition, but rejects the extreme Stoic definition of "good men".

prune ... back to the very limit Literally "cut back to the quick"; Cicero's image would be puzzling in English, and I have adopted what seems to be the nearest intelligible equivalent. The meaning, as far as can be seen from the context, is that Cicero (or Laelius), having just said that only the good can be friends, does not now wish to adopt the Stoic definition of the good, and consequently reduce the class of potential friends to virtually nothing. Reid translates "probe the question to its roots", and *OLD* follows him; but *reseco* means "cut back", not "probe", and Laelius is surely not saying that his treatment of the question will be superficial! For similar phrases cf. *Verr.* II 3.118, *Flacc.* 91, Schol. Pers. 5.15 (where the phrase is used in the specific context of surgical excision); Otto, *Sprichwörter* 377-8.

more subtly i.e. displaying a cleverness above the level of common sense; Cicero elsewhere characterises the arguments of the Stoics as "subtle", cf. *Fin.* 3.3; *De Or.* 3.66.

nobody is a good man who is not wise The Stoics identified virtue with wisdom and knowledge, and believed that only the complete virtue of the perfect sage qualified to be called virtue at all.

no human being has ever yet attained it The Stoic Chrysippus (ap. Plut. *De Stoic. repugn.* 31) said that neither he nor any of his contemporaries or predecessors was a good man. Seneca, speaking as a Stoic, said (*Ep.* 42) that the good or wise man was as rare as the phoenix, appearing perhaps once every five hundred years; and (*Tranq.* 7.4) that one should not seek only wise men for one's friends, since they are so rare.

we should pay attention to those things which are available in our own experience This can easily strike the reader as simple, unphilosophical common sense, but in fact there were in later Stoicism signs of a reversion to an attitude like this one: Panaetius (with whom Laelius studied) had concentrated on real problems of morality, removing the ideal of the perfect sage to a relatively unimportant position (cf. Sen. *Ep.* 116.5); and Peripatetic morality had always firmly begun from the real world. The same attitude is apparent in Cicero, *Off.* 1.46.

Gaius Fabricius, Manius Curius, Tiberius Coruncanius A favourite Ciceronian triad of Roman heroes from the time of the Pyrrhic war; see my note on *Cato Maior* 15. They were noted for simple life and upright dealings.

keep for their own use In fact Stoics did not lay claim to perfect wisdom themselves; Cicero presumably means only that they may use the word in their own way if they like. On *sibi habeant* – here, as often, dismissive – see my note on *Cato Maior* 58.

19. in rough common-sense terms The Latin *pingui Minerva*, literally "with a fat Minerva", baffles the translator, though its general meaning is clear enough. It is a phrase like *aequo Marte* "with equal Mars", i.e. (of a battle) equally matched; *invita Minerva* "with Minerva unwilling", i.e. against the grain. Minerva (in her primitive Roman form, not in her mythological identification with Athena) is the *numen* or tutelary spirit of mental activity and craftsmanship, her name perhaps connected with *mens* "mind" (Romans connected it with the related verb *moneo* "to remind, advise", Paul. Fest. 123); we are not to think literally of a fat goddess, nor yet should we simply label the phrase as an instance of "metonymy". *Pinguis* is presumably in this context meant as the opposite of *subtilis*, coarse-grained as opposed to fine or subtle. The adjective *pinguis* applied to the mind is often derogatory, meaning "slow" or "sluggish", but that would not be appropriate here; Cicero's meaning is much like that of Horace *Sat.* 2.2.3 *crassaque Minerva*, cf. *Priapea* 3.10, Macrob. *Sat.* 1.24.13, Otto, *Sprichwörter* 224-5. Columella 1 praef. 33 and 11.1.32 probably derives the phrase from Cicero.

Those who behave and live, etc. Laelius defines "good men" by reference to a list of individual virtues. The list seems to be based on a version of the canonical four "cardinal virtues" (which Cicero used as the basis for his discussion in the *De Officiis*): "honesty, integrity, fairness and generosity" correspond to the cardinal virtue of justice; the absence of "greed, intemperance or shamelessness" corresponds to temperance, and "great strength of character", presumably, to fortitude; the fourth, wisdom or prudence, is omitted in this context for obvious reasons. The idea that moral virtues could thus be separated from wisdom would be countenanced only by the Peripatetics among the Greek philosophical schools; Aristotle follows this sort of division in the *Ethics*. So much for the content: the presentation of the definition has about it a certain Roman legal atmosphere (cf. Introd. §7). The initial *qui*, the strings of near-synonyms with asyndeton, and the reference to example and precedent, combine to suggest Roman legal formulae, albeit delicately. "Good men" are defined in a similar way in *Tusc.* 5.28.

strength of character *Constantia*: see above on §8.

whom I have just named Laelius here uses an old-fashioned turn of phrase, *modo quos nominavi* (Ciceronian Latin would normally have *quos modo nominavi*): see Fedeli, *RhM* 1972, 164. Other mild archaisms are occasionally to be observed in this dialogue; cf. Introd. §7.

follow ... Nature The idea of following Nature as a guide for life (whatever precisely that may involve) is very common in Cicero: see *Cato Maior* 4 and my note, with parallels there cited. It recalls Greek philosophy, particularly Stoicism, but here the point is (as also in *Fin.* 3.11 and *CM* 4) that the old Roman heroes were virtuous by the light of nature, not by philosophical wisdom; and insofar as they followed nature, they were actually (without knowing it) fulfilling one of the Greek philosophical definitions of virtue.

a certain natural bond of association The idea that human society is a consequence of human nature, and that there is a hierarchy of relationships from the widest (common humanity) to the narrowest (friendship between two, or the husband-wife relationship), seems straightforward enough and hardly needs to be traced to a particular philosophical source. It was held by both the Peripatetics and the Stoics. However, the Stoic belief involved in addition the idea that moral duties arise from these forms of kinship, and that men (and indeed other living creatures) feel a natural impulse of kindness towards those who are thus related to them. Whether, or to what extent, the Peripatetics also believed this, is the subject of considerable dispute: it has been thought that Theophrastus's views approached those of the Stoics on this point, and either influenced them or were influenced by them. On the other hand, our evidence for any such Peripatetic doctrine is late and incomplete, and it may be that those who report it (particularly Arius Didymus ap. Stob. *Ecl.* 2, pp. 119-21 W.-H. – a passage similar in many respects to Cicero) were themselves affected by Stoic influence in their interpretation. On this question, see particularly C.O.Brink, "Theophrastus and Zeno on Nature in moral theory", *Phronesis* 1.2 (1956) 123-45 esp. 135-9.

The Stoic teaching was known as the doctrine of οἰκείωσις (a verbal noun meaning being or becoming or realising oneself to be οἰκεῖος, related or akin or familiar to another): Cicero's Latin equivalent of οἰκειοῦσθαι is *conciliari*, and here he uses *conciliare* of Nature effecting the bond of relationship. Cicero puts forward the full Stoic doctrine in *Fin.* 3.62-3, 66-7; similar opinions are attributed to the Academy in *Acad.* 1.21 and *Fin.* 5.65, but this probably reflects the Stoicising tendencies of Antiochus of Ascalon. The idea of the hierarchy of human relationships is developed at much greater length in *Off.* 1.50ff. (also inspired by Stoicism). Friendship duly appears there (1.55-6) and is praised in similar terms to those of this passage, but it does not form a part of the natural hierarchy as first stated; there, as expected, the family takes precedence. Here in the *Laelius*, Cicero emphasises the advantages of friendship at the expense of family relationships (using an argument that turns purely on the meanings of words: for a similar argument cf. Dio Chrysostom *or.* 3.113), and does not mention the husband-wife relationship at all. That is largely due to the rhetorical exigencies of the context; in writing on friendship, Theophrastus also placed it at the top of the list (Jerome on Micah 2.7 = *Corpus Christianorum, Series Latina* 76 p. 509). On the other hand, Stoics valued marriage and the family; Antipater of Tarsus, *SVF* III p. 255, put marriage above friendship; cf. Musonius Rufus περὶ γάμου; Sen. *Ep.* 104. This context should not necessarily lead us into thinking that Cicero undervalued the family in general, though in his doubly-divorced state in 44 BC he may not have felt disposed to sing the praises of marriage.

fellow-countrymen are closer ... strangers   These words are translated from Xenophon, *Cyropaedia* 8.7.14; the passage is from the last speech of Cyrus, in which he exhorts his two sons not to quarrel with each other after his death, arguing from the natural closeness of the relationship between brothers. This speech was also drawn on by Cicero in the *Cato Maior*, 79-81, and, it seems, by Sallust in *Jug.* 10. For other passages in this dialogue derived from Xenophon, see on §62. The presence of this adaptation from Xenophon should caution us against automatically assuming a Stoic source for ideas that look vaguely Stoic.

20. However ... a small number   This sentence is rhetorically impressive on a first reading, but what does it mean? Presumably that in the hierarchy of human relationships, the bond of affection is stronger in inverse proportion to the size of the group; consequently the closest relationship, that between two people only, is also (potentially) the strongest and most genuine in terms of affection. A similar phrase is used in *Off.* 1.53 (of the family as the smallest unit of society). For the thought behind this, one may compare Aristotle, who believed that any individual could have only a few real friends (*NE* 8.1158a 10, 9.1171a 8; *EE* 7.1245b 20); cf.

also Plutarch, περὶ πολυφιλίας 2. The canonical examples of friends (cf. §15 above) are of course pairs, and Cicero always sees friendship as primarily a one-to-one relationship rather than as membership of a circle or group.

community of views on all matters human and divine Cf.§§15 and 100; here the idea functions as a formal definition of friendship. The idea that agreement or community of desires is the essential feature of friendship is commonplace. Aristotle, *NE* 9.1166a mentions it as a popular view; it appears also in the rhetorical tradition, as in Aristotle, *Rhet.* 2.4.1381a; cf. Cic. *Inv.* 2.166, *Planc.* 5, *Fam.* 5.2.3, and the epigrammatic statement in Sallust *Catiline* 20, *idem velle atque idem nolle, ea demum firma amicitia est*; this phrasing became proverbial (see Otto, *Sprichwörter* p. 19 and *Nachträge* p. 52 and 130). The idea was useful in rhetoric as a means of exhorting the listener to agreement or loyalty. The Stoic definition of friendship was based on shared life and activities (Sen. *Ep.* 48.2; Diog. Laert. 7.124; Stob. *Ecl.* II p. 74 W.) as well as agreement (Stob. *Ecl.* II.7 p.105 W.); the proverbial κοινὰ τὰ φίλων was supposed to be Pythagorean (cf. *Off.* 1.51). Cf. also Aristotle *NE* 8.1161b 11, 9.1171b 32; Plutarch, *Quomodo amicus* 51b; Sen. *Ep.* 109.16; Dio Chrysostom *or.* 4, p. 155R. Aristotle *EE* 7.1241a distinguishes the agreement that is essential in friendship from that which is accidental or not even desirable: as so often, Aristotle sees further and more acutely than others. See also *NE* 9.1167a on the concept of ὁμόνοια, "concord" - more than simple agreement, but less than friendship.

together with goodwill and affection Cicero has shown above that goodwill must be part of the concept of friendship. The style of definition, "X is an A of type B together with C", follows the pattern of the philosophical definitions *per genus et differentiam*, to be found in Aristotle and elsewhere.

leaving aside wisdom Plato had said that wisdom was the greatest gift of gods to man, *Timaeus* 47b; Cicero echoes him in *Leg.* 1.58, *Acad.* 1.7, *Tusc.* 1.64. Regarding friendship, the idea is repeated below, §47.

Some put wealth before it Cicero is talking here, not about philosophical definitions of the highest good (no philosopher made wealth the *summum bonum*!), but about the practical attitudes of ordinary people. Nevertheless, it is true enough that this way of talking about aims of human action derives from the philosophers; cf. Aristotle, *NE* 1.1095b-96a.

fit only for animals Cf. §32 below *pecudum ritu*; *Paradoxa* 14; *Tusc* 5.73. Cicero never tires of expressing his contempt for the life of pleasure, and for the Epicureans who believed that pleasure (in however refined and intellectualised a form) was the chief end of human activity.

uncertain and unstable Aristotle in *NE* 1.1095b had used this type of argument against supposing that honour and reputation should be counted as the highest good.

blind chances *temeritas*: this word is derived from *temere*, an adverb meaning "at random" but originally, it is hypothesised, "in the dark" (compare the related Sanskrit word *tamas* "darkness": for the *s - r* change cf. *genus - generis*; Latin *tenebrae* "darkness" is thought to derive from *temes-rae). Though *temeritas* in Latin often does mean the same as English "temerity", i.e. rashness or audacity (cf. §37 below), the sense here is nearer to the etymological meaning: Cicero is not saying that Fortune is overbold, but that she acts capriciously, randomly or blindly.

regard virtue as the highest good The Stoa, the Academy and the Peripatos of Cicero's time all agreed that virtue was the *highest* good, though the Stoics alone said that it was the *only* good. The English translation "virtue" is perhaps a little misleading. *Virtus* is, in usage, simply the abstract noun corresponding to the adjective *bonus* "good" when used of persons, as Greek ἀρετή corresponds to ἀγαθός (*bonitas* is more restricted in meaning, referring to what we call "good nature"). In different contexts, *virtus* may be translated as "virtue", "[human] goodness", "[human] excellence", "good character", or "fine qualities [of character]". Etymologically *virtus* meant "manhood", and in Latin it very often has the sense of "courage", but in a philosophical context like this one it should be understood in the widest possible sense. The essential meaning of the philosophical doctrine is that the proper reason for carrying out any action is that it is a good action, the sort of thing that a person of good character would do; and that it is better to possess good character than to have wealth or power or pleasure.

virtue ... produces ... friendship Expanded on in §§27ff. below. Good men (says Cicero) are naturally attracted to each other.

maintains *OLD* s.v. *continere* 3; not "contains".

nor can friendship exist ... without virtue As said above, §18: friendship can only exist properly in the good, i.e. those endowed with *virtus*.

21. the word virtue Cicero resumes his argument against the narrow Stoic definition of "good men", as above, §18. Here he implies that the Stoics pervert the use of language: an argument of a type that was used against them particularly by Antiochus of Ascalon (who belonged to the Academy).

Paulus, Cato, Galus, Scipio or Philus For Paulus, Cato and Galus see §9 above. L.Furius Philus, consul 136 BC, was a friend of Scipio and Laelius and one of the speakers in the *De Republica*; cf. §§14, 69, 101. His name is simply the Greek φίλος, "friend"; no doubt that was a factor in Cicero's choice of the example in this context. The names are plural in Latin, as we might talk about "Newtons and Einsteins"; see my note on *Cato Maior* 13.

22. such great advantages Laelius now embarks on a rhetorical encomium of friendship. Aristotle had listed some of the obvious advantages of friendship in *NE* 8.1155a; Xenophon, *Mem.* 2.4.5-7 made Socrates praise the ideal friend, in more concrete terms than Cicero's here. Seneca, *Tranq.* 7.3 perhaps had Cicero in mind when writing in a similar vein. Nor should one forget St. Paul's encomium of ἀγάπη ("charity") in I *Corinthians* 13: with this passage compare particularly verses 4-8.

"lively life" "Lively" in the translation represents the form of the adjective *vitalis*, rather than the meaning, which in this context is uncertain. Usually the word means simply "of or pertaining to life". Without more of Ennius's words it is impossible to see what exactly he meant by it (Skutsch, *Ennius* p. 759). From Cicero's use of the phrase here, it might mean "life that is truly life". However, it is perhaps more likely that *vitalis* was intended as a (makeshift) equivalent for the Greek word βιωτός "livable"; this would also make good sense for Cicero here. Cf. Aristotle, *NE* 8.1155a 5 ἄνευ γὰρ φίλων οὐδεὶς ἕλοιτ' ἂν ζῆν ἔχων τὰ λοιπὰ ἀγαθὰ πάντα ("nobody would choose to live without friends even if he had all the other good things in life"); §§52 and 55 below.

just as with yourself cf. Seneca *Ep.* 3.2 *tam audaciter cum illo loquere quam tecum* (this letter is perhaps influenced by the *Laelius*); Pliny *Ep.* 5.1.12 *non aliter tecum quam mecum loqui soleo*; also Cic. *Fin.* 2.85.

good fortune ... adversity The advantages of friendship in both situations are discussed by Aristotle, *NE* 9.1169b 14ff.; cf. also Arist. *Rhet.* 2.4.1381a; Xen. *Symp.* 8.18; Cic. *Fin.* 1.67; Dio Chrysostom *or.* 3.100-1; 41.13. Isocrates, *Ad Demonicum* 26 points out that the real test of a friend is not whether he sympathises with you in misfortune, but whether he takes pleasure in your success without being envious. Cf. also §64 below.

fire and water The proverb recurs (whether from Cicero or independently, is not clear) in Plutarch, *Quomodo amicus* 51b; cf. Otto, *Sprichwörter* p. 19.

common or incomplete sort ... true and perfect friendship The distinction recurs below, §§76, 77, 100. "Perfect" corresponds to Greek τέλειος: cf. Aristotle *NE* 8.1156b 6 τελεία δ' ἐστιν ἡ τῶν ἀγαθῶν φιλία.

both pleasurable and profitable Aristotle's two inferior forms of friendship are based on pleasure and on profit. Cicero's point is a rhetorical one: if even the inferior forms of friendship are pleasant and useful, then how much better must true friendship be.

the few who are remembered §15 above.

23. a beacon of hope So our idiom has it, but the image of *praelucet* is actually of a torch carried in front of one to light the way; we are envisaged as journeying into the future. "Nor does it allow the human spirit to weaken or stumble" continues this image.

a reflection of himself The idea that a friend is another self is Aristotelian (*NE* 9.1166a ἐστὶ γὰρ ὁ φίλος ἄλλος αὐτός; ibid. 1170b 6; *EE* 7.1245a esp. 36-8; MM 2.1213a) and Stoic (Zeno in Diog. Laert. 7.23); Cicero alludes to it also in §80 below. He had long before called Atticus his "second self", *me alterum* (*Att.* 3.15.4); the phrase was used in conventional protestations of (political) friendship, as by Cicero to Caesar in *Fam.* 7.5.1 or Pompey to Cicero as reported in *Att.* 4.1.7; see F.Lossmann, *Cicero und Caesar im Jahre 54: Theorie und Praxis der römischen Freundschaft* (Wiesbaden 1962) 33-51; cf. also Cic. *Fam.* 2.15.4; Pliny, *Ep.* 2.9.1; Otto, *Sprichwörter* 26.

those who are absent are made present A similar rhetorical excursion was employed by Cicero in speaking of glory in *Pro Milone* 97 *quae efficeret ut absentes adessemus, mortui viveremus.* Presumably he means (if "means" is not too strong a word) that an absent or dead person is present or alive in the thoughts of his friend. The idea that the dead live in the memory of those who survive them is commonplace; for an early instance cf. Simonides *epig.* 121 Diehl (= *AP* 7.251) οὐδὲ τεθνᾶσι θανόντες. The topic is reverted to in the peroration of this dialogue, §§102-4.

no house or city will be able to stand Cf. Aristotle, *NE* 8.1155a 22 ἔοικε δὲ καὶ τὰς πόλεις συνέχειν ἡ φιλία; Matthew 12.25 "A house divided against itself cannot stand".

nor even will the tilling of the land continue Presumably because it requires co-operation and respect for property.

24. a wise man of Agrigentum Empedocles; his cosmological speculations are here referred to, for which see his Περὶ φύσεως, frr. 17, 18-21, 26, 35 Diels-Kranz; see also Diels-Kranz 31 A 28ff. "Friendship" here corresponds to φιλότης, conventionally translated "love"; "discord" to νεῖκος, usually translated "strife"; for Empedocles these were the two principles that determined the expansion or contraction of the universe. Aristotle, *NE* 8.1155b also refers to this cosmological theory of Empedocles in the context of human friendship, but (unlike Cicero) admits that it is hardly relevant. From a rhetorical point of view it i, clearly meant to demonstrate the universality of friendship. Note that Empedocles is not named here: cf. Introd. §7.

declared *vaticinatum*, literally "prophesied": Empedocles is represented as an inspired poet rather than a rational philosopher, as also by Cicero in *Acad. Pr.* 2.14; cf. Lucretius 1.731.

circumstances call for some action *exstitit officium*, "an *officium* [conventionally "duty"] has arisen". *Officium amici* is not simply the duty of a friend, but also any action to perform which, in a given set of circumstances, would be characteristic of a friend.

Pacuvius The first of a number of references to the Roman theatre; cf. Introd. §§5 and 7. M.Pacuvius was a tragic playwright, nephew and pupil of Ennius; he enjoyed the patronage of Laelius (see Beare, *Roman Stage* 69-74). This episode from his works is also mentioned in *Fin.* 2.79 and 5.63; in the latter passage the actual words are quoted, *Ego sum Orestes ... Immo enimvero ego sum, inquam, Orestes* (Pacuv. trag. 365 Ribbeck). The passage comes most probably from a play entitled *Chryses* (cf. O.Jahn, *Hermes* 2 [1867] 233), from which the grammarian Nonius Marcellus quotes a line *Inveni, opino* [sic], *Orestes uter esset tamen* (trag. 101), clearly referring to the same event. The episode apparently belongs during the flight of Orestes and Pylades from the land of the Taurians, narrated by Hyginus (*Fab.* 121) as the sequel to the events of Euripides's *Iphigenia in Tauris*. The two friends, having found Iphigenia (who was, according to this version, miraculously saved by Artemis from the sacrifice at Aulis, and deposited among the Taurians) and escaped with her, were pursued by the Taurian king Thoas. They were given protection by Chryses, son of Agamemnon and Chryseis; Thoas, having tracked them down, was outwitted and killed. It is possible that this story formed the plot of Sophocles's lost play *Chryses* (Jebb-Pearson JI. pp. 327-30), but only if the Iphigenia in Tauris story existed before Euripides's treatment of it (cf. Wilamowitz, *Hermes* 18 (1883) 257), or if the *Chryses* itself was composed later than Euripides's play (i.e. in the last few years of Sophocles's life). If that is the case, Pacuvius's play may have been based on Sophocles.

The audience stood up to applaud Cf. *Att.* 2.19.3; J.Gwyn Griffiths, *CR* 66 = N.S. 2 (1952) 72, takes this as evidence that Roman theatres had seats in Laelius's time, on the assumption that an anachronism on this point would be uncharacteristic of Cicero; cf. Beare, *Roman Stage* Appendix A; F.L.Lentz, *N. Jahrb. Kl. Phil.* 101 (1870) 17-18. On the reaction of the Roman audience, cf. also E. Rawson in *Homo Viator: classical essays for John Bramble*, ed. M.Whitby and others (Bristol 1987) 80.

those who lecture on those subjects Laelius again contrasts himself with the professional Greek philosophers: cf. Introd. §7.

25. The following brief conversational exchange, in which Laelius's show of reluctance is overcome with surprising ease, serves to mark off the preceding generalised praises of friendship from the rather more analytical discussion which follows.

the texture of your argument is somehow different The Latin metaphor, *filum*, literally means "thread"; it is not uncommon in such contexts; cf. Cic. *Orat.* 124, *Fam.* 9.12.2, *De Or.* 2.93; 3.103; Hor. *Epist.* 2.1.225; etc. Unlike English "thread", it refers to the texture rather than the direction of an argument. Probably Cicero means to characterise his own treatment as more generously rhetorical, more practically and moralistically biassed, and less subtle and abstract than that of the Greek philosophers.

conversation on politics   I.e. the (imaginary) conversation narrated in Cicero's own *De Republica*, already alluded to above in §14. In the third book of the *De Rep.*, Philus presented the view of Carneades that government requires injustice; Laelius undertook to refute this view, and was thus the "defender of justice" (*patronus*, legal term for defence advocate). For the problem of whether Fannius was present at the conversation, see above on §14.

for maintaining it   The language here, *ob eam ... servatam,* is dignified and formal, and calls to mind the style of a citation for a public honour; cf. the legend *ob cives servatos* on Augustan coinage.

26. force   *Vim adferre* is used in technical legal contexts (*OLD* s.v. *vis* 3) to mean "to apply force" or "compulsion", and it is this usage that is doubtless in question here. Most usually, however, the word *vis* (sometimes with the verb *adferre*) refers to actual physical violence (*OLD* ibid. 2). For locutions like *vim hoc quidem est adferre*, cf. Plaut. *Capt.* 750, Ter. *Ad.* 943, Suet. *Div. Jul.* 82; Otto, *Sprichwörter* p. 374.

26-32. Second main speech of Laelius: the problem of the origins of friendship.   Ancient speculation on friendship seems to have concerned itself to a large extent with the question of how friendship came to exist in the first place; this was related to the wider issue of the origin of human society (cf. *Rep.* 1.39, where the question of the origin of political associations is posed in similar terms, and – the *locus classicus* for Epicurean ideas on this point – Lucretius 5), while opinions on the origin of friendship also had implications for the treatment of moral questions concerning it.

The view that friendship arises from weakness or insufficiency in the individual parties is to be found in Plato, *Lysis* 214e-215c, and more or less the same is said of love (*eros*) in *Symposium* 201d-204e, where the personified Eros is said to be the son of *Penia* (poverty: for the genealogical image see §29 below). The related idea that, as Cicero puts it here, "each man receives from another what he could not achieve for himself", occurs in Aristotle *NE* 9.1169b τὸν δὲ φίλον ... πορίζειν ὃ δι' αὑτοῦ ἀδυνατεῖ (the friend provides for a man what he cannot himself provide), but Aristotle concludes that this is more characteristic of the lower and imperfect form of friendship that is based on utility, rather than the true and perfect sort based on the harmony of personalities. The Epicureans' view is succinctly expressed by Lucretius (5.1019-20): friendship, like other forms of human association, was originally a sort of contract for mutual protection, thus based entirely on expediency. Compare also Diogenes Laertius 10.120 τὴν φιλίαν διὰ τὰς χρείας γίγνεσθαι, Cic. *Fin.* 1.66ff. (which presents a more moderate Epicurean view in addition), and the Epicurean sayings in *Gnom. Vat.* 32 and 39 (cf. Introd. §2 for bibliography on Epicurean views of friendship); before Epicurus, the Cyrenaics had held similar views (Diogenes Laertius 2.91). The problem formulated here was clearly well-worn, as appears from Cicero's previous discussions of it (*Inv.* 2.167, *Leg.* 1.49, *ND* 1.122); cf. Introd. §2. Cic. does not draw a distinction between the idea that one acquires friends because one *needs* them (owing to a weakness in oneself), and the view that one acquires them because it is *advantageous* to have them (though one may be able to manage perfectly well without them); this constitutes a considerable looseness in his argument, but it seems that the same confusion may have been present in the Epicurean views which he attacks. The argument also squares rather badly with §§22, 52-5 and 88, where he says that life without friends is hardly tolerable. Cf. also §§29 and 51 below.

often had occasion to think A standard rhetorical opening formula; cf. *De Or.* 1.1 *Cogitanti mihi saepenumero.*

love, from which friendship derives its name Cicero is fond of etymologising for philosophical purposes; here he makes the obvious point that the Latin word *amicitia* comes from the root *am-* meaning "love"; cf. below, §100, and *ND* 1.122.

cultivated ... under the pretence of friendship The ancients were much preoccupied with the topic of flattery and insincerity in friendship; see §§53 and 91ff. below.

27. animals, which love their offspring Cf. Aristotle *NE* 8.1154a; the topic is treated by Plutarch in his essay Περὶ φιλοστοργίας. For the parallel between humans and animals cf. also §81 below.

parents and children The parallel between friendship and natural family affection is drawn by Aristotle, *NE* 8.1155a; *EE* 7.1241b.

some abominable crime Cicero is no doubt thinking of the ancient horror of parricide.

affinity in character Cf. above, §§20 and 23; below, §§50 and 82. One often finds the idea that friendship is based on similarity; the philosophers sometimes qualify this as meaning similar attainments in respect of virtue. Cf. Plato *Lysis* 214e ff.; *Gorgias* 510b; *Laws* 8.837a; Thuc. 3.10; Aristotle, *NE* 8.1155a 32, 1157b 7, 1159b 1, *EE* 7.1235a; Plutarch, *Quomodo amicus* 51b; Cic. *Off.* 1.55-6.

28. excellence of character excites affection cf. §20 above, and observation ad loc. on the concept of *virtus*. Cicero's phrase *nihil est virtute amabilius* occurs also in *ND* 1.121, where he cites the Stoic belief that all good and wise men are friends to each other, even if they do not know each other, owing to the natural and inevitable attraction of one virtuous man for another (though Aristotle pointed out, with rather more justification, that since friendship is properly speaking mutual, goodwill is the most one can have towards those one does not know). The same idea is alluded to below, §50.

Gaius Fabricius or Manius Curius Cf. above, §18.

Spurius Cassius, Spurius Maelius These two characters were both alleged to have attempted to establish personal domination at Rome during the fifth century BC; the former was supposed to have been condemned to death for treason, the latter to have been killed by C. Servilius Ahala at the instance of the dictator Cincinnatus. It is difficult to think that Romans of the late Republic felt as strongly about these semi-legendary figures as Cicero implies, yet the memory of Cassius and Maelius may have been revived in the controversy over the Gracchi, whom they resembled in some respects (and indeed features of the Gracchi may have been read back into the stories of Maelius and Cassius). For Cassius see Livy 2.41 and Ogilvie's commentary, pp. 337ff.; Cic. *Rep.* 2.49 and 2.60; for Maelius, Livy 4.12 and Ogilvie pp. 550ff.; the example of Maelius is referred to a number of times by Cicero: *Rep.* 2.49; *CM* 56; *Mil.* 72; *Catil.* 1.3; *Phil.* 2.114; in none of these passages does it constitute more than a stock example of what happens to someone who tries to make himself tyrant at Rome. Cf. also A.W.Lintott, 'The Tradition of Violence in the Annals of the Early Republic', *Historia* 19 (1970) 12–29.

Pyrrhus and Hannibal Cf. *Off.* 1.38. Pyrrhus was regarded by the Romans as an honourable man, while Hannibal's cruelty was proverbial.

29. the receiving of kindnesses ... the building up of familiarity The three factors mentioned here may perhaps reflect the threefold classification of friendship κατ' ἀμοιβήν (by exchange of favours), ἐκ συνηθείας (from habitual association) and κατ' ἀρετήν (because of virtue), given by Clement of Alexandria (*Strom.* II p. 483) from an earlier source, either Stoic or Peripatetic. The first two of these certainly correspond to two of Cicero's items here, and the third too corresponds if one bears in mind Cicero's statement that friendly interest is excited in the first place by the observation of the other's good character. This threefold scheme is evidently an alteration of Aristotle's division of friends and friendships into good, useful and pleasurable; for similar triplets see Plutarch περὶ πολυφιλίας 94b, Stob. *Ecl.* 2 p. 94 W.-H. (Stoics).

mean origin ... no aristocratic lineage Cicero's language here refers explicitly to genealogy, and no doubt he had in mind the Platonic fancy that Love was born of Poverty (*Symp.* 203c). There is however no reference to the other parent specified in the Platonic passage, *Poros* (abundance); this would not have suited the argument. See above on §26.

30. regarding ... as within his own control The self-sufficiency of the wise or good man is here stressed. The phrasing is the same as in §7 above where Fannius compliments Laelius on his philosophical bearing.

some opinion Note Laelius's characteristic modesty.

31. as we practise kindness ... If it were done for a reward it would not be strictly speaking kindness or generosity. Aulus Gellius 17.5 discusses this passage, defending it against a critic who had alleged it to be illogical. On the virtues of *beneficentia* and *liberalitas*, cf. *Off.* 1.42-60; Sen. *Benef.* 4.3.3.

it is by nature that we are disposed to generosity cf. *Leg.* 1.43 *natura propensi sumus ad diligendos homines*; *ND* 1.122.

32. who, in swinish manner, refer everything to pleasure A virtually explicit attack on the Epicureans, for whom pleasure was the aim of all human action. For the characterisation of hedonism as "swinish" (*pecudum ritu*, literally "in the manner of farm animals") cf. §20 above; also Horace's jocular *Epicuri de grege porcum* (*Epist.* 4.16).

cannot look up This continues the idea of hedonism as a "swinish" philosophy. Cicero is here probably recalling a passage of Plato's *Republic*, 9.586a, where it is said that lovers of commonplace pleasures οὔτε ἀνέβλεψαν πώποτε ... ἀλλὰ βοσκημάτων δίκην κάτω ἀεὶ βλέποντες ... βόσκονται, i.e. feed with their heads downwards like cattle, and never look up (towards philosophic truth). Ancient writers often contrast the erect posture of man, which enables him to look up towards heaven, with the less privileged position of quadrupeds whose eyes are directed downwards towards their source of food: cf. Xen. *Mem.* 1.4.11, Cic. *Leg.* 1.26, *ND* 2.140 (the latter a Stoic context), Sallust, *Cat.* 1, Ovid, *Met.* 1.84-6.

that affection that consists in goodwill Lit. "the affection of goodwill", i.e. the state of being well-disposed to another, which, when it becomes mutual, turns into friendship.

more disposed to do favours   Cf. Aristotle, *NE* 1169b 11;   for an expansion of the theme, Seneca *Ep.* 9.

each competing honourably with the other   cf. Sen. *Benef.* 1.4.3;   Musonius περὶ γάμου.

If it were simple expediency   Cf. *Fin.* 3.70 (an explicitly Stoic context) *minime vero probatur huic disciplinae de qua loquor, aut iustitiam aut amicitiam propter utilitates adscisci aut probari; eaedem enim utilitates poterunt eas labefactare atque pervertere.*

since nature itself cannot be changed   All this implies is that good qualities of character do not change their nature; the Stoics thought that virtue, once acquired, could not be lost.   One should beware of taking this as evidence that Cicero believed that human character or personality was by nature immutable;   indeed he says in the very next paragraph that men's characters often change for certain reasons; see ad loc., and cf. §54 below.

true friendships are ... everlasting   Aristotle believed that true friendships (i.e. those based on goodness of character and natural affinity) were permanent or likely to be so (*NE* 1156b), while the inferior sorts were easily dissolved, because based on impermanent things (utility or pleasure).   The idea however is commonplace;   even nowadays people are prone to think that if a friendship comes to an end, it was never a true one.   See e.g. Cic. *Rab. Post.* 32; Livy 40.46.12; Isocrates, *Ad Demonicum* 1; Otto, *Sprichwörter* 19.

who is younger than I am   Cicero makes his characters observe conventions of precedence according to age;   Laelius similarly speaks on behalf of Scipio in *Cato Maior* 6.

33-104. Third main speech of Laelius
33-44. The difficulty of maintaining friendship, leading into discussion of the moral choice between loyalty to a friend and loyalty to one's country.

33. Listen then   It is a standard device in dialogue to make a character quote from an absent person, or report a discussion held at some other time.   Not only does it make for literary variety, but it also allows the expression of a wider range of views.   Here it appears that the practical and worldly thoughts on friendship that follow are being attributed to Scipio, in order to avoid collision with the idealistic and philosophical doctrines which Laelius puts forward in his own person.   In particular, Laelius has just said that true friendships are permanent, but he now turns to discuss the various reasons why friendship may not (in practice) last.   The change of viewpoint is neatly signalled by the conjunction *quamquam* (here translated "yet now that I think of it"), and the emphatic *ille quidem* ("he used to say").   The device is paralleled in the *Cato Maior*, §§39ff., where Cato is made to reproduce arguments attributed to Archytas of Tarentum;   there are Platonic precedents (e.g. Socrates's recounting of his conversation with Diotima in the *Symposium*).   In the present dialogue, Laelius quotes Scipio again below in §§59-60 and 62: the former passage is more or less a parenthesis in the main argument, the latter marks the transition between one major section and the next;   cf. on those passages.

that men's characters changed   Literally their ways of behaving (*mores*), but the normal English equivalent of *mores* is "character";   it is irrelevant to argue in this connection whether the Romans thought each individual had a basic character which could not change however much his outward manner of behaviour might alter or seem to do so; probably most of us intuitively hold some such belief, but it does not affect our ability to say that a person's character can change, nor did it stop the Romans from saying things such as Cicero says here. It is high time that the phantom of the "Roman belief in the immutability of character" was laid to rest; on this point see also my review of J.M.May, *Trials of Character: the Eloquence of Ciceronian Ethos* (Chapel Hill 1988), *CR* 39 (1989) 225; C.Gill, *CQ* 33 (1983) 469ff.

with advancing age In *CM* 10 Cicero makes the contrasting point, in a laudatory passage, that the *mores* of Q. Fabius Maximus did not deteriorate with age.

with the *toga praetexta* The purple-bordered toga, which was (by idiosyncratic Roman custom) confined to boys under military age and to curule magistrates. It was ceremonially laid aside (*deponere*) normally at the age of sixteen, when the adolescent boy would assume the plain woollen *toga virilis*. Cicero imagines boys laying aside their adolescent friendships at the same time; of course he does not imply that *all* friendships formed in boyhood are impermanent.

34. competition ... over a marriage arrangement i.e. rivalry for the hand of one woman.

in the top ranks of society literally "the best men"; the distinction between the majority, who desire money, and the aristocracy, who desire honour and glory, reflects the nature of most ancient society, Greek as well as Roman.

35. would do anything for the sake of a friend with implication of wrongdoing, cf. Greek πανοῦργος and Catullus 75.4 *omnia si facias*.

36. how far love for a friend ought to be taken Cicero never really answers this question precisely. He gives in the following sections (up to §44) an emphatically negative answer to the question whether one should prefer loyalty to a friend over loyalty to one's country. Yet in a later passage (§61) he seems ready to admit that some compromise of principles for a friend's benefit is permissible; see on that section.

Coriolanus Cf. §42 below; for the story of Coriolanus see Livy 2.33 and Ogilvie's commentary, pp. 314ff.; Dion. Hal. 6-7; Plutarch *Coriolanus* (the source of Shakespeare's play).

Vecellinus or Maelius see above, §28; "Vecellinus" was supposed to be Spurius Cassius's *cognomen*.

37. Tiberius Gracchus This dialogue is set four years after the tribunate of Tiberius Gracchus. It was quite natural for Cicero to make Laelius speak with lively concern of these events; it is not so certain whether the Laelius of the dialogue represents the views of the historical Laelius, although evidence outside Cicero to support or disprove this is largely lacking. Cicero makes Laelius speak in much the same vein in *De Rep.* 1.31. He himself regarded the Gracchi very unfavourably, and he may be projecting his own views back on to Laelius to some extent. On the other hand, there is no reason to suppose that Cicero indulged in deliberate distortion on a factual level, or that his evidence is automatically less credible because it is embodied in a philosophical dialogue rather than a work of historical narration (cf. Appendix 3 of my edition of the *Cato Maior*). In assessing the historical evidence for the Gracchan period, the *Laelius* should be treated as a source like any other, with due regard to the fact (a) that it was composed some ninety years after the events described (though still earlier than most of the other extant sources), and must therefore have relied on earlier sources now lost to us, which may well have been tendentious or inaccurate; and (b) that Cicero's own political preoccupations are bound to have coloured his presentation of the Gracchan period, consciously or unconsciously. The fact that he makes so much of these events here indicates how important he thought they were; they could be seen as the beginnings of the historical process that culminated in the civil wars of Cicero's own lifetime, and it is fairly clear from several of Cicero's remarks below that this is how he intended the reader of the *Laelius* to regard them. Cicero obviously could not refer directly in the dialogue to events later than 129 BC, when the conversation of the *Laelius* was supposed to take place, but he could comment indirectly on them by reference to parallel events in the past, and by making Laelius indulge in a certain amount of discreet political prognostication. The reader should not be troubled by the dramatic irony of Laelius's allusions to later events; see notes below and Introd. §3.

There is an immense bibliography on the history of the Gracchan period; those new to the subject should begin with Stockton, *Gracchi*; E.Badian *ANRW* I.1, pp. 668ff.; D.Earl, *Tiberius Gracchus* (Coll. Latomus 66, 1963). Of particular relevance to the following passage is J.Briscoe, "Supporters and opponents of Tiberius Gracchus", *JRS* 64 (1974) 125ff.; on Cicero's presentation of the Gracchi in general, see J.Béranger, *ANRW* I.1. pp. 732-63. The main ancient sources for Tiberius Gracchus's tribunate, and related events, are the Livian Epitome (58ff.), Plutarch's life of Tiberius Gracchus, and Appian *BC* I; see also A.H.J.Greenidge and A.M.Clay, *Sources for Roman History 133-70 BC* (ed.2, revised by E.W.Gray, Oxford 1960) 1-23. On Laelius's political position in 129 cf. also Astin, *Scipio* 230 n.2; Münzer, RE XII, 404-10.

37. Quintus Tubero He was a nephew of Scipio Aemilianus, his mother being an Aemilia, daughter of Aemilius Paulus. He had philosophical interests, and appears as a character in Cicero's *De Republica*. Cf. §101 below; Briscoe art. cit. p. 131.

Gaius Blossius of Cumae The Blossii were a distinguished (cf. Cic. *Leg. agr.* 2.93) and widespread Campanian family, belonging to the Hellenised native Italian aristocracy of the region; the name is attested not only at Cumae but at Puteoli, Capua, Herculaneum, Aquinum and in Sardinia (*CIL* 10 index); cf. *Année Épigraphique* (1980) 67, no. 242. The family seem originally to have been Capuan (Livy 23.7.8-9; 27.3.4-5).

This Gaius Blossius had studied Stoic philosophy with Antipater of Tarsus, and he is often supposed to have influenced Tiberius Gracchus's policies; yet it is difficult to pin this down to anything specific. See D.R.Dudley, "Blossius of Cumae", *JRS* 31 (1941) 94-9; Plutarch *TG* 8, 17 and 20; Val. Max. 4.7.1 (following the present passage); Badian *ANRW* I.1.679, Béranger, ibid. 755-6, Earl, *Tiberius Gracchus* (cited above on §36) 96, C.Nicolet, *Les Gracques* (Paris 1967) 149, Astin, *Scipio* 229-30 and 349. Montaigne, *Essais* 1.28, takes issue with Cicero over his judgement on Blossius.

a guest of your family This passage is the only evidence for ties of *hospitium* between Blossius and the Mucii Scaevolae. However, P. Mucius Scaevola, consul in 133, cousin of Scaevola the Augur (the Scaevola of this dialogue), was an associate of Tiberius Gracchus, and acquiesced in his policies (though later defended Scipio Nasica for killing Gracchus). There is little evidence as to Scaevola the Augur's relations with Gracchus; Cicero makes him critical of the Gracchi in *De Oratore* 1.38. See Briscoe, *JRS* 64 (1974) 129, E.S.Gruen, Roman *Politics and the Criminal Courts 149-78 BC* (Cambridge, Mass., 1968) 112-4.

Laenas and Rupilius P.Popillius Laenas and P.Rupilius, the consuls of 132. For Rupilius's friendship with Scipio cf. §§69; 73; 101.

in an advisory capacity *in consilio*: the consuls' *consilium* was an informal advisory body chosen by themselves.

the new tribunal A tribunal (*quaestio*) was set up by decree of the Senate in 132 to try the supporters of Tiberius Gracchus. See Sallust *Jug.* 31.7, Vell. Pat. 2.7.3, Plutarch *TG* 20, Stockton, *Gracchi* 90.

fled to Asia Plutarch *TG* 20 tells us that Blossius went to Asia Minor to join Aristonicus. Attalus III of Pergamum, who died in 133, had bequeathed the kingdom to Rome, and Aristonicus, who may have been an illegitimate half-brother of Attalus, led a rising against the Romans in 133-130. On his defeat, Blossius committed suicide.

38. nothing wrong ... laying down The Latin phrases *nihil habeat res viti* and *si statuerimus* have a legal flavour, as often in this dialogue: cf. Introd. §7.

supposing that we were equipped with perfect wisdom Cicero again contrasts the theoretical perfection of the Stoic sage with the wisdom that is found in practice in everyday life (cf. §18 above), and in doing so he seems rather to break the flow of his argument. Having said that there can be no conflict between friendship and morality if the friends are perfectly wise, he then amends this in order to assure us that perfect Stoic wisdom is not necessary for such a situation to obtain.

39. Aemilius Papus Q.Aemilius Papus and C.Fabricius Luscinus (for whom see above, §18) were consuls together in 282 and 278 BC, and censors in 275 (Broughton, *MRR* I, 189, 194, and 196). One should beware of taking this passage to imply that colleagues in magistracies were always, or even in general, friends. There were notable instances of colleagues who were indeed friends (such as Cato the Elder and Valerius Flaccus, colleagues both as consuls and as censors), but there were also notable examples of colleagues failing to see eye to eye. The triple coincidence of Aemilius Papus and Fabricius would no doubt be noteworthy, but Cicero is careful to make it clear that the assertion of their friendship is not merely an inference from this, but was vouched for by independent tradition ("so we have heard from our fathers"). Cicero's argument here is quite different: it is that close personal association between politicians does not necessarily result in conspiracy against the public interest. He contrasts the instance of Blossius and Gracchus, in which the friends did (in his view) lead each other astray, with that of Aemilius Papus and Fabricius, who were equally close friends, holding high office together, but who never acted against the interests of the state (despite the ample opportunities they might have had for doing so).

Manius Curius and Tiberius Coruncanius see above, §§18 and 28.

their duty The Latin word is *fides*, conventionally "good faith", referring, in the context of political office, to the duty or responsibility entrusted to a magistrate and his good faith in carrying it out; to act *contra fidem* is to commit a breach of trust. For the combination *fides magistratusque* in official formulae, see Hellegouarc'h, *Vocabulaire* 30-31; cf. e.g. Cic. *Pro Murena* 1, Varro *LL* 6.86.

Gaius Carbo cf. below, §§41 and 96. C. Papirius Carbo was tribune in 131 or 130, a strong supporter of Gracchan policies; as tribune he proposed a law explicitly allowing tribunes to be elected for a second term (§96 below), thus legitimising Tiberius Gracchus's attempt at re-election; and he was a member of the Gracchan land commission in 130. Cf. Stockton, *Gracchi* 91-2; [Livy] *Epit.* 59; Appian *BC* 1.21.

Gaius Cato His father was Cato the Censor's elder son M.Porcius Cato Licinianus, his mother a daughter of Aemilius Paulus and sister of Scipio Aemilianus; thus he was a cousin of Q.Tubero, mentioned above, §37. He later became consul in 114 BC. Little seems to be known of his political activities. Cf. Astin, *Scipio* 87.

his brother Gaius Gaius Gracchus, while absent on the Numantine campaign, was made a member of Tiberius Gracchus's land commission. In *TG* 21, Plutarch records that Gaius Gracchus questioned Scipio in public about Tiberius Gracchus's death, presumably soon after returning from Numantia; in the life of Gaius Gracchus, Plutarch says that he withdrew from public life after his brother's death (but does not say for how long). He spoke in favour of Carbo's law in 131 or 130 (cf. above, and §96 below; Malcovati, *Oratorum Romanorum Fragmenta* pp. 178-9); thereafter we hear little of his activities until 126 when he stood for the quaestorship, but this passage may be taken as evidence that he was politically active in 129.

40. enact this law This anticipates the fuller legalistic summary in §44. For the phrase, see also *Planc.* 5.

Indeed ... the Republic Cicero makes Laelius digress on the political situation in 129 and likely future events; the passage is of course written with scarcely disguised hindsight. Laelius is made to look forward with trepidation to Gaius Gracchus's tribunate, six years in the future, as though it were already a certainty; and in §43 below, Laelius more or less prophesies the civil wars of the next two generations.

veered ... off the straight course The metaphor, in the Latin, is explicitly from chariot-racing; similar images occur in §§45, 63, 67, 85 and 101.

41. tried to establish a tyranny This was the standard accusation against Tiberius Gracchus, however ill-founded it may seem from a modern historian's point of view; see Plutarch *TG* 14.1; Sallust, *Jug.* 31.7; Stockton, *Gracchi* 69-70. Since "tyrannicide" was regarded as justifiable, the accusation had the effect of justifying the killing of Gracchus; cf. Scipio Aemilianus's remark as reported in Vell. Pat. 2.4.4, *si is occupandae rei publicae animum habuisset, iure caesum videri* (though the "if"-clause is probably Velleius's expansion; Cicero, *De Or.* 2.106 and *Pro Mil.* 8, reports only the last three words).

Had the people of Rome seen or heard anything like it before? The Gracchan sedition, involving mob violence, was persistently seen as a new departure, despite partial precedents (cf. L.R.Taylor, "Forerunners of the Gracchi", *JRS* 52 [1962] 19-27).

Publius Nasica On the textual problem here, see Appendix. P. Cornelius Scipio Nasica Serapio, a cousin of Scipio Aemilianus, was the killer of Tiberius Gracchus. After the events of 133 Nasica was sent to Pergamum on an embassy: Plutarch says that this was an attempt by members of the senate to keep Nasica safe from possible reprisals in Rome. However, Nasica died at Pergamum soon afterwards, and Cicero implies here that his death was not accidental. Cf. Val. Max. 5.3.2e, Plutarch *TG* 21; H.Dessau, *Inscriptiones Latinae Selectae*, no. 8886 is his epitaph.

Carbo cf. above, §39. *Sustinuimus* only makes sense as meaning "we kept in check", i.e. by threatening him with a similar fate to that of Gracchus. It could also mean simply "put up with", and is sometimes so interpreted (e.g. in Combès's Budé edition), but it is then very difficult to see what the logic of the sentence might be.

the ballot The introduction of the secret ballot was regarded with grave suspicion by conservative Roman politicians; previously it had been possible for the aristocrats to keep a check on the way their clients and tribesmen were voting. Voting in elections was made secret in 139 BC by a law of the tribune A. Gabinius; L. Cassius Longinus, tribune in 137, extended the secret ballot to juries; Carbo, in 131, extended it still further to voting on legislation. See Cicero *Leg.* 3.35ff. on all these laws; in §37 of that passage he records a view that Scipio Aemilianus was partly responsible for the passing of the law of Cassius (a view which Cicero here discreetly fails to mention: Laelius could hardly criticise Scipio in this context); but Badian (*ANRW* I.1.698-700) has argued that Scipio did not really support the bill, but only opposed the unconstitutional use of the veto against it. Cf. Astin, *Scipio* 130f., Briscoe, *JRS* 64 (1974) 127 n.3 and 130; Staveley, *Voting and Elections* 158.

42. Why all this? This marks the return from the digression; cf. *Cato Maior* 13, 42, 44.

Themistocles ... Coriolanus The comparison of Themistocles and Coriolanus was standard (although not adopted by Plutarch in his *Parallel Lives*). This was not the only instance in which Roman antiquarians tried to establish a chronological connection between apparently similar events in Greek and Roman history. Cf. Cic. *Brutus* 42-4 and A.E.Douglas's notes, Gellius 17.21.12, E.Fantham *LCM* 6 (1981) 7-17. Cicero had used the examples of Themistocles and Coriolanus when debating what to do at the outbreak of civil war in 49 BC: see *Att.* 7.11.3; 9.10.3. On Cicero's use of Themistocles as an example in various contexts, see H.Berthold, *Klio* 43 (1965) 38-48 esp. 46-7; on Themistocles's exile in general, A.J.Podlecki, *The Life of Themistocles* (Montreal & London 1975) 115-6, R.J.Lenardon, *The Saga of Themistocles* (London 1978) ch. 7-9. On Coriolanus see §36 above, and E.T.Salmon, *CQ* 24 (1930) 96-101.

43. this sort of conspiracy of bad men This refers to what has gone before, and indeed is rather awkward after the two examples of Themistocles and Coriolanus where the point was the notable absence of conspiracy.

so as to prevent anyone from thinking Again (cf. §§40, 44) we have a quasi-legal formulation, and the language here (*ut ne quis*) is correspondingly official-sounding.

which I am not sure will not happen The reader is of course meant to think of Sulla and especially Caesar.

XIII:44. So then ... should be heeded This paragraph acts as a summary of the preceding section (cf. Introd. §6), but also introduces the new topic of advice between friends, to be returned to in §§88ff. below.

law of friendship cf. above, §40.

45-61. Refutation of a number of Greek doctrines on friendship A fairly clearly-defined section follows, in which Cicero examines various views of Greek origin − not all necessarily philosophical − and refutes them one by one. The connection of this part of the treatise with what precedes is loose; it is artificial to try to link the two sections into one, as do some commentators. The first of the points raised in this section (the idea that one should not be too closely involved in friendships) may perhaps be linked with the previous discussion, in that avoidance of close friendships might suggest itself as a way of avoiding the conflict of friendship and public duty; but the connection is not made explicit by Cicero. The conjunction *nam*, "for", need not in general imply a strict logical connection, and can hardly do so here; but it may indicate some such progression of thought.

45. strange doctrines ... exercise their subtleties Laelius is made to affect an overtly disdainful attitude to the authors of the doctrines to be refuted; this is not to be taken as disdain for Greek thought in general, but only for the wrong type of Greek thought. One may compare the tone of the reference to the subtleties of the Stoics in §24 above, but the point is slightly different.

that excessively close friendships are to be avoided ... This whole passage is a paraphrase of Euripides, *Hippolytus* 253ff. (the Nurse's speech): "χρῆν γὰρ μετρίας εἰς ἀλλήλους | φιλίας θνητοὺς ἀνακίρνασθαι | καὶ μὴ πρὸς ἄκρον μυελὸν ψυχῆς, | εὔλυτα δ'εἶναι στέργηθρα φρενῶν | ἀπό τ'ὤσασθαι καὶ συντεῖναι. | τὸ δ'ὑπὲρ δισσῶν μίαν ὠδίνειν | ψυχὴν χαλεπὸν βάρος, ὡς κἀγὼ | τῆσδ'ὕπερ ἀλγῶ. | οὕτω τὸ λίαν ἧσσον ἐπαινῶ | τοῦ μηδὲν ἄγαν | καὶ συμφήσουσι σοφοί μοι." ("It were better that mortals should temper their friendships towards one another in moderate proportion, and not to the very marrow of the soul; that the mind's bonds of love should be loose, so as to be pushed away or tightened together. But for one soul to be in labour on behalf of two, as I suffer pain for her [i.e. Phaedra], is a sore burden: so it is that I praise the extreme less than the law of "Nothing in excess", and wise men will agree with me.") For the dramatic context and meaning of these lines, see W.S.Barrett's commentary on lines 261-3.

Particular points of contact are the image of tightening or loosening the bonds of love, which in Cicero become reins (*habenas amicitiae*), and the image of one soul being in labour (ὠδίνειν, *parturiat*) on behalf of another. It is possible also that the reference to *sapientes*, "wise men", at the beginning of this paragraph, is meant to reflect Euripides's mention of σοφοί at the end of the passage quoted above; but it should be quite clear that the endorsement of the σοφοί in Euripides is claimed only for the saying "nothing in excess" (one of the trite maxims attributed to the Seven Sages), and is not meant to cover the ideas put forward in the rest of the passage. Alternatively it may be that Cicero means to include Euripides himself among those who are "considered in Greece to be wise men"; it would not be surprising if Cicero were treating the views expressed by the character in the play as if they were the playwright's own opinion. The idea that the philosophic precept of moderation should be applied to friendship is, indeed, a typically Euripidean paradox, and the paradoxical quality is increased by the fact that this idea comes from the lips of the loyal and unintellectual Nurse: she does not, after all, propose to put it into practice, but will continue to suffer on behalf of Phaedra; still less should we believe that Euripides himself meant to endorse these ideas.

keep the reins of friendship as loose as possible The Latin seems to have an etymological play on *habenas habere* (*habenae* "reins" being derived from *habere* in the sense of "hold"). The chariot-driving image (for which cf. §40 above) is not explicit in Euripides.

freedom from care Latin *securitas*, meant to represent Greek ἀταραξία or ἀπάθεια. In general this was a common ideal among ancient philosophers of various persuasions, but the idea that close friendships are inimical to tranquillity of mind is apparently not found in the teachings of the major philosophical schools. Seneca (*Ep*. 9) attributes the idea to Stilbo (or Stilpo) the Megarian, who was criticised by Epicurus for his view that the wise man, being self-sufficient, did not need friends. Similar views are reported by Diogenes Laertius for the Cyrenaic school: see esp. Diog. Laert. 2.98 for Theodorus, who said that the wise did not need friendship, whereas the non-wise were incapable of it (cf. E.Mannebach, *Aristippi et Cyrenaicorum fragmenta* [Leiden 1961] nos. 232-8). There is a passage of Diogenes Laertius (10.120) where the transmitted text presents abstention from friendship as part of Epicurean doctrine; but this is so out of tune with all the other evidence for Epicurean views on the subject that the manuscript reading is generally agreed to be wrong (Bignone's correction φίλον τε οὐδένα προήσεσθαι, "<the wise man> will never abandon a friend", is generally accepted instead of φίλον τε οὐδένα κτήσεσθαι "<the wise man> will never acquire a friend"). Altogether (though of course it is impossible to be certain of this) there is some suspicion that Cicero is here attacking a view that had not been held by any reputable philosopher for a long time. However, it suits his rhetorical purposes well. Under the pretext of refuting this view, he emphasises his belief that friendship is an essential part of human nature (and especially the nature of virtuous human beings), that friends necessarily and rightly feel sympathy for each other, and that one is sometimes required to put oneself to trouble for the sake of one's friends. The argument about sympathy involves an attack on the Stoic idea of the wise man who is impervious to pain and emotion, but it need not be supposed that Cicero is otherwise attacking Stoicism (cf. below on §48).

46. friendships should be sought for the sake of protection This is slightly different from the version of the doctrine discussed above, §§26 and 29-32; there Cicero was discussing the origins of friendship as a feature of human society, but here the question is why friendships are desirable in general; thus Cicero is not quite repeating himself. In both cases, however, he is clearly attacking the views of the Epicureans (cf. on §26 above).

women It is difficult to reproduce in English translation the patronising diminutive *mulierculae*.

47. wisdom Picks up "wise men" from the previous paragraph, and alludes sarcastically to the "wisdom" claimed by the Epicureans (cf. *CM* 43).

tear the sun out of the sky Cf. *Att*. 9.10.3 *Sol, ut est in tua quadam epistula, excidisse mihi e mundo videtur:* Cicero there endorses Atticus's comment on Pompey's departure from Italy in 49 BC, that it is as if the sun had fallen out of the sky. Otto, *Sprichwörter* (s.v. *sol*, p. 327) records neither the present passage nor any other parallel. The phrase sounds proverbial, but was perhaps an idiosyncrasy of Atticus; if so, the use of it here in a work dedicated to Atticus would have special point.

no better ... gift cf. §20 above.

in truth The Latin *reapse* is a slightly old-fashioned usage, suiting Laelius's generation (cf. Introd. §7); cf. Sen. *Ep*. 108.32 commenting on Cicero's use of it in the *De Republica* (set at about the same time).

48. if distress of mind is permissible *Cadit in*, literally "falls to", often equivalent to "is predicable of". Cicero here makes Laelius attack the peculiarly Stoic idea of the wise man who is above all distress of mind, from a common-sense humanistic point of view: the same common-sense position is presented in *Tusc.* 3.12, but only as an object of refutation; the rest of *Tusc.* 3 is an exercise in defending the Stoic doctrine. In that passage of the *Tusculans*, Cicero also refers to the arguments of the Academic philosopher Crantor against the Stoic ideal of impassivity, but the argument quoted there from Crantor bears no significant resemblance to the present one. Epicureans also believed that the wise man should be prepared to suffer for his friends (cf. J.M.Rist, *CPh* 75 [1980] 121-9).

spread itself ... contract Apparently both Stoics and Epicureans sometimes preferred to talk of συστολή (contraction) instead of λύπη (pain, grief, any unpleasant feeling), presumably in an attempt to separate the objective sensation of pain from its psychological or moral aspects. This way of talking may have its origin in the theory of sensation in Plato's *Timaeus*. Here of course it is mental pleasure or pain that is in question, but Cicero uses the physical metaphors in order to emphasise the idea that sympathy with friends is something natural and unavoidable.

as I said before §27 above.

sign of good character Cf. *Off.* 1.46; 2.32; *Tusc.* 2.58; Aristotle, *NE* 1167a 18-21. Presumably these ideas have their ultimate antecedent in Plato's theories about love (principally in the *Phaedrus*).

49. (if I may use the word) reciprocating love Cicero apologises for the neologism *redamare* "to love back", representing Greek ἀντιφιλεῖν, as used by Plato *Lysis* 212c, Aristotle *EE* 7.1235a, *Rhet* 2.4.1381a, etc.

50. likeness Cf. §§20, 27, 74.

as far as good men are concerned Contrasts with "yet this same goodness extends also to groups of people collectively" below. Again, Cicero summarises the argument of the preceding section, i.e. the refutation of the first point stated above in §45, but adds an entirely new point while doing so; cf. above §44.

to watch over whole peoples Cicero regards the relationship between the citizen and his country (or, what is much the same thing, his attitude towards his fellow-countrymen collectively) as analogous to love or friendship; and, since the "good" man, or man of excellence or virtue, is seen as a member of the governing classes, the relationship is seen in terms of the Roman statesman's responsibility to his people. Cicero may here be indirectly attacking the Epicurean belief that the wise man should keep out of politics.

the affection of the multitude It is not quite clear whether *vulgi* here is a subjective or objective genitive, "affection for the multitude" or "affection shown by the multitude". Cicero often uses *caritas* in the sense of "popularity", and this may incline one towards the latter; on the other hand, this section has so far been about the affection shown by the statesman in looking after his people. Perhaps Cicero meant to leave it vague, implying that the affection was reciprocal.

51. utility Cicero now turns to the second point raised in §§45-6.

the kindest and most generous cf. §30 above.

follow from the pursuit of utility Lit. "follow utility". For the idea, cf. Plutarch, *Quomodo amicus* 5 ἣ χρεία τῇ φιλίᾳ παρέπεται; for the form of the sentence, [Aristotle] *Magna Moralia* 1209b 36 οὐ γὰρ ἀκολουθεῖ τῇ ἡδονῇ ἡ ἀρετὴ ἀλλὰ τῇ ἀρετῇ ἡ ἡδονὴ ἀκολουθεῖ; Plut. *Adv. Coloten* 9.

52. persons who overflow with self-indulgence This is usually taken as a paraphrase for "Epicureans", but Cicero knew as well as anyone that this would have been grossly unfair. Rather, Cicero is deliberately avoiding the explicit mention of the Epicurean school; cf. Introd. §8.

For who ... loved by anyone? Cf. Aristotle *NE* 8.1155a 5; 9.1169b.

tyrants That tyrants lived an unhappy life, and in particular were incapable of friendship or of trusting anybody, was a commonplace; cf. Plato, *Gorgias* 510b; *Republic* 8.576a; Xen. *Hiero* 3; Aesch. *PV* 226-7; Ennius ap. Cic. *Off.* 1.26; Cic. *Tusc.* 5.57-63.

53. for who loves a person ... whom he fears? Cf. Arist. *Rhet.* 2.4.1381b 33 οὐδεὶς γὰρ ὃν φοβεῖται φιλεῖ.

Tarquin i.e. Tarquinius Superbus, the last king of Rome, treated here as an example of a tyrant; cf. Ogilvie on Livy 1.49-60. The anecdote seems not to be known elsewhere.

54. with his arrogance *superbia*, alluding to Tarquin's usual epithet *Superbus*. Cf. also *Rep.* 1.62.

not only is Fortune herself blind Proverbial: cf. Pacuvius 366 Ribbeck (ap. [Cic.] *Ad Herenn.* 2.36), Cic. *Phil.* 13.10, Menander fr. 417 Kock, monost. 718, Theophrastus fr. L70 Fortenbaugh, [Cato] dist. 4.3, Otto *Sprichwörter* 141-2. The personified Wealth is blind in Aristophanes *Plutus*, and is said also to make others blind by Menander fr. 83 Kock and Antiphanes fr. 259 Kock.

a man who is stupid and successful *Insipiente fortunato*: *fortunatus* is a person favoured by *Fortuna*, hence basically "lucky", but with much stronger implications of wealth, power and success than our word "fortunate". Cicero's phrase reproduces Aristotle's characterisation of the wealthy man in *Rhetoric* 2.1391a ἀνοήτου εὐδαίμονος ἦθος πλούτου ἐστίν.

changed by power On change of character, cf. above §33.

55. furniture Friends are compared with various types of property by Xenophon, *Mem.* 2.4.1; cf. below, §62. In Greek, the word κτῆμα ("piece of property", originally "thing acquired") is used to refer to friends, with little or no sense that it is a metaphor; the Latin *supellex* ("furniture" or "household equipment") is more strikingly metaphorical.

belong in the end to whoever can lay his hands on them by force *qui vicit viribus*, an alliterative phrase suggesting either a proverb or a poetic quotation, though no direct source seems to be identifiable (*vicit viribus* would comfortably form the end of an iambic line from tragedy or comedy). Cicero's insistence on the insecurity of household possessions, and the fact that they may be won from their possessor by force, should be read against the background of the Civil Wars. For the thought, cf. also Theognis 918.

undisputed possession The language recalls the legal terminology for ownership and possession of property.

But that is enough on that point Cicero has indeed strayed rather far from the point which he set out to refute. The line of thought is that if friendship is sought because of utility, there can be no disinterested affection; if there is no disinterested affection, there can be no friendship properly so called; but life without friendship, even if provided with wealth, is intolerable; and such a situation does in fact often exist because wealth and power are inimical to friendship; though of the two, friendship is preferable by far.

56. definition of the scope of friendship *fines et quasi termini*: a *finis* is a boundary-line, a *terminus* a boundary-stone; the metaphorical use derives from the use in Greek philosophy of ὅρος "boundary-stone" to mean "definition", and survives etymologically in our words *define* and *determine*. (*Finis* is also used in a different philosophical sense, as in the title *De Finibus Bonorum et Malorum*, to represent the Greek τέλος "end or aim of action", but this is not relevant here.) See also Appendix on the text of this passage.

three opinions These are three different aspects of one basic principle, that of exact reciprocity in friendship. Cicero objects to them because they appear to restrict excessively the notion of what is proper behaviour for friends.

should have the same attitude towards a friend as we have towards ourselves This doctrine is adumbrated in Aristotle, *NE* 9.1166a 30 (with reference to the idea that a friend is a second self, cf. §23 above with note, and §80 below); cf. Arist. *NE* 1168a-69a. It was part of Epicurean doctrine on friendship (see Cic. *De Fin.* 1.68ff. and 2.83). In *Tusc.* 3.73, Cicero seems to approve of the principle that one should love one's friends to the same degree as one loves oneself, and he draws the line at loving them more than oneself. Why then does he object to the very similar formulation here? In the third book of the *Tusculans*, he is pleading a specific case against the desirability of mourning for one's friends when they are dead, and he does so from a deliberately contrived Stoic point of view (we have already seen an instance above (§48) in which Cicero makes Laelius in this dialogue take a line which is opposed to the Stoicism of *Tusc.* 3). In that context, additionally, he is only talking about the general level of affection for a friend. Here he is thinking of how the principle would work out in practice when applied to particular actions. From this practical point of view, he treats the formulation as liable to exclude the possibility of doing kindnesses to a friend at one's own expense, or of doing for a friend what one might not do on one's own behalf.

To us, the doctrine which Cicero rebuts here seems reminiscent of the Judaeo-Christian "Love thy neighbour as thyself". This, however, was never meant as a definition of friendship. Its original context was in Leviticus 19.18, "Thou shalt not avenge, nor bear any grudge against the children of thy people, but thou shalt love thy neighbour as thyself"; cf. ibid. 19.34, "But the stranger that dwelleth with you shall be unto you as one born among you, and thou shalt love him as thyself". Taken out of context it was expanded (by both Jewish and Christian interpretation) into a law of universal charity.

57. perfectly honourable to do so on behalf of a friend Cicero is perhaps thinking particularly of his activities as advocate.

58. calling friendship to account, etc. This passage consists of a sustained financial metaphor: *calculos*, originally the beads on the abacus used for accounting; for *exigue* used in financial contexts, cf. Ter. *Heaut.* 207 and Caes. *BG* 7.71.4 (and note the etymological connection of *exiguus* and *exilis* with *exigere* "demand payment"); *ratio acceptorum et datorum; divitior et affluentior; ne plus reddat quam acceperit; excidat, in terram defluat* (it should be borne in mind that ancient finance was more concretely based on coinage than ours); *congeratur*, lit. "pile up" (of savings or investments). Cf. §31 *neque enim beneficium feneramur.*

59. but first This opinion is really a fourth definition of the "boundaries of friendship" – this time an entirely worldly and cynical one – to be set alongside the three philosophical definitions already mentioned; clearly Cicero thinks it more objectionable than any of those.

make known Latin *edixero*: the verb *edicere* (whence the word "edict") normally means "to announce", and is rare in Classical Latin outside official contexts. Here it suits the context and the personality of Laelius, because of its formal or old-fashioned tone. There is no need to resort to the banal alternative reading *dixero* ("say").

love as if one were some day going to hate This sentiment is attributed to Bias or Chilon among the Seven Sages, and is found also in Sophocles *Ajax* 680-2; cf. Aristotle *Rhet.* 2.1389b (attributing it to Bias), ibid. 1395a; Diog. Laert. 1.87; Gellius *NA* 1.3.30 (attribution to Chilon); Demosthenes *In Aristocratem* 122 (660); Otto, *Sprichwörter* p. 21. It does not appear in the collection of Bias's sayings in Diels-Kranz I⁶, 61ff.

handles The Latin metaphor *ansas* is exactly the same as the English, but the Latin has an extra twist in that the word for "complain", *reprehendere*, is derived from *prehendere* "to grasp", and still sometimes preserves its literal meaning of pulling someone back.

60. care in forming friendships This anticipates the fuller discussion of the choice of friends in the remainder of the dialogue; see below §§62ff., 78, 85.

endure it, rather than ... start a quarrel cf. §§76ff. below.

61. This, then ... a source of popularity This paragraph begins by rounding off the preceding section of the argument. It gives a definition of friendship, of which Cicero approves in preference to those previously discussed; this is in fact the same as that already put forward in §§15 and 20. However, Cicero realises that his notion of perfect community of aims between friends will not work in cases where the friends are not endowed with perfect moral goodness: one member of the partnership may do wrong, and the other must then decide how to react. Cicero has already treated the extreme example of this in §§36-44, but he has not so far said anything about lesser instances, not serious enough to cause a complete break between the friends, but where to follow the precept of community of actions and aims would lead to some loss of integrity. He discusses this question most cursorily here; Aulus Gellius, *NA* 1.3.14, apparently quite rightly, criticises this passage for being vague and unhelpful in comparison with the discussion in Theophrastus's treatise on friendship. The brevity and vagueness are made worse by obscurity: in the passage from "However, one's reputation ..." to "... source of popularity" it is difficult to work out the logical connection of thought. One can see that Cicero is thinking of times when it seems necessary to compromise principles for the sake of maintaining a friendship or political alliance. Presumably his thought then moves from compromise of principles (implied in *declinandum de via* and *turpitudo*) towards compromise of reputation. He seems to be saying that the public will forgive one to some extent if one departs from the straight path for the sake of a friend. Then he says that one must not neglect reputation, i.e. presumably by going too far from the straight path, to the extent that the public will no longer pardon you. A politician must always consider it important to retain the goodwill of the people. Then Cicero seems to correct himself again: the politician must not court public goodwill by flattery (this subject recurs, §§96-7). The effect of the last sentence of the paragraph is to imply that what Cicero really meant by "one must not neglect one's reputation" was "one must not depart from virtue, which is the source of good reputation". Yet his previous remarks imply that he thinks a certain degree of departure from virtue is permissible, and that this need not affect one's reputation. It seems either that Cicero is muddled, or that he is in some way trying to tread a tightrope.

How can one explain this? There is a natural temptation to assume that Cicero was thinking primarily of his own past career, and in particular of times when he felt that he himself had to compromise his principles. On this assumption, the paragraph can be read as a piece of self-justification, albeit rather confused and ineffective, perhaps even disingenuous. But there is another possibility: we must remember after all that this is Cicero speaking in the authoritative persona of Laelius, purporting to lay down general rules of conduct. He may have been thinking of people other than himself, who had in his eyes compromised themselves, e.g. by following Caesar: it will be remembered that C.Matius, in writing to Cicero in 44 BC, justified his support of Caesar on grounds of personal friendship. (This does not necessarily imply that the *Laelius* was written after the correspondence with Matius; there will have been other instances of the same attitude among Caesar's supporters; cf. Introd. §3.) If one reads it in this way, the passage makes rather more sense. Cicero is declaring that he accepts the arguments of such as Matius to some extent, since he says that it is permissible to leave the straight path on behalf of a friend. He thus qualifies what might have seemed the extreme and categorical position of §§36-44. On the other hand, he does not give in to their arguments entirely: a fault is still a fault even if it was committed for the sake of a friend, and if one goes too far wrong there may be an irremediable loss of reputation. The apparent oscillation of the argument is then easily explicable: Cicero wishes on the one hand to appear tactfully indulgent towards those whom he believes to have taken the wrong course in politics, but on the other hand he does not wish to admit that they were in the right, or to lose sight of his own declared principles. For this interpretation cf. K.Heldmann, *Hermes* 104 (1976) 72-103.

62-88. Advice on the forming and maintaining of friendships   On the structure of this section see Introd. §6.

62. Scipio   A reference to Scipio again introduces a more practical, less philosophical section of the discussion, as above, §§3 and 59. But the complaint here attributed to Scipio is directly translated from Xenophon, *Memorabilia* 2.4.4, where it is put in the mouth of Socrates. Cicero may have thought this appropriate, in that Scipio was said to have been fond of reading Xenophon (cf. my note on *Cato Maior* 59). (One sometimes meets with the idea that there were those who thought of Scipio as a Roman Socrates, but this is absurd: it derives from a fragment of Fannius's histories quoted in Cicero's *Academica*, which said nothing more than that Scipio had the quality of εἰρωνεία, as Socrates did.)

signs and marks   Cf. Euripides *Hippol.* 925, *Medea* 516-9; Xen. *Mem.* 2.6. The word "character" originally meant a "mark" (as for instance an assay mark on metal).

shortage   cf. below, §§64 and 78-9; Theognis 79ff.; Aristotle, *NE* 8.1156b 24; *EE* 7.1237b 35; Theophrastus περὶ φιλίας (referred to by Jerome on Micah 2.7) fr. L93 in Fortenbaugh, *Quellen zur Ethik Theophrasts*, p.66.

63. Therefore, it is a wise man's duty ... before pursuing friendship   The text is somewhat doubtful here (see Appendix), but the meaning is clear enough:

one must be cautious in the early stages of friendship, and try out one's friends, as one would try out a team of horses. The image comes from Theognis 1.125-6 Bergk οὐδὲ γὰρ εἰδείης ἀνδρὸς νόον οὐδὲ γυναικός Ι πρὶν πειρηθείης ὥσπερ ὑποζυγίου. On the necessity for caution and for testing friends, see also Aristotle, *NE* 8.1156b; *EE* 7.1237b-38a; Isocr. *Ad Demonicum* 25; Plut. *Quomodo amicus* 49d; §§78 and 85 below.

64. Ennius *scaen.* 210 Vahlen = 185 Jocelyn. "A friend in need is a friend indeed". The line contains a triple etymological play on *certus, re incerta, cernitur*: originally *certus* "sure" was the past participle of *cernere*, cf. *decernere* "decide"; the words are related to Greek κρίνειν "judge" (for the sound-change *ri > er* cf. *tertius*/τρίτος), whence our "critic", etc., and Latin *discrimen* "difference" or "point of decision", whence our "discrimination". The idea is among the most commonplace; cf. Eur. *Hec.* 1226, Aristotle *EE* 7.1238a, Plaut. *Epid.* 113, Publil. Syr. 41, Petron. 61.9, Otto, *Sprichwörter* 21-2.

desert them when they fail The opposite idea to that mentioned in the previous note, viz. that one's friends desert one in disaster, is also very common; cf. Petron. 38.13; Ovid *Trist.* 1.9.5-6; *Pont.* 2.3.23-4; Lucan 8.535; Ter. *Eun.* 237-8.

65. good faith *fides*, in the most general sense, trustworthiness and honesty.

Besides this, it is reasonable to choose ... This whole paragraph (§§65-6) appears to be based (perhaps directly) on Aristotle, *Rhetoric* 2.4.1381a-b, where the qualities of character that tend towards friendship are defined. That passage is primarily written not from the standpoint of philosophical analysis, but from that of the part of rhetorical theory which dealt with human character and psychology (*ethos* in Aristotle's terminology). Here in Cicero, as in Aristotle, we find the idea that natural sympathy is necessary as a precondition of friendship (cf. also Arist. *NE* 9.1166a, Plut. *Quomodo amicus* 51b), that potential friends should not be liable to make complaints and accusations, and that they should have a pleasant and easy-going manner.

sympathetic *consentiens*: the Latin *consentire* means "to agree", but etymologically "to feel with [someone]"; Cicero is clearly trying to provide an exact Latin equivalent of the Greek συμπαθής, as is clear from his explanation *id est qui eisdem rebus moveatur*: without this, *consentiens* would naturally have been taken in its more usual meaning of "agreeing", and would thus have been obscure. Cf. *consensio* in §20 above.

should not be eager to make accusations Cf. Arist. *Rhet.* 2.4.1381a 30 (see above on §65 init.).

cannot exist except in good men §18 above.

66. seasoning Aristotle, *Rhet.* 2.4.1381a 30ff. (referred to above) says that an easy-going nature and sense of humour is a desirable quality in a friend; Cicero has the additional problem of balancing this with the Roman ideal of dignity and severity. The resulting compromise is typically Ciceronian: he is fond of expressing it by means of the image of "seasoning", for which see *Cato Maior* 10 and my note.

67. question Latin *quaestio*, with the nuance of a problem set for an expert to solve: equivalent to Greek ζήτημα. Cf. §17 above.

whether ... one should prefer new friends cf. Aristotle, *EE* 8.1237b.

the oldest should be the most pleasant cf. Plaut. *Truc.* 174 *certe hercle quam veterrimus homini optimust amicus*; Otto, *Sprichwörter* p. 23. For the comparison with wine, cf. *CM* 65 and my note; for the specific use of the image in the context of friendship, cf. Ecclesiasticus 9.10. Quintilian, *Inst.* 5.11.26, in a similar context, makes a comparison with a ship.

one must eat many bags of salt together This was a Greek proverb; it is referred to as such by Aristotle, *EE* 7.1238a and *NE* 8.1156b 27; cf. Plutarch, περὶ φιλαδελφίας 8.482b; περὶ πολυφιλίας 3.94a; Otto, *Sprichwörter* 19-20. However, Cicero seems to alter its original import. Aristotle says that one must eat many bags of salt together before one can get to know a person properly, and ensure that he is reliable; whereas Cicero seems to take the saying to mean that long association is necessary in order to fulfil the potential of friendship. The present editor has come across the same proverb in a modern Irish context – "You'ld eat a bag of salt before you'ld get to know a Kerryman".

68. like a healthy green cornfield lit. "as in the case of green shoots that are not deceptive"; for *fallax* used of corn-shoots that do not mature to produce grain, cf. Tibullus 2.1.19, Virgil, *Georg.* 1.195, etc.

the force of habit prevails cf. the similar argument in *Fin.* 1.69. Aristotle refers to the possibility of feeling affection for inanimate objects in *NE* 8.1157b 29.

even mountainous and wild ones *silvestris*, here translated "wild", is literally "wooded" or "forested". Cicero is here thinking of his own love for the country surrounding his native town of Arpinum, of which we hear more in the *De Legibus* which is set there. It would not have been usual for an ancient Italian to feel any interest in mountains and forests as such, other than a patriotic attachment to those of his own native area; hence the addition of *etiam* "even". The modern tendency to take pleasure in wild countryside for its own sake is largely a product, in the first place, of the Romantic movement, and subsequently, of reaction against industrial or suburban development. Romans were much more prone to admire well-cultivated land, and to regard mountainous areas as backward and inhospitable. Cf. A.Foucher, "Cicéron et la nature", *Bull. Assoc. Budé*, 4ème série, no. 3, 1955, pp. 32-49; J.C.Davies, *G. & R.* 18, 1971, 152ff.

69. to treat inferiors as equals Aristotle discussed at some length the question whether true friendship implied equality, or whether it could exist between persons who were unequal in some respect; see *NE* 8.1162a 34, 1163a 24ff.; *EE* 7.1238b, 1242b. We learn from Aspasius's commentary on *NE* (p. 141) that the subject was also treated by Theophrastus. Cf. also Jerome on Micah 2.7 (*CCSL* 76, p. 510). Aristotle inclined towards the view that true friendship existed only between (approximate) equals. Cicero admits friendship between unequals, saying that the friends themselves should try to minimise the inequality. Naturally enough for a Roman consular, he starts from the point of view of the superior partner. The "common touch", *comitas* or *communitas*, was not perhaps so universally admired and demanded among Romans as it is in our supposedly egalitarian society, but it certainly did occasion admiration when it existed; cf. Cic. *Off.* 1.109.

it happens that one person stands out over others *excellentiae quaedam sunt*, literally "there are certain excellences", "instances of excellence". Cicero's *excellentia* is doubtless meant to translate the Greek ὑπεροχή, as used by Aristotle in the passages cited above.

our flock Cicero liked to think of Scipio and his friends as a distinctive and harmonious group; he portrays them as such in the *De Republica*, and this has given rise to the notion of the "Scipionic Circle" (cf. Introd. §5).

He never put himself before ... The phrase *numquam se anteposuit* is perhaps deliberately reminiscent of Terence, *Andria* 65 *numquam praeponens se illis* (Bentley deleted that line, but probably wrongly).

Philus cf. §§14 and 21; **Rupilius** P.Rupilius, cos. 132; cf. §§37 and 73; **Mummius** Sp. Mummius, brother of the Mummius who sacked Corinth; the same three are mentioned together in 101, and Philus and Mummius appear in the *De Republica*.

Quintus Maximus his brother i.e. his brother by blood, elder son of Aemilius Paulus, adopted by a Q. Fabius Maximus, and hence called in full Quintus Fabius Maximus Aemilianus (consul 145 BC, cf. §96).

70. **shepherds** There are a number of mythological instances of heroes brought up by shepherds: Paris, Amphion and Zethus, Asclepius, Oedipus, Romulus and Remus; cf. also the story of Cyrus in Herodotus I. It is not clear whether Cicero was thinking of a particular treatment of one of these myths in which the hero retained an affection for his foster-parent; one possible candidate is Ennius's tragedy *Alexander*, which dealt with Paris's upbringing.

71. **who turn their services into a reproach** Almost certainly again reminiscent of Terence, *Andria* 43-4 *nam istaec commemoratio quasi exprobratiost immemori benefici* (i.e. "... a reproach to one unmindful of a kindness"). Cf. also Demosthenes *De Corona* 269 and 316, Aristotle *EE* 7.1243b, *Rhet.* 2.4.1381b 3; Sen. *Benef.* 2.10.4.

72. - 73. as much as one can manage oneself cf. Sen. *Benef.* 2.15.3.

Scipio could make Publius Rupilius consul, but not his brother Lucius Rupilius Of course Scipio had not the power to "make" anyone consul; it was the Roman People that made consuls; but in this informal context, with an aristocratic readership in mind, the looseness was no doubt permissible. A man in Scipio's position could without doubt exercise a considerable influence over the electorate. But the point here is that even Scipio could not always get his own way. Publius Rupilius was consul in 132 BC, cf. §37 above; L.Rupilius, who had been praetor in 133, presumably stood unsuccessfully for the consulate of 131, 130 or 129. According to Cicero in *Tusc.* 4.40, the historian Fannius recorded that P.Rupilius was so grieved at his brother's failure to be elected that he soon afterwards died. Cf. also Pliny *NH* 7.122.

74. one cannot judge friendships Montaigne, *Essais* 1.28 quotes this passage in a context disapproving of Greek pederasty.

hunting or ball-games Characteristic adolescent sports, cf. Ter. *Andria* 55-7, and *Cato Maior* 58 with my note.

one does not have to keep as one's friends cf. §33 above.

but ... in some other way ... otherwise stable friendships cannot last It is probable that something has dropped out of the text here (cf. Appendix).

difference of interests pushes friendships apart cf. §27 above and note.

75. It is also right to warn ... It is not quite clear how this section fits logically into the context; the end of this paragraph (§76 init.) repeats the end of §72, providing superficial cohesion, and perhaps the relationship of Lycomedes and Neoptolemus is meant as a further example of unequal friendship, the inequality in this instance being in age. However, there is no difficulty in the content: a warning against "excessive concern" is clearly in place. There may be a distant connection with a saying of Theophrastus quoted in Plutarch, *Cato Minor* 37, that excessive love or friendship may sometimes turn into hatred.

Lycomedes   Neoptolemus was the son of Achilles by Deidameia, daughter of Lycomedes, king of Scyros. After Achilles left for the Trojan war, Neoptolemus was brought up by Lycomedes. After the death of Achilles, the Greeks were informed that Troy would never be taken unless Neoptolemus was brought there to fight. Lycomedes tried to prevent him from going (Neoptolemus would still have been very young at the time) but without success, and Neoptolemus duly played a crucial part in the sack of Troy. For the ancient sources of the myth, see P.Grimal, *The Dictionary of Classical Mythology* (English translation, Oxford 1986), notes s.v. "Lycomedes" and "Neoptolemus". The Roman tragedian Accius wrote a play on Neoptolemus, which may be alluded to here: Ribbeck, *Tragicorum Fragmenta* pp. 196-7.

76. now our discussion is slipping ... ordinary friendships   True and perfect friendships, said Cicero in §32, last for life; but the more common sort may come to an end, as already noted in §§33-5. The distinction occurs in §22 above, and is repeated in §§77 and 100 below. On the breaking of friendships, cf. Aristotle *NE* 9.1165b; Chrysippus also discussed the subject in his second book περὶ φιλίας, according to Plutarch, *Stoic. Repugn.* 1039b.

Cato   This saying attributed to Cato (*dict.* 70 Jordan) does not seem to be recorded elsewhere; cf. below, §90, for another instance.

unpick the seam rather than tear it apart   cf. *Off.* 1.120 *ut amicitias quae minus delectent et minus probentur, magis decere censent sapientes sensim diluere quam repente praecidere*; and below, §78. The saying is alluded to by Jerome, *Ep.* 8.

intolerable ... wrong: cf. Aristotle, *NE* 9.1165b 36.

77. change of character or interests   cf. above, §§33 and 54.

Nothing is more unbecoming ... friendly terms   cf. §60 above.

Quintus Pompeius   The grandfather of the Q. Pompeius of §2; he was consul – the first of his family to hold that office – in 141 BC. It was on that occasion that he incurred the enmity of Scipio and Laelius; he was supposed to have promised Scipio that he would not stand for the consulate himself, but support Laelius instead; but he went back on his word, and was himself elected. See Astin, *Scipio* 85 and 311-2; Briscoe, *JRS* 64 (1974) 133.

Metellus   Q. Metellus Macedonicus, consul 143; he is called "our colleague" because, like Laelius, Scaevola and (perhaps already at the dramatic date of the dialogue) Fannius, he was a member of the augural college. For his quarrel with Scipio, cf. *De Rep.* 1.31, *Off.* 1.87; Briscoe, *JRS* 64 (1974) 133; Astin, *Scipio* 85 and 312-5.

78. burnt out ... quenched   cf. §76 above. Note that *exstingui* means "to go out" (of its own accord), not "to be extinguished"; see my notes on *CM* 39 and 71.

the former friendship should be respected   This is very similar to Aristotle, *NE* 9.1165b 31-6.

one should not start a friendship too quickly   Cf. Solon's saying φίλους μὴ ταχὺ κτῶ· οὓς δ᾽ ἂν κτήσῃ, μὴ ἀποδοκίμαζε (Diog. Laert. 1.60 and Diels-Kranz I⁶, p.63, cf. B.Radice in *The Translator's Art*, cited above on §7); Isocrates *Ad Demonicum* 24.

79. a rare breed   cf. §62 above.

all fine things are rare   cf. *Fin.* 2.81; Otto, *Sprichwörter* p. 294.

many people This is sometimes taken by editors as a further attack on Epicureanism, but it is surely not: Cicero is talking about the behaviour of ordinary people in everyday life. Cf. Ovid, *Pont.* 2.3.8 *vulgus amicitias utilitate probat.*

cattle cf. §62 above for a similar comparison.

80. every person loves himself cf. Aristotle, *NE* 9.1168a-b on love of self. That self-love is natural and instinctive is a Stoic idea; cf. *Fin.* 3.16; 5.28; Chrysippus, *SVF* 3.178 = Diog. Laert. 7.85.

another self cf. on §23 above.

81. animals For the comparison with animals cf. §27 above.

turn the two into one cf. §92 below; also §23 above for the idea of the friend as another self.

82. Yet many people... This does not necessarily refer to philosophical doctrines about friendship arising from dissimilar natures that complement each other, but simply to the way ordinary people behave when they seek friendship purely for their own profit, without thinking what they can provide in return. Cf. above on §79.

are in control of those desires Cf. Xenophon *Mem.* 2.6.1 for this as a qualification for friendship. The image of being enslaved to desires is common, especially in Plato and Xenophon; cf. also *Somn. Scip.* 21 (29).

respect *verecundia*, the quality that makes people ashamed to do wrong; Greek αἰδώς or αἰσχύνη. Cf. Cic. *Off.* 1.148, *Part. Or.* 79, Sen. *Ep.* 11; F.Lossmann cited on §23, pp. 69-111 esp. 95.

83. a helper in virtue cf. *Fin.* 1.66; also *Leg.* 1.58, where the law is described as *vitiorum emendatricem commendatricemque virtutum*; Plutarch, *Quomodo amicus* 9.

84. to learn from experience cf. Euripides fr. ap. Plut. *Fabius Maximus* 17; Philemon fr. ap. Stob. *Flor.* 30.4. See also above, §54.

85. judge before making friends, and not make friends before judging them This formulation of the sentiment already expressed at §§62 and 78 above reproduces a saying of Theophrastus (probably from his treatise on friendship) quoted by Plutarch, περὶ φιλαδελφίας 8.482b, and referred to by Seneca, *Ep.* 3.2 *contra praecepta Theophrasti, cum amaverunt iudicant, et non amant cum iudicaverunt.* Cf. also Amm. Marc. 26.2.9 (without attribution to Theophrastus or Cicero); Max. Tyr. 20.3; Stob. Flor. 84.14; Rutilius Lupus *De figuris* 1.6; and the gnomological collections quoted by Fortenbaugh, *Quellen zur Ethik Theophrasts*, fr. L98.

the old proverb *Actum ne agas*, "don't re-open a closed case" (assuming the legal meaning of *agere*), or more literally, "don't do [all over again] what has [already] been done". The proverb is alluded to a number of times in Latin literature: cf. Cic. *Att.* 9.6.6; 9.18.3; Plaut. *Cist.* 703, *Pseud.* 260; Ter. *Phorm.* 419; Livy 28.40.3.; Otto, *Sprichwörter* p. 9.

86. unanimously for *uno ore* "with one voice" see Otto, *Sprichwörter* p. 259.

Virtue Friendship is here again compared with other things that are normally thought desirable, as in §20 above.

those who take part in politics ... The classification of ways of life was familiar in Greek philosophy; Cicero's four categories here correspond to the Greek βίος πολιτικός, θεωρητικός, χρηματιστικός and ἀπολαυστικός. Cf. *Off.* 1.70-1;

R.Joly, *Le thème philosophique des genres de vie dans l'antiquité classique*, Mém. Acad. Royale de Belgique 51 (1956).

uninvolved in public life *otiosi*, lit. "leisured": Cicero would no doubt have been thinking of members of the equestrian order who deliberately chose not to have a political career, such as Atticus; such men were however often active in financial or business concerns, and their "leisured" status was more of a social convention than a reality. Cf. Cic. *Cluent*. 153, *Rab. Post.* 13; Sallust *Hist.* 1.55.9 M.; R.Syme, *The Roman Revolution* 13-14; J.-M. André, *L'Otium dans la vie morale et intellectuelle romaine des origines à l'époque augustéenne* (Paris 1966) 281ff.; W. Kroll, *Die Kultur der ciceronischen Zeit* (Leipzig 1933) I, p. 5. (Note that although *negotium* "business" was in origin simply the negation of *otium*, meaning "not-leisure", Cicero can here say *suum negotium gerunt otiosi* without any apparent sense of contradiction.) This aspect of the classification is distinctively upper-class Roman; the Greeks were less ashamed to admit to being businessmen.

in a civilised fashion lit. "in a way befitting a free man".

87.   Timon of Athens On this character, the subject of Shakespeare's play (the material for which was drawn from Plutarch's *Life of Antony* 70 and Lucian's *Timon*), see Aristophanes *Lysistrata* 808 (the first substantial reference to him in extant literature) with J.Henderson's note. Cf. also *Tusc.* 4.25.

spew out The image is Terentian, *Adelphi* 510 *ibo ac requiram fratrem ut in eum haec evomam*.

steely ... steal away This is an attempt to reproduce the (admittedly rather strange, and possibly accidental) assonance in the Latin, *ferreus - ferre - auferret*.

88.   Archytas of Tarentum   A contemporary and friend of Plato, prominent in Tarentine politics in the fourth century BC, and well known as a mathematician and philosopher. Cicero's account of the oral transmission of the saying is implausible (even if not impossible); it should be seen as little more than a way of fitting the supposed saying of Archytas into the dialogue; a very similar account of an alleged oral tradition occurs in *CM* 43, and in *CM* 39-41 Cato the Elder is made to quote a discourse attributed to Archytas, which he is supposed to have heard from a Tarentine when on campaign at Tarentum as a young man; see my notes on those passages.

Human nature The Latin just says *natura*, "nature", but it is clear enough that it is human nature that is chiefly in question here. To say "nature", *tout court*, in English could be misleading, because of the modern tendency to take "nature" to exclude mankind. The argument from nature is characteristic of Greek philosophy, whether Stoic or Peripatetic, though the particular insistence that mankind cannot bear solitude recalls the latter rather than the former school. Cf. above, §§22 and 52-5.

88-100.   The place of advice and criticism in friendship: the true friend distinguished from the flatterer   The topic of advice and criticism among friends was introduced, but not properly discussed, in §44; now it receives fuller treatment, and leads on to the topic of flattery contrasted with true friendship. The possible methods of distinguishing the two were discussed by a number of ancient authors; cf. §95 below; [Q.Cic.] *Commentariolum Petitionis* 39; Isocr. *Ad Demonicum* 30; essays were devoted to the topic by Plutarch (*Quomodo amicus*) and Maximus of Tyre.

89. my friend i.e. Terence; the quotation is line 68 of the *Andria*. Other citations of the line are listed by Otto, *Sprichwörter* p. 368. "Friend" here translates *familiaris*, not *amicus* (the English word has to do duty for both): originally, *familiaris* meant a member of someone's household, while in later usage it came to imply any reasonably close acquaintance or association, but without the connotations of affection and respect that the word *amicus* had. The tradition of Terence's association with Laelius and Scipio was well-established in Cicero's time; cf. Cic. *Att.* 7.3.10; on this matter, see W.G.Arnott, *Menander, Plautus, Terence* (Greece & Rome New Surveys in the Classics 9, Oxford 1975) 46-7.

which poisons friendship cf. Tac. *Hist.* 1.15; Pliny, *Paneg.* 89 (*Paneg.* 91 and 92 also pick up phrases from this passage).

90. Cato cf. §76 above.

enemies do ... better service The germ of this saying (*dict.* 69 Jordan) is in Aristophanes, *Birds* 375ff. ἀλλ' ἀπ' ἐχθρῶν πολλὰ μανθάνουσιν οἱ σοφοί κτλ.; cf. also Ovid *Met.* 4.428 *fas est et ab hoste doceri*; Plutarch, *De utilitate ex inimicis capienda* 6; *Quomodo amicus* 36. However, there is no need to doubt that this saying, as given, is genuinely Catonian: the antithetical sentence-structure, combined with the rather laborious-sounding *eos amicos qui dulces videantur* and above all the abruptness of *hos numquam*, is characteristic of Cato's style.

91. flattery The flatterer, who says what the object of flattery wants to hear, is contrasted with the true friend, who gives advice and criticism when it is needed, even if it is unwelcome. The various words for flattery in the Latin have slightly differing connotations; *adulatio* originally and literally meant "fawning" as applied to dogs and other animals; *blanditia* means wheedling or ingratiating talk; *assentatio*, the most relevant for this context, means constant agreement with everything the object of flattery says, as exemplified by Gnatho in §93.

92. substitutes a counterfeit version Latin *adulterat*. In Cicero, *adulterare* in its metaphorical use means "counterfeit"; the meaning corresponding to the English word "adulterate" (i.e. debase or contaminate) is not found before Ovid (*OLD* s.v.). The counterfeit version is substituted for the truth as an adulterer substitutes himself for the true husband.

turning a number of minds into one This is said to be a Pythagorean definition of friendship by Cicero in *Off.* 1.56. Cf. §81 above.

93. one who alters himself Cf. [Q.Cic.] *Comm. Pet.* 42, *opus est magnopere blanditia, quae etiam si vitiosa est et turpis in cetera vita, tamen in petitione necessaria est ...*; ibid., *petitori ... cuius et frons et vultus et sermo ad eorum quoscumque convenerit sensum et voluntatem commutandus et accommodandus est.* Those who debate the authenticity of the *Commentariolum* should take this passage into account: is it real advice given by Quintus to Marcus Cicero in 64 BC? In which case how is the similarity with the *Laelius* to be explained? Or is it more likely that a later fabricator remembered the *Laelius*, and consequently, in attempting to rebut what Cicero says here, was trapped into an anachronistic allusion? On some other difficulties in accepting the *Commentariolum* as genuine, see R.G.M. Nisbet, *JRS* 51 (1961) 84-7. With this passage of Cicero compare also Juvenal's description of Greek flatterers in Satire 3.100-108.

"A man says no ... to agree with everything" Terence, *Eunuchus* 252-3. Gnatho, whose name derives from γνάθος "jaw" (implying gluttony, not loquacity), is an example of the "parasite" of New Comedy, who lives (or tries to live) on the patronage of others, employing his wit to entertain his patrons, and practising the arts of flattery to maintain his position; he is typically a man who will do anything to win a dinner invitation. Terence's character of Gnatho was apparently based on a character of the same name in Menander's play *Kolax* ("The Flatterer").

94. there are many people like Gnatho We must believe Cicero; for the parasite would not have been such a constant feature of Greek and Roman comedy if the type had not been found entertaining, and it would not have been entertaining if it had corresponded to nothing in real life.

95. a demagogue *popularis.* As is now generally realised, this word does not refer to a party or an ideology, but simply to any politician who courted the favour of the popular assembly, and used it in preference to the Senate as his political base. Like many political labels, *popularis* could be used either favourably or pejoratively; Cicero, in the latter part of his career at least, tends to use it with a nuance of disapproval, and here he refuses to admit that a *popularis* can be anything other than a demagogue who flatters the people insincerely in order to build up his own power. It is a far cry from Cicero's own claim to be a *popularis consul* nineteen years earlier. See R.Seager, "Cicero and the word *popularis*", *CQ* 22 (1972) 328-38.

reliable, serious and consistent *constans, severus, gravis* - all characteristically Ciceronian terms of approval.

96. Gaius Papirius Carbo: see on §39 above.

not merely going along with them The use of *comes* here is rather puzzling: what is a "companion of the Roman people"? The nearest usage seems to be Cic. *Phil.* 7.22 where he refers to having the Roman people as one's *comes*, i.e. on one's side. A *comes* is literally "one who goes along with". But one suspects that Cicero used the word here more as a contrast with *dux* than for its intrinsic meaning. Cf. also *Sull.* 9, *Flacc.* 5.

Gaius Licinius Crassus's law on priesthoods This Crassus was tribune in 145 BC (the consulship of Q.Fabius Maximus Aemilianus and L.Hostilius Mancinus). The priestly colleges (pontifices, augurs, etc.) were previously self-electing bodies; Crassus proposed a bill to open them to popular election, but as Cicero says here, the attempt failed. A later law of Cn. Domitius Ahenobarbus in 104 BC provided that the pontifices should be elected by seventeen out of the thirty-five voting tribes, chosen by lot: this curious procedure was a sort of compromise between the old system and the normal democratic elections that had been proposed by Crassus (cf. L.R.Taylor, *Roman Voting Assemblies* [Ann Arbor 1966] 82). Cicero's Laelius regards the proposal of Crassus as an offence against traditional religion. It was in fact politically important, since the pontifices and augurs had considerable powers to obstruct legislation. For Laelius's speech, which Cicero admired, cf. *Brut.* 83, *ND* 3.5; 3.43.

He was the first to stand facing the Forum The original *Rostra* faced away from the body of the Forum, towards the *Comitium* and the Senate House. The *Comitium* was the historic meeting-place of the Roman people (cf. the word *comitia* for the popular assembly itself), but it was limited in area; a much larger crowd could gather in the Forum. Julius Caesar replaced the old *rostra* with a new construction, which faced away from the Senate House down the length of the Forum, and thus embodied the new practice mentioned here. The new *rostra* were completed in 44 BC, and their construction would thus have been topical at the time when Cicero wrote the *Laelius*; consequently, this passage is not a piece of gratuitous antiquarianism, since the origin of the new convention whereby magistrates faced the Forum when presiding over the Assembly would have been a matter of live interest. The *Rostra* we now see are largely Augustus's extension of those of Julius Caesar.

Cicero's information here about Crassus coincides with that of Varro, RR 1.2.9, where it is said that Crassus was the first to "lead the people out from the *Comitium* to the Forum to vote on legislation". Cicero's phrase *agere cum populo*, here translated "to preside over the Assembly", refers to the transaction of the formal business of the *comitia*, and particularly the taking of votes; Cicero does not necessarily imply that nobody had previously turned towards the Forum when merely making a speech at a public meeting (*contio*). Doubtless the change in official procedure initiated by Crassus was meant as a popular gesture; Cicero certainly implies as much here. Plutarch, *Gaius Gracchus* 5.2, says that C. Gracchus was the first to face the Forum when addressing the people. However, it seems likely that Plutarch mistook "Gaius Crassus" for "Gaius Gracchus": the more famous name would attract anecdotes of this sort. See L.R.Taylor, *Roman Voting Assemblies* (cited in previous note) 23-5; Staveley, *Voting and Elections* 152.

97. the public stage   For the comparison of a public meeting with a theatrical performance, cf. *De Or.* 2.338 *quia maxima quasi oratoris scaena videatur contio esse*, Caelius ap. Cic. *Fam.* 8.11.3, Cic. *Ad Brut.* 17.2; for the more generalised use of theatrical images for public life, cf. Cic. *Brut.* 290, *Att.* 1.18.2, *Verr.* II 5.35, *Q.F.* 1.1.42, *Rab. Post.* 42; Fantham, *Imagery* 34-5.

see into the other's heart   lit. "see an open breast and show your own". Cf. Seneca *Ep.* 59.9; Pliny *Ep.* 6.12.3; Otto *Sprichwörter* p. 270.

opens his ears ... to flatterers   cf. *Off.* 1.91.

98. braggart soldiers   The *milites gloriosi*, such as the one after which Plautus's *Miles gloriosus* is named; but here particularly Thraso, the soldier in Terence's *Eunuchus*, who is the victim of Gnatho's flattery. The quotation is from *Eunuchus* 391-2; Thraso is hoping to ingratiate himself with the courtesan Thais, and Gnatho plays on this.

99. "The tribe of senile idiots ..."   Quoted from a lost play of Caecilius Statius, incert. fr. 3, p. 243 Ribbeck. Cicero also quotes the phrase *comicos stultos senes* on its own in the *Cato Maior*, §36, where see my note. A literal translation of the lines would be "... with the result that you have twisted me around and fooled me most neatly today, more than all other stupid old men in comedy".

100. wise men   cf. §§18 and 36.

those of no value   This is a stronger distinction than that made above in 76 and 77: the relationships between flatterer and victim, just described, are only pretended friendships, and do not even qualify as *vulgares amicitiae*.

100-104. Conclusion

Gaius Fannius, and you, Quintus Mucius   Laelius addresses his two companions by name, to mark the climactic point in the dialogue, as does Cato in the peroration of the *Cato Maior*.

harmony   Cicero's word *convenientia* represents the Greek term ὁμολογία, "agreement" or "concord".

Whenever it rises up ... This passage repeats and summarises the content of §§26ff. above.

light ... **blazes forth** Though in the previous passage these images were separated, their conjunction here perhaps suggests a coherent metaphor of one lamp being lit from another, as in Ennius ap. Cic. *Off.* 1.51; Lucr. 6.900-5.

advantage cf. §51.

101.   Lucius Paulus, Marcus Cato, Gaius Galus cf. §21; Publius Nasica P.Cornelius Scipio Nasica Corculum, the father of Nasica Serapio (§41); this Nasica was a much more cultivated and affable character than his son (cf. *Off.* 1.109). Cf. Briscoe, *JRS* 64 (1974) 134.

Tiberius Gracchus The father of the brothers Tiberius and Gaius. He had close connections with the Scipio family: his wife was Cornelia, sister of the Scipio who adopted Scipio Aemilianus, and Scipio Aemilianus himself married Sempronia, Gracchus's daughter.

Lucius Furius Philus; **Publius Rupilius, Spurius Mummius** cf. §69 above.

Quintus Tubero cf. §37 above.

Publius Rutilius P.Rutilius Rufus, consul 105 BC. He had served under Scipio at Numantia, and studied philosophy with Panaetius. Later, in 94 BC, he was legate of Q. Scaevola (the Pontifex) in Asia, was prosecuted for mismanagement, and went back as an exile to Asia, where he became a citizen of Smyrna. There Cicero apparently met him, and in the *De Republica* Cicero makes Rutilius the intermediary through whom he heard of the alleged conversation there narrated.

Aulus Verginius Little is known of him except that he was a lawyer; Pomponius in the Digest (1.2.40) mentions him together with Rutilius.

reach the finishing-line Cf. the similar chariot-racing metaphor in *CM* 83; Otto *Sprichwörter* p. 67.

102. still lives Imitated by Pliny, *Ep.* 2.1.11.

103. In the characteristic manner of "ring composition", Laelius reverts to the topic of the friendship of Scipio, with which he began in §§10 and 15.

one house See note on §15 above.

travels and country holidays cf. *De Or.* 2.22.

104. far from the public eye cf. Horace *Sat.* 2.1.71-4.

any suffering that is short-lived should be tolerable This is reminiscent of the Epicurean ideas about suffering that are put forward in *De Finibus* 1.40, but this type of approach need not have been peculiar to the Epicureans.

That is what I had to say cf. the end of the *Cato Maior* (85) *haec habui de senectute quae dicerem.*

SOMNIUM SCIPIONIS: INTRODUCTION

1. The *De Republica*: transmission What we know as the *Somnium Scipionis* ("The Dream of Scipio") was not meant to be a separate work. It was simply the concluding section of Cicero's dialogue in six books entitled *De Republica* ("On the Republic"). The *De Republica* was one of Cicero's most ambitious literary works, and perhaps had a claim to be considered his greatest; but we are not now able to judge this conclusively, since we possess no complete text of it. It is estimated that between a quarter and a third of the *De Republica* is extant today. Our knowledge of it comes from three sources: first, the single Vatican manuscript discovered in 1820, dating originally from the fourth or fifth century AD, which provides us with an almost complete text of the first two books (though with considerable gaps), and short fragments of the third, fourth and fifth; secondly, the medieval manuscript tradition of the *Somnium Scipionis*, which was at an early stage excerpted from the full text; and thirdly, a considerable number of quotations, some quite lengthy, in later Latin writers. The survival of the *Somnium Scipionis*, independently of the rest of the text, is to be attributed to the fact that it was attached to copies of the commentary written on it by the fourth-century AD Latin writer Macrobius, which survived to become widely read in the Middle Ages. Cf. Introd. §§7-8 below; L.D.Reynolds in *T. & T.* 131-2.

2. The date and circumstances of writing We have, as it happens, particularly good evidence for the composition of the *De Republica* from Cicero's letters. The project is first mentioned, in general terms, in two letters of May 54 BC (*Q.Fr.* 2.12 and *Att.* 4.14). The *dramatis personae* are listed in a letter to Atticus written in June or July of the same year (*Att.* 4.16); Cicero tells Atticus that the setting of the dialogue in the past, as in the *De Oratore* which he had recently written, excluded the mention of Varro that Atticus had suggested. However, he says, it may be possible to address Varro in the prologue to one of the books. This refers to an early version in which each individual book had its own preface; in the final version, it seems, only books I, III and V had prefaces. The fullest information on the process of composition, however, comes in a letter to Cicero's brother Quintus, written in October or November 54 (*Q. Fr.* 3.5). There he says that he had completed two books of the dialogue, with the characters as previously mentioned and as they eventually appeared in the final version. At this stage, it appears, Cicero intended that the complete dialogue should occupy nine books. Cicero tells Quintus that he had the two finished books read to him in the presence of one Sallustius, who suggested that the work should be recast with Cicero himself as the main speaker. This apparently he started to do, although he says that he was reluctant to abandon the previous project.

Evidently, Cicero in due course reverted to something more like his former scheme; the *De Republica* as we have it is a dialogue between Scipio Aemilianus and his friends, as originally projected. The number of books has however been reduced to six, from the nine originally projected. The final version was clearly published by May 51, when Caelius reports to Cicero that his *politici libri* (i.e. the six books of the *De Republica*) are enjoying universal popularity. In April 50, finally, Cicero replies to some criticisms of details in *Rep.* II that Atticus had made (*Att.* 6.2), and asks Atticus to correct a mistaken form of a Greek name (the Vatican manuscript however preserves Cicero's original error). The *De Republica* was thus composed between 54 and 51 BC; Cicero clearly expended much labour on it, and it went through a number of versions before he reached one that finally satisfied him.

*   *   *

Cicero's decision to embark on the writing of the *De Oratore* and *De Republica* (followed closely, it appears, by the *De Legibus*) must be seen against the background of his political position at the time. As consul in 63 BC he claimed to have "saved the Republic" from the conspiracy of Catiline, and some of his influential contemporaries, at least temporarily and on the surface, supported his claim; but he had also made enemies. In the years following his consulship, Cicero tried to align himself with conservative and aristocratic elements in the Senate, but meanwhile the informal combination of Pompey, Crassus and Caesar, known traditionally but misleadingly as the "First Triumvirate", was concentrating more real political power in its own hands than Cicero seems to have realised. As tribune in 58, Cicero's enemy Clodius drove him into exile; his recall a year later was due largely to Pompey, and placed him greatly in Pompey's debt. Cicero returned to a triumphant welcome from the people of Italy, and there were signs of dissension between the Triumvirs. Cicero tried to pursue an independent and broadly conservative line in politics, but he suffered a major setback in 55 BC, when the Triumvirs reached a new agreement (at the "Conference of Luca"), and it became clear that there was now little room for Cicero as an independent politician. (For more detailed accounts of Cicero's position at this time, see Rawson, *Cicero* 128-163, Stockton, *Cicero* 211-224).

In the letter to Quintus referred to above (*Q.Fr.* 3.5), Cicero expresses disgust with the state of the Republic, and says that he will devote himself entirely to literature. This is a rhetorical outburst in a private context, and should not be taken too seriously. It is clear that Cicero still had much to occupy him in public life; he was much in demand as an advocate in the courts, not least in the defence of various friends of Pompey whom Cicero had previously attacked. In *Att.* 4.16, he says that he is short of the leisure that he needs for his literary work, and in *Q.Fr.* 3.3 (November 54) that he is daily occupied as a defence counsel. This period should certainly not be seen as one of retirement from public life, like the years 46-44 BC under Caesar's dictatorship; his complaints about the state of the Republic are those of one who is still involved in it, and even an active politician was entitled to a summer vacation, particularly in the extremely hot summer of 54 BC. Indeed, in the later *De Divinatione* Cicero refers to the *De Republica* as written when he still sat at the helm of the state – not as strange a remark as some have thought; and the prologue of the *De Republica* itself contains a vigorous defence of Cicero's participation in public life, which would be not so much hypocritical as senseless if its author thought of himself as retired from politics. (On this topic see Leeman-Pinkster on Cic. *De Oratore*, I, pp. 17ff.)

Nevertheless, it is clear that Cicero was politically dissatisfied, and his main impulse towards the literary work that issued in the *De Oratore*, the *De Republica* and the *De Legibus* was no doubt the feeling that his strictly political influence now counted for less than it had done, and that he must find other ways of publicising his views and adding to his personal reputation. Attempts to discern a definite practical aim behind the composition of the *De Republica* and *De Legibus* rest on shaky foundations. Whether or not Cicero really thought that his idealised picture of the Roman constitution and of Roman law could produce any improvement in the state of Rome in the 50's, nevertheless there is no doubt that these works would provide an effective contrast to the reality of which he complained in the letters; they would constitute an escape, perhaps, for Cicero and his readers, into something better; and if anyone were to choose to take practical notice of Cicero's views on how a state ought best to be run, then Cicero would be the last person to object. Some believe that Cicero's political theories did in fact have an influence on the formation of the Augustan regime; but that is another open question, on which it would be inappropriate to expand in this context.

3. The *De Republica*: content   As a literary work, the *De Republica* was (explicitly) Cicero's answer to Plato's *Republic*; but it was no mere imitation. The subject-matter and setting were entirely Roman, although naturally there is much Greek philosophical influence to be detected. The dialogue was supposed to have taken place between Scipio Aemilianus, his friend Gaius Laelius, and a number of other friends and contemporaries – Philus, Manilius, Sp. Mummius; and from the younger generation, Fannius and Scaevola, Q.Tubero and P.Rutilius Rufus, the last being in imagination the intermediary who narrated the conversation to Cicero. The conversation is set at the *Feriae Latinae* in 129 BC, soon before the death of Scipio.

In the first book, the friends gather and discuss the contemporary political situation. The theme of the dialogue is stated, and Scipio makes some general observations on the theory of constitutions. In the second, Scipio gives an outline of Roman history, and of the development of the Roman constitution to its most perfect form. In the third, the role of justice in government was evidently discussed: Philus undertook to defend Carneades's position that government was based on injustice, while Laelius took the opposite line (cf. *Lael.* 25). The third book also included discussion of the various constitutions – democracy, oligarchy, tyranny. The fourth book appears to have contained a discussion of education, while the fifth was apparently concerned with the delineation of the ideal citizen (or statesman, as *civis* is perhaps more appropriately translated in this context); that is, the person best fitted to take part in government. Little survives of the sixth book apart from the *Somnium* itself, which apparently formed the conclusion of the whole dialogue (*Lael.* 14; cf. note on §21 [29]); but it appears that more was said there about the ideal ruler (*rector rei publicae*).

In connection with this, there has been endless debate as to whether Cicero intended his ideal statesman or ruler to be a monarch. The loss of crucial parts of Cicero's argument makes it impossible to resolve the problem certainly, but the present editor inclines to believe that Cicero envisaged his "ruler" as able to operate equally well as a leader in a democratic state, or as one of a number of leaders with equal influence, and that he did not think it necessary or even desirable that the "ruler" should occupy a permanent position of supreme power. Such a thing would have been against all the principles of the Roman Republican constitution, which Cicero took as his ideal both in theory and in practice. On the other hand, it must be realised that the Roman constitution was not quite like that of a modern democracy. A Roman consul in his year of office was subject to various checks, such as the tribunician veto and the citizen's right of appeal to the people, but his powers were more far-reaching than those of any modern government official, and could be seen as virtually regal. A man who was capable of acting well in the highest public office when called upon to do so, and, when not in office, of directing the course of events by his advice and influence – that is to say, a successful and conscientious Roman statesman – could surely qualify as a "good ruler", and it is this sort of man who is rewarded by eternal happiness in the heaven described in the *Somnium Scipionis*.

4. The *Somnium Scipionis* and its Platonic model   Plato's *Republic* ends with the so-called Myth of Er (614b-621d): the story (told in the dialogue by Socrates) of Er the son of Armenius, a Pamphylian, who was found on the field of battle, assumed dead, and taken home for cremation. On the twelfth day, as he lay on the funeral pyre, he came back to life, and recounted his vision of the fate of the soul after death. The events of which he tells were located in a version of the mythical Underworld or Hades.

The Myth of Er is pure fiction; and it was criticised as such by some ancient writers, particularly Colotes, a follower of Epicurus (4th/3rd century BC; cf. Macr. *SS* 1.2.4; Proclus *In Plat. Rep.* pp. 105ff. Kroll). Cicero in the *De Republica* (either in the preface to the fifth book, as Bréguet thinks, or in the dialogue of book VI, as more commonly thought) referred both to the Myth of Er itself (Favon. Eulog. p. 1 = *Rep.* V fr. 2 Bréguet, VI.3 Ziegler) and to the criticisms of it (Macr. *SS* 1.2.1 = *Rep.* V fr. 3 Bréguet, VI.7 Ziegler). Augustine, *Civ. Dei* 22.28 (= *Rep.* V fr. 4 Bréguet, VI.4 Ziegler) quotes Cicero as saying that Plato was not serious about the content of the Myth.

The position of the *Somnium* at the end of the *De Republica*, and its general subject, parallel those of the Myth of Er. Just as the Myth was introduced by Plato with a discussion of the rewards of virtue, in which Socrates said that the rewards after death were more certain and permanent than any in this life, so Cicero introduced the *Somnium* in a passage which Macrobius reproduces as follows (*SS* 1.4.2-3, = *Rep.* VI fr. 4 Bréguet, VI.8.8 Ziegler; cf. R.Knab, *Hermes* 112 [1984] 501-4):

> *Cum enim Laelius quereretur nullas Nasicae statuas in publico in interfecti tyranni remunerationem locatas, respondit Scipio post alia in haec verba:* "Sed quamquam sapientibus conscientia ipsa factorum egregiorum amplissimum virtutis est praemium, tamen illa divina virtus non statuas plumbo inhaerentes nec triumphos arescentibus laureis, sed stabiliora quaedam et viridiora

praemiorum genera desiderat." – "Quae tandem ista sunt?" inquit Laelius. Tum Scipio: "Patimini me," inquit, "quoniam tertium diem iam feriati sumus ..." *et cetera quibus ad narrationem somnii venit, docens illa esse stabiliora et viridiora praemiorum genera, quae ipse vidisset in caelo, bonis rerum publicarum servata rectoribus.*

["For when Laelius complained that no statues of Nasica had been set up in public as a reward for killing a tyrant, Scipio answered (after saying other things) as follows: "But although for wise men the very consciousness of having accomplished fine deeds is the noblest prize of virtue, nevertheless, Virtue, divine as she is, longs not for statues fixed together with lead or for triumphs with their fading laurels, but for prizes of a fresher and more permanent kind." – "Tell us what those are," said Laelius. Then Scipio said: "Allow me, since this is now the third day of our holiday ..." and the rest which leads up to the narration of the dream, making it clear that the prizes of a fresher and more permanent kind are those which he had himself seen in heaven, reserved for good rulers of commonwealths."]

Cicero replaced Plato's tall story of Er, who died (or appeared to die) and came to life again, by an equally fictitious but much more realistic account of Scipio's dream (cf. Macr. *SS* 1.1.2ff., Favon. Eulog. p. 1). Of the content of the Myth of Er, Cicero retained virtually nothing. The Myth does indeed contain an account of the structure of the cosmos and the arrangement of the planets, cast in a highly mythologised form; but Cicero's cosmology owes much more to Plato's *Timaeus* and to the current speculations of real astronomers. Cicero's Scipio encounters not a poetic image of celestial mechanics, but a vision of the actual universe as it was thought to be, at least by one influential school of ancient thought.

5. The *Somnium Scipionis*: structure, content, style (1 [9]) Scipio Aemilianus narrates how, when on campaign in Africa at the start of the Third Punic War, he was entertained by Massinissa, king of Numidia. (2 [10]) After a long evening's conversation, mainly about Scipio Africanus his adoptive grandfather, Scipio fell into a deep sleep. In his dream, Africanus himself appeared to him. (3-4 [11-12]) Africanus points out Carthage and prophesies its destruction, together with Scipio's future career and (ambiguously) his death in 129, the year of the dialogue itself. (5-6 [13-14]) He then reveals that there is a place in heaven set apart for the souls of virtuous statesmen; the life after death, in which the soul is freed from the body, is the only true life. (6-8 [14-16]) Then Scipio's father Aemilius Paulus appears, and explains to Scipio that the journey to heaven cannot be hastened artificially by suicide. By now the earth has retreated into the distance and is visible as a sphere; Scipio sees the Milky Way, the home of departed souls, and the true sizes of the stars and the comparative insignificance of the earth.

(9-11 [17-19]) Africanus then shows Scipio the ordering of the planets, and explains the cause of the "Music of the Spheres" which Scipio can hear as the planets revolve in their orbits. (12-17 [20-25]) Scipio, however, cannot stop himself from looking at the earth, and Africanus then delivers a discourse on the fragility of earthly glory. The fame of a Roman statesman, he says, is confined to a small portion of the globe, and can never reach some parts of it at all; nor, by geological or astronomical standards, can it last long in time. (18-20 [26-28]) Then Africanus speaks of the immortality and divinity of the soul, reproducing Plato's "proof" of immortality from the *Phaedrus*. (21 [29]) With a final exhortation to Scipio to work for his country and set his mind on heavenly things, and a warning of the fate of those who give themselves up to the desires of the flesh, Africanus departs.

*   *   *

It should never be forgotten, when one reads the *Somnium*, that it is the concluding and climactic section of the *De Republica*. Its subject, as already intimated, is quite clearly the rewards of the good statesman after death; all the cosmology and geography is there to illustrate aspects of this theme. The narrative is articulated by four separate mentions of the rewards of political virtue, at §§13, 16, 25-6, and 29. The first of these is supported by the statement that of all earthly things, nothing is more pleasing to God than states and commonwealths; the second, by the doctrine that men were created and placed on the earth in order to watch over it; the third is the conclusion of the argument on the vanity of earthly glory, stressing as a contrast the real rewards that consist in heavenly immortality; the fourth follows the proof of the immortality of the soul, and it is said that the best occupation for a man's immortal soul is to care for his country.

The *Somnium* also contains clear echoes of passages of the first book of the *De Republica*: it is natural that the concluding passage of the work should revert to themes stated at the beginning. (Cf. M.Ruch, "La composition du *De Republica*", *REL* 26 (1948) 157-71; M.Pohlenz, "Cicero de re publica als Kunstwerk", in *Festschrift R.Reitzenstein* (Leipzig & Berlin 1931) 70-105 esp. 99; Büchner, *Ciceros Somnium Scipionis* 111-6). The very beginning of Book I is lost, but Nonius preserves a fragment (fr. 2 Bréguet), probably to be assigned to the opening section, which says that one's debt to one's country is greater than that to one's parents; this is mirrored in *Somnium* 8 (16). *Rep.* 1.2 states that the greatest use of virtue is in governing one's country (cf. also 1.12), clearly the same sentiment as that of *Somnium* 21 (29). In *Rep.* 1.39, a definition of the state is given, which is echoed in *Somnium* 5 (13).

The subject of astronomy is raised at the beginning of the dialogue, when Scipio and his friends discuss the alleged portent of the double sun, and Philus talks of the sphere of Archimedes, a model of the solar system which was used to predict eclipses (1.21ff.) Further on, Scipio talks of the moral and psychological effects of astronomical and philosophical study, in terms which strongly anticipate the *Somnium*. (It is possible that these sentiments are owed to Aristotle: see the fragment of his *Protrepticus*, 10a Ross, and possible imitation of it in the pseudo-Aristotelian *De Mundo*.) The passage (1.27) is worth quoting:

Quid porro aut praeclarum putet in rebus humanis, qui haec deorum regna perspexerit? aut diuturnum, qui cognoverit quid sit aeternum? aut gloriosum, qui viderit quam parva sit terra, primum universa, deinde ea pars eius quam homines incolant, quamque nos in exigua eius parte adfixi, plurimis ignotissimi gentibus, speremus tamen nostrum nomen volitare et vagari latissime?

["Again, what would he think splendid among human affairs, when he has seen these realms of the gods? Or long-lasting, when he has realised what is eternal? Or glorious, when he has seen how small the earth is: in the first place the whole of it, but then still more that part of it in which men live; and in what a small part of it we are confined, unknown to great numbers of races, yet still hoping that our fame will fly abroad and be spread far and wide?"]

A few lines later, Scipio says that the wise man will regard public office not as something desirable, but as something that he is compelled to undertake for the sake of duty, not in order to achieve personal reward or glory. This virtually sums up the negative side of the message of the *Somnium*: the positive side, the doctrine of immortality, is reserved for the revelation in the *Somnium* itself. In this whole preliminary discussion in Book I, Scipio represents the high-minded attitude of the Platonic philosopher-ruler; and it is this feature of the personality of Scipio, as presented in the dialogue, that finds its consummation in the narrative of the Dream. How much it has to do with the historical Scipio, is a question which perhaps can never be answered, and for purely literary purposes need not trouble the reader. The Scipio of the *De Republica* speaks for the idealistic, intellectual, Platonic side of Cicero's own personality. The other side, the more practical one, is also amply represented, e.g. by Laelius in I.31-2: Laelius in the dialogue has a down-to-earth air about him which recalls Socrates's preference for moral enquiry over cosmological speculation. (It should be noted that this contrast is not merely the conventional ancient dichotomy between the active and contemplative ways of life. It is Scipio, the active military leader and statesman, who puts forward the other-worldly philosophical view, while Laelius, who was less eminent in politics and more given to intellectual study, represents the more practical attitude.)

Thus seen, the *Somnium* is not an uneasy mixture of Ciceronian patriotism with Platonic other-worldliness. Many have seen a tension or even a contradiction here; but if one observes the articulation of the narrative and its close links with the rest of the *De Republica*, the message is clear. It is that our existence on earth, taken as a whole, is transitory and insignificant. Whatever we achieve in this life, any merely earthly reward will in the end be unsatisfactory. The pursuit of earthly rewards – power, fame, wealth or pleasure – reduces men to the level of slaves of their own desires, and leads to dishonour, injustice and crime. There are, however, better things in human life. Philosophic contemplation is one; to live a life of justice and courage and selfless service to one's country is another. Nations and commonwealths are established, within the framework of earthly life, as an embodiment of natural justice and the social virtues; and men were put on earth for a purpose, to guard and rule the world in the closest possible approach to the order and consistency of the Cosmos itself. By practising virtue in both action and contemplation, the good statesman can free himself from earthly contagion and achieve eternal life and happiness after death.

This message may be incredible to a sceptical modern reader, but it is not self-contradictory or contemptible.

Among scholarly literature on the "themes" or "message" of the *Somnium*, the following may be referred to in particular here: R.Harder, "Über Ciceros Somnium Scipionis", *Schriften der Königsberger Gelehrten Gesellschaft, geisteswissenschaftliche Klasse*, 6.3 (1929), = *Kleine Schriften* (Munich 1960) 354-95; A.J.Festugière, *Eranos* 44 (1946) 370ff.; L.Alfonsi, *Latomus* 9 (1950) 149-56; Büchner, *Ciceros Somnium Scipionis*; id., *Gymnasium* 69 (1962) 220-41 = *Studien zur römischen Literatur II* (Wiesbaden 1962) 148-72.

* * *

As a mere literary artefact, the *Somnium* has been admired sufficiently often and sufficiently warmly to make it unnecessary to argue about its stylistic merits. It is one of those great pieces of writing whose greatness consists above all in simplicity, economy and consistent dignity of tone. Cicero rivals his Platonic models in fluency and vividness; perhaps he lacks Plato's exuberance of poetic imagination, but on the other hand he mostly avoids imitating Plato's occasional retreats into hierophantic obscurity.

The Ciceronian purity of language and dignity of style is partly a negative quality – a matter of avoiding lapses into unsuitable colloquialism or into awkward phraseology. The language of the *Somnium* contains nothing that is exaggeratedly poetic or grandiose, but some items of old-fashioned or high-flown vocabulary may easily be noted: *grates ago, caelites, his tectis, excelso, anfractus, Grais, nuncupatis, extimus, stellifer, proles.* Some turns of phrase and images verge on the poetic: *somnus complexus est, cum eris curru in Capitolium invectus, ancipitem video quasi fatorum viam, summam tibi fatalem confecerint, impias propinquorum manus effugeris, aevo sempiterno fruantur, flere prohibebat, quid moror in terris?* There is an occasional touch of the alliteration characteristic of Republican poetry, as in *luce lucebat aliena* (also exemplifying what is called "figura etymologica", the juxtaposition of words etymologically connected). There have been attempts to show that Cicero's style in the *Somnium* was specifically influenced by Lucretius (J.Fontaine, *Mélanges A.Piganiol* III [Paris 1966] 1711-29). The phrase *aevo sempiterno fruantur* is compared with Lucr. 2.647 *immortali aevo summa cum pace fruatur*; *vestigiis ingressus* with 5.55 *ingressus vestigia*; *digito demonstrari* with 5.1032 *ut digito quae sint praesentia monstrent*. Cicero, as is known, read Lucretius soon before he wrote the *De Republica*, and it would not be surprising if some phrases from Lucretius's poem stuck in his mind. But those parallels that are quoted are not sufficient even to show specific dependence on Lucretius, as opposed to generalised influence from the language of Latin poetry, and they certainly cannot be used to prove deliberate imitation.

The introductory narrative and connecting passages of dialogue are notably simple in style, and the grandeur of the vision is balanced by Scipio's modesty and urbanity as he introduces the story. In the speeches of Africanus and Paulus, the style is more rhetorical, and the sentence-structure more periodic. There are some notable effects of balance: *ad quam tu oppugnandam nunc venis paene miles – hanc hoc biennio consul evertes; id tibi per te partum – quod habes adhuc a nobis hereditarium; hinc profecti – huc revertuntur; ultima a caelo – citima a terris; angustata verticibus – lateribus latior.* The longer descriptions of the series of the planets and the surface of the earth are orderly in arrangement, but subtly varied in expression. Two climactic passages of the Dream, the end of the initial prophecy and the pronouncement of the divinity of the soul, are marked by anaphora: *te senatus, te omnes boni, te socii, te Latini intuebuntur, tu eris unus ...;* and *deum te igitur scito esse, si quidem est deus qui viget, qui sentit, qui meminit, qui providet, qui tam regit et moderatur,* etc. Throughout, as is customary for Cicero, the ends of sentences and phrases fall into rhythmical patterns (clausulae). It is not so much an accumulation of analysable "effects" that makes the style of the *Somnium* impressive, as the lucid diction, measured rhythm and sentence-structure, and harmonious ordering of material in the extract as a whole. (For further detail on the language of the *Somnium*, see C.Brakman, *Mnemosyne* n.s. 51 (1923) 381-9; A.Ronconi in *Studi in onore di G. Funaioli* (Rome 1955) 394-405.)

Finally, a word should be said of the *Somnium* as a narrative. This aspect has been sadly ignored by most commentators since Macrobius pronounced that Scipio is immediately taken up to the Milky Way at the beginning of the dream, and stays there (presumably immobile) throughout. This is wrong in any case, but certainly does not do justice to the subtlety of the narration. Since the episode is a dream, we do not expect detailed descriptions of movement from one place to another; we all know how the parts of a dream succeed each other imperceptibly, and how the point of view can change like the changes of angle in a film. If we read attentively, we can see how Cicero catches this. First, Africanus appears. He points out Carthage "from some high place full of stars": we are to imagine Scipio first looking upwards and seeing the pointing Africanus surrounded by stars, and then seeing a landscape spread out in front of him, with Carthage and the Mediterranean beyond. This may be imagined as the view from the top of a mountain, or from some reasonably low region of the sky; we do not need to know which. (The modern reader should perhaps beware of thinking in terms of the view from an aeroplane!) Then comes the conversation with Paulus: by the end of this, Scipio has clearly ascended into heaven, since he can see clearly first the Milky Way (much brighter than we normally see it), then the Southern stars; the stars appear as they actually are, much greater than the earth; and now (*iam* - surely to be given its temporal sense here) the earth looks very small. Clearly Scipio is now much higher up than he was when he could see Carthage. Then we have the central portion of the narrative, containing the description of the planets: Scipio watches the revolutions of the planets in amazement, and hears their music. This marks the zenith of his ascent. Then he looks back at the earth, which Africanus proceeds to describe. We are to imagine, now, a gradual descent. First, Scipio can see the whole sphere of the earth, with the five zones, and Europe, Asia and Africa in one corner. (The references to vision – *vides, cernis* – should surely be taken literally in all this.) Then Africanus's rhetoric homes in on the habitable world; he points to its boundaries, the Ganges and Caucasus, with the deictic pronouns *hunc* and *illum*. This, however, is only a temporary (and very dream-like) geographical "close-up". Africanus himself never leaves the upper reaches of heaven, which he refers to as "this place" several times in what follows, including the last line of his closing speech. At the end, Africanus "departs": this does not necessarily mean that he disappears in a flash like an epic divinity, but may only imply that he recedes into the distance.

Roughly speaking, therefore, the Dream takes the form of an ascent followed by a descent, from the dreamer's point of view; while Africanus and Paulus, as is proper for departed spirits, appear for the first time among the stars, and presumably return there when they have said their piece.

6. The question of "sources"   There is in the present editor's mind no doubt that the *Somnium*, like the rest of the *De Republica*, is a substantially original literary work. It bears the same relation to Plato's Myth of Er as, say, the sixth book of the *Aeneid* does to Homer's *Nekyia*, or the Shield of Aeneas in *Aeneid* VIII to the Shield of Achilles in *Iliad* 18.

In the past, much scholarly effort has been devoted to the search for a "source" or "sources" for the *Somnium*. It is not always made precisely clear what, in such a context, is being looked for. The *Somnium* certainly has a literary model, the Myth of Er: that is common knowledge. The various ideas contained in the *Somnium* certainly have their respective sources, and very often we know what they are. The ideas on the soul, its immortality and the after-life come either directly from Plato himself or from some adaptation or interpretation of Platonic doctrine. The inspiration for the cosmological excursus is also Platonic; the astronomical and geographical content is, on the whole, based simply on current scientific ideas, and some of it is very similar to what is found in Greek geographical or cosmographical works. There is some reasonably clear influence from Pythagoreanism, or what passed for Pythagoreanism in Cicero's time, in the account of the Music of the Spheres (though it is difficult to see as much Pythagorean influence on the rest of the *De Republica* as is postulated by R.G.G.Coleman, "The Dream of Cicero", *PCPS* NS 10 [1964] 1-14).The reference to the periodic conflagrations of the world possibly (though not certainly: see ad loc.) owes something to Stoic ideas; the whole topic of the insignificance of earthly glory was apparently a philosophic commonplace. Most of the individual ideas in the work can be traced to their origins in this way, with a greater or lesser degree of precision. What, then, remains to be accounted for?

Nobody now believes (at least, one hopes not) that Cicero's philosophical works are all transcribed from lost Greek sources. Yet even so, it seems, there remains a vestigial idea that something about the *Somnium* still needs to be explained, even when one has accounted for its individual elements as described above. One still meets with attempts to identify a sort of Greek proto-*Somnium*, or two or three prototypes for the different sections, which Cicero could have taken over more or less ready-made. Even in the recent commentary on the *De Republica* by K.Büchner, who is in general opposed to the search for "sources", there is a very flimsily supported attempt to identify a section of Aristotle's *Protrepticus* as the prototype of the speech on the vanity of glory (see note on

§12 [20]). But no agreement has ever been reached on the identification of a proto-*Somnium*, and only two alternative conclusions are possible: either it has disappeared leaving so little trace that we cannot hope to identify or reconstruct it; or, the more likely alternative, it never existed at all.

Naturally, Cicero may have been influenced by lost Greek works in ways we cannot now determine. He may have made his first acquaintance with Platonic cosmology through intermediate sources now lost, or through personal association with philosophers. However, such things are relatively of little importance; one wonders how many readers of this book can now remember precisely how they first learnt about (say) the Copernican theory of the solar system, or Newton's theory of gravitation. There may also have been literary influences apart from Plato himself. One possible parallel is Heraclides Ponticus's *Vision of Empedotimus* (cf. Gottschalk, *Heraclides* 98ff.), which seems to have resembled the *Somnium* superficially in some respects; but there is no evidence to suggest that Cicero followed it closely. It is possible that some of the astronomical or geographical lore may have come from Posidonius of Apamea: the ground for supposing this consists in the similarity between the astronomy of the *Somnium* and that of the astronomical treatise of Cleomedes, which, according to an ancient note appended to the end of the text, is largely derived from Posidonius. However, there are some differences in detail between what is said in the *Somnium* and what we know of the doctrines of Posidonius (see notes on §§9 [17] and 13 [21]); and whatever may be the truth about this, the parallels with Cleomedes can only show that Cicero may have used Posidonius as an authority for scientific information: they do not show in the least that Posidonius was the source of Cicero's literary or philosophical inspiration. There is even less ground for believing (as G.Luck attempted to establish, *Harvard Theological Review* 49 [1956] 207ff.) that the literary framework of the *Somnium* may be traced to Antiochus of Ascalon, an Academic philosopher contemporary with Posidonius and Cicero who had great influence in more strictly philosophical matters. There is in fact no evidence to show that either Antiochus or Posidonius went in for this sort of writing at all.

To continue the search for a "source", in the absence of more certain evidence, is equivalent to admitting that Cicero was incapable of inventing for himself the narrative framework of the *Somnium*, and of combining its various ingredients into a unified whole. This, to speak plainly, is absurd. Admittedly, we do not elsewhere see much of Cicero's abilities as a writer of literary fiction; but as an orator he was a master of the art of arranging and presenting ideas, and he certainly knew how to compose a cogent narrative. His gifts for rhetorical composition were quite sufficient to account for the creation of the *Somnium* out of the materials and models that we can identify. The postulation of a lost literary "source" or "sources", over and above these, is an unnecessary hypothesis. This has been seen by some modern scholars, P.Boyancé being the most notable among them; if due attention had been paid to Boyancé's work, the question might by now have been regarded as closed. (See Boyancé, *Études*; id., *L'Ant. Class.* 11 [1942] 5-22, repr. in *Études sur l'humanisme cicéronien*, Coll. Latomus 121 [1970] 276-93.)

*   *   *

It is, however, quite appropriate to raise the rather wider question of the origin of Cicero's interest in the Platonic doctrines which appear in the *Somnium*. A number of factors are relevant here. One is simple literary emulation of Plato (it was doubtless principally the *De Republica* that Quintilian had in mind when he called Cicero *Platonis aemulus*). Another is Cicero's political disappointment: it is a common view that this led him to take refuge in the imagined idea of an afterlife, in which he would himself be rewarded for his services to the Roman state; the idea could be comforting, even if he never seriously believed it (and we do not know that he did not).

He may have been influenced by contemporaries, such as Varro or Nigidius Figulus, who had interests in Platonism and Pythagoreanism. At some time in his life, though it is uncertain when, he dedicated to Nigidius a translation of Plato's *Timaeus*, of which part survives. There has long been a tendency among scholars to attribute a sort of Platonic revival to certain Greek philosophers of the first century BC, particularly Posidonius the Stoic; but the evidence for this is really very slight, and it is more a hypothesis to explain Cicero's apparent interests than a securely based theory. The existence of Platonic and Aristotelian pseudepigrapha, such as the *Axiochus* and *De Mundo*, both of which contain doctrines derived from Plato and elsewhere which are very similar to those of the *Somnium*, has sometimes been used to support the idea of a first-century BC Platonic revival; but the conventional first-century dating of these works itself depends on the hypothesis of such a revival, and so the argument is circular. H.Dörrie, *Revue de Théologie et de Philosophie*, III sér., 24 (1974) 13-29, attributes the "Platonic revival" of Cicero's time to the Romans themselves, or at any rate to persons who were not professional philosophers. That these ideas were current and aroused interest among Romans other than Cicero, we need not doubt (cf. P.Boyancé, "Le Platonisme à Rome", *Actes Congrès Budé* 1953).

Finally, it has been suggested that the *De Republica* was conceived as a reaction against the Epicurean preachings of Lucretius, whose poem came into Cicero's hands in February of 54 BC, the very year in which he began the composition of the *De Republica*. This is quite uncertain; but it is certainly true that the *De Republica* was partly directed against Epicureanism in general, and the doctrines of the *Somnium* are clearly opposed to the Epicurean insistence on the finality of death. (See J. Fontaine, in *Mélanges A. Piganiol* III [Paris 1966] 1711-29.) As said above, the linguistic parallels between the *Somnium* and Lucretius prove nothing: they are not substantial enough for it to be said that Cicero was deliberately using Lucretian language to put forward anti-Lucretian doctrine.

7. Cicero's other allusions to the doctrines of the *Somnium*, and the work's later influence   Cicero, having produced in the *Somnium* what one might call a potted Platonic creed, reverted to the ideas contained in it fairly constantly in his later philosophical writing. These ideas even turn up in a law-court speech, the *Pro Scauro*, delivered in September 54 when the composition of the *De Republica* was evidently on Cicero's mind. The reference there is not at all serious in tone; Cicero provides a glaringly inaccurate summary of the *Phaedo*, which is really more like a summary of the *Somnium*, in the context of a discussion of a Sardinian woman who had committed suicide (in the course of which he also produces a horrid pun about a salted sardine). However, there is no reason to believe that his references in the later philosophical works – *De Legibus, Hortensius, Consolatio, Tusculans, De Natura Deorum, Cato Maior, Laelius* – were not meant seriously. There are too many of them for this to be a mere literary conceit. Whether or not Cicero gave the doctrines his full intellectual assent (cf. *Tusc.* 1.24), they were clearly important to him; probably for two reasons. First, they were useful as ammunition against the Epicureans: the idea of a blissful afterlife for the virtuous was easy to present as more attractive than the Epicurean belief that death was annihilation. Secondly, they provided Cicero himself with consolation, probably more so at this later stage of his life than when he wrote the *De Republica* itself. By the time he came to write his later series of philosophical works, the Republic had broken down apparently beyond repair, and Cicero's personal life was also beset by troubles, chief among which were the death of his daughter Tullia in February 45, and his unsuccessful second marriage around the same time. The prospect of a just reward for his efforts as a statesman, of reunion in heaven with Tullia, and of meeting the heroes of Rome's past there as well (cf. *Cato Maior* 84) cannot have seemed to him anything other than pleasant.

*   *   *

The *Somnium Scipionis* did not have a separate life in the Roman world; it was simply a part of the *De Republica* (which was, of course, widely read), and as long as the works of Plato himself were commonly read in the original, it had no particular significance as a source of ideas. E. Norden saw influence from the *Somnium* on the sixth book of Virgil's *Aeneid*, and the idea has proved popular among scholars (cf. Boyancé, *Études* 39ff.; id., *Hommages Dumézil* [Brussels 1960] 60ff.; Ronconi's edition, 25ff.; J.Hubaux, in *Hommages à L.Herrmann*, Coll. Latomus 44 [Brussels 1960] 436-45; R.Lamacchia, *RhM* 107 (1964) 261-78). But if such influence is there, it is very generalised, and there is not much (if there is anything) that cannot be accounted for by a combination of Virgil's epic models and his reading of Plato and other Greek philosophers in the original. There are occasional echoes of the *Somnium* in the works of Seneca (cf. *Cons. Marc.* 18, *Cons. Polyb.* 9), for whom Cicero's philosophical writings were a source of literary, rather than doctrinal, inspiration.

The *Somnium* may be seen as a relatively early manifestation of the process of extracting from Plato, by interpretation, extension and summary, a set of beliefs that amounted virtually to a religious system. The full development of this is to be seen in the Neoplatonists of late antiquity. Naturally enough, many of their basic doctrines were similar to those which Cicero had acquired from the Platonic philosophy current in his time; but these ideas were subjected to a vast degree of elaboration and systematisation, and the mystical or contemplative side of Platonism (which naturally had not been very prominent in Cicero, nor indeed in any of Plato's immediate Greek successors) became by far the most important characteristic of the philosophy. It was as a follower of Neoplatonism that Macrobius wrote his commentary on the *Somnium* (see the useful annotated translation by W.H.Stahl, New York 1952). Macrobius's work is not perhaps as bad as some modern critics have held it to be: he had a basic sympathy with his subject, and he makes some useful observations. However, he interprets Cicero very much in the light of the Neoplatonism of his time, and he digresses at great length on subjects such as numerology, cosmology and the Aristotelian objections to Plato's doctrine of the soul. We also possess another, much less extensive, late-antique commentary on the *Somnium*, written by one Favonius Eulogius (ed. R.E. van Weddingen, Coll. Latomus 27 [1957]; A. Holder, Leipzig 1901). This is largely devoted to numerology and the Music of the Spheres.

Macrobius's commentary was one of the encyclopaedic works from the late Roman empire that were passed on to the Middle Ages as the chief source of ancient learning. It was itself widely read, and it was the vehicle whereby the *Somnium* became known as a separate text, at a time when the rest of the *De Republica* was lost. The cosmology and geography of the *Somnium* and of Macrobius became, more or less, that of all Western Europe in the Middle Ages. Much of it had, in any case, become the common property of pagans and Christians alike by the time of the fall of the Western Empire; it did not, by and large, conflict with orthodox Christian teachings, and the Platonic doctrines on immortality and the after-life were easily assimilated to the Christian conceptions of these matters. (For the use of the *Somnium Scipionis* by Christian writers, see P. Courcelle, *REL* 36 [1958] 205-34.) Hence, throughout medieval and Renaissance literature, we find references to the planetary spheres, their music and astrological influences; the contrast between the imperfect sublunary world in which we live and the regions beyond the moon where all is perfect and eternal; the zones of the earth, the impossibility of reaching the southern hemisphere, and the stream of Ocean that surrounds the world. The influence of the *Somnium*, and of other works in the same tradition, on medieval and Renaissance literature has been well described by C.S.Lewis in *The Discarded Image* (Cambridge 1964) esp. 23-28.

It is probably true to say that the prevailing acceptance of some of these ideas retarded the development of scientific geography and astronomy. Yet the late-antique and medieval world picture was not as erroneous as is often popularly thought. Medieval writers believed that the earth was round, not flat; they believed that the sun and stars were larger than the earth, and that they were situated at a great distance from us. They believed that the moon shines by light reflected from the sun. They may have thought that the earth was the mathematical centre of the universe, but they certainly did not think that it was the most important place there was. They believed these things largely because they had read them in the *Somnium Scipionis*. We happen still to believe some of them, because scientific observations have confirmed them; but the other elements of the older "model" (as Lewis calls it) were equally rational beliefs in their time. It is quite wrong to suppose that the older model is merely mythical; it was a theoretical construct which was thought to explain the observed phenomena, so far as they were known.

Among the manifestations of the more specifically literary influence of the *Somnium* in the medieval and Renaissance world may be mentioned Petrarch's Latin poem *Africa*, which paraphrases several passages; while Chaucer, in *The Parlement of Foules*, narrates a dream brought on by a reading of the *Somnium*, and paraphrases many of its doctrines. A Greek translation was made by the Byzantine scholar Maximus Planudes (cf. G.Alberti in *Studi Ronconi* [Florence 1970] 7-15, M.Gigante, *P. del P.* 59-60 [1958] 173-94). In the eighteenth century, finally, the *Somnium* achieved the distinction of being set (in a very free Italian adaptation) to music – by Mozart in *Il Sogno di Scipione*.

8. Text and manuscripts The text of the *Somnium* comes to us by two routes: the full text appended to manuscripts of Macrobius's *Commentary* or, sometimes, occurring by itself in medieval manuscripts; and the quotations in the body of the Commentary itself, which between them cover about two thirds of the *Somnium*. (For the translation from Plato in §§19-20 (27-8), we also have the version in *Tusculans* I.) All the medieval texts of the complete *Somnium* descend from a single archetype, which had the mistake *parum rebus* for *parumper* (Bouhier's virtually certain correction) in §4 (12); this error (REB: for PER) would happen most easily in uncial script (like that of the Vatican palimpsest of *De Republica*). The text of the Macrobian quotations diverges in some details from the consensus of the medieval manuscripts, although the picture is obscured by the fact that some of the medieval manuscripts appear to incorporate corrections from the Macrobian tradition: for example, the earliest manuscript (A, Paris nouv. acq. lat. 454, 9th century) contains corrections by a second hand which sometimes agree with the readings of Macrobius. Thus it happens that all the good readings from Macrobius also appear somewhere in the manuscript tradition: there is no place where Macrobius preserves a clearly correct reading not found in the medieval manuscripts. On the whole there are hardly any important variants in the manuscript tradition itself, and it is unnecessary to include details of it here. We may be reasonably confident that we have the text as Cicero wrote it. Three relatively minor problems are discussed in the Appendix. The following articles on the text and manuscripts may be cited: G.Alberti, "Macrobio e il testo del *Somnium Scipionis*", *SIFC* 33 (1961) 163-84; L.Castiglioni, *Rend. Ist. Lomb.* 68 (1935) 301-20 and 331-51; E.Hauler, *WS* 42 (1920-21) 90-95 and 182-6; M.Sicherl, *RhM* 102 (1959) 266-86 and 346-64; K.Ziegler, *Hermes* 66 (1931) 268ff.; B.C.Barker-Benfield (on the MSS. of Macrobius and the *Somnium*) in *T. & T.* 224-32.

THE DREAM OF SCIPIO
SOMNIVM SCIPIONIS

MARCI TVLLI CICERONIS SOMNIVM SCIPIONIS
EXCERPTVM EX LIBRO VI DE RE PVBLICA

[I:1 (= *De Rep.* VI.9)] [SCIPIO:]   Cum in Africam venissem hoc Manilio consule*, ad quartam legionem tribunus, ut scitis, militum, nihil mihi fuit potius quam ut Massinissam convenirem, regem familiae nostrae iustis de causis amicissimum. Ad quem ut veni, complexus me senex conlacrimavit, aliquantoque post suspexit ad caelum, et "Grates," inquit, "tibi ago, summe Sol, vobisque reliqui caelites, quod antequam ex hac vita migro, conspicio in meo regno et his tectis Publium Cornelium Scipionem, cuius ego nomine ipso recreor: ita numquam ex animo meo discedit illius optimi atque invictissimi viri memoria." Deinde ego illum de suo regno, ille me de nostra re publica percontatus est, multisque verbis ultro citroque habitis, ille nobis est consumptus dies; [2 (10)] post autem, apparatu regio accepti, sermonem in multam noctem produximus, cum senex nihil nisi de Africano loqueretur, omniaque eius non facta solum sed etiam dicta meminisset. Deinde ut cubitum discessimus, me et de via fessum et qui ad multam noctem vigilassem, artior quam solebat somnus complexus est. Hic mihi (credo equidem ex hoc quod eramus locuti; fit enim fere ut cogitationes sermonesque nostri pariant aliquid in somno, tale quale de Homero scribit Ennius, de quo videlicet saepissime vigilans solebat cogitare·et·loqui) Africanus se ostendit, ea forma quae mihi ex imagine eius quam ex ipso erat notior; quem ubi agnovi, equidem cohorrui; sed ille "Ades," inquit, "animo, et omitte timorem, Scipio, et quae dicam trade memoriae.

[II:3 (11)] "Videsne illam urbem, quae parere populo Romano coacta per me, renovat pristina bella nec potest quiescere," (ostendebat autem Carthaginem de excelso et pleno stellarum, illustri et claro quodam loco), "ad quam tu oppugnandam nunc venis paene miles? Hanc hoc biennio consul evertes, eritque cognomen id tibi per te partum, quod habes adhuc a nobis hereditarium. Cum autem Carthaginem deleveris, triumphum egeris, censorque fueris et obieris legatus Aegyptum Syriam Asiam Graeciam, deligere iterum consul absens, bellumque maximum conficies: Numantiam exscindes. Sed cum eris curru in Capitolium invectus, offendes rem publicam consiliis perturbatam nepotis mei: [4 (12)] hic tu, Africane, ostendas oportebit patriae lumen animi ingeni consilique tui. Sed eius temporis ancipitem video quasi fatorum viam. Nam cum aetas tua septenos octiens solis anfractus reditusque converterit, duoque hi numeri quorum uterque plenus alter altera de causa habetur, circuitu naturali summam tibi fatalem confecerint, in

THE DREAM OF SCIPIO
FROM BOOK VI OF THE *DE REPUBLICA*

[I:1 (=De Rep. VI.9)] [SCIPIO:] When I arrived in Africa, in the year that Manilius here was consul - as you know, I was military tribune with the fourth legion - my first duty was to meet Massinissa, the king, with whom our family had for good reasons a strong bond of friendship. The old man embraced me with tears in his eyes as we met, and after a time he looked up to heaven, saying, "I give you thanks, highest Sun, and you other heavenly ones, that before I depart this life, I have seen in my kingdom and in this house Publius Cornelius Scipio, at whose very name I regain my strength: so true is it that the memory of that best and most invincible of men is never absent from my mind." Then I made enquiry of him about his kingdom, and he of me about our republic; we spent that whole day in conversation, and there was much talk on either side. [2 (10)] After this we were royally entertained, and we carried on the conversation far into the night: the old man talked of nothing but Africanus, recalling all his deeds and his sayings as well. Then the company broke up and we went to bed; and I, since I was tired from the journey and had stayed awake very late, fell into a deeper sleep than is usual for me. Then – (I think myself that it was because of what we had been speaking of; for it often happens that our thoughts and conversations give rise to something in our sleep, similar to what Ennius writes about Homer, about whom no doubt he very often used to talk and think when awake) – Africanus himself appeared to me. His appearance was more familiar to me from his effigy than from real life. I was seized with fear when I recognised him, but he said, "Attend and cast off your fear, Scipio, and remember what I shall say to you.

[II:3 (11)] "Do you see that city, which, once compelled by me to be obedient to the Roman people, now renews its old wars and cannot stay quiet," (he pointed out Carthage from some high place full of stars, brilliant and clear) "which you now come to attack, little more than a common soldier? Within these two years, as consul you will destroy it, and you will have earned for yourself by your own merits the name which you have until now had as an inheritance from me. When you have destroyed Carthage and celebrated a triumph, and when you have been censor and travelled as legate through Egypt, Syria, Asia and Greece, you will be chosen consul a second time in your absence, and you will bring to its end a great war: you will sack Numantia. But when you have ridden up to the Capitol in your chariot, you will come upon a republic troubled by the plottings of my grandson: [4 (12)] here, Africanus, you must show to your country the light of your mind, your intelligence and your wise counsel. But at that time I see, as it were, a fork in the road of destiny. For when your life has accomplished eight times seven revolutions and returnings of the sun, and these two numbers, which are both for diverse reasons thought to be perfect, have in their natural circuit completed for you the

te unum atque in tuum nomen se tota convertet civitas: te senatus, te omnes boni, te socii, te Latini intuebuntur; tu eris unus in quo nitatur civitatis salus, ac ne multa, dictator rem publicam constituas oportet, si impias propinquorum manus effugeris."

Hic cum exclamavisset Laelius, ingemuissentque vehementius ceteri, leniter arridens Scipio, St! quaeso, inquit, ne me e somno excitetis, et parumper audite cetera.

[III:5 (13)] "Sed quo sis, Africane, alacrior ad tutandam rem publicam, sic habeto: omnibus qui patriam conservaverint adiuverint auxerint, certum esse in caelo definitum locum, ubi beati aevo sempiterno fruantur. Nihil est enim illi principi deo, qui omnem mundum regit, quod quidem in terris fiat, acceptius, quam concilia coetusque hominum iure sociati, quae civitates appellantur: harum rectores et conservatores hinc profecti huc revertuntur."

[6 (14)] Hic ego, etsi eram perterritus non tam mortis metu quam insidiarum a meis, quaesivi tamen viveretne ipse et Paulus pater, et alii quos nos exstinctos esse arbitraremur.

"Immo vero," inquit, "hi vivunt, qui e corporum vinclis tamquam e carcere evolaverunt. Vestra vero quae dicitur vita, mors est. Quin tu aspicis ad te venientem Paulum patrem?"

Quem ut vidi, equidem vim lacrimarum profudi; ille autem me complexus atque osculans flere prohibebat, [7 (15)] atque ego ut primum fletu represso loqui posse coepi, "Quaeso," inquam, "pater sanctissime atque optime, quoniam haec est vita, ut Africanum audio dicere, quid moror in terris? Quin huc ad vos venire propero?"

"Non est ita," inquit ille; "nisi enim deus is cuius hoc templum est omne quod conspicis, istis te corporis custodiis liberaverit, huc tibi aditus patere non potest. Homines enim sunt hac lege generati, qui tuerentur illum globum quem in hoc templo medium vides, quae terra dicitur; eisque animus datus est ex illis sempiternis ignibus quae sidera et stellas vocatis, quae globosae et rotundae, divinis animatae mentibus, circulos suos orbesque conficiunt celeritate mirabili. Quare et tibi, Publi, et piis omnibus, retinendus animus est in custodia corporis, nec iniussu eius a quo ille est vobis datus, ex hominum vita migrandum est, ne munus* assignatum a deo defugisse videamini. [8 (16)] Sed sic, Scipio, ut avus hic tuus, ut ego qui te genui, iustitiam cole et pietatem, quae cum magna in parentibus et propinquis, tum in patria maxima est: ea vita via est in caelum et in hunc coetum eorum qui iam vixerunt, et corpore laxati illum

appointed sum of years, then the whole state will turn towards you and call upon your name; the senate, all good citizens, the allies and the Latins will look to you; you will be the one man on whom the salvation of the state can rest, and not to say more, you must re-establish the republic as dictator, if only you can escape the impious hands of your relatives."

At this point Laelius cried out and the others murmured loudly; but Scipio, smiling gently, said, "Hush, please! don't wake me from my sleep, and wait a little while I tell you the rest."

[III:5 (13)] "But, Africanus, so that you may be the keener to protect the Republic, be sure of this: for all those who have saved or helped or increased the power of their native land, there is a place set apart in heaven, for them to enjoy eternal life in happiness. For, of all at least that is done on earth, there is nothing more pleasing to that supreme God who rules the whole universe, than the communities and gatherings of men, held together by law, which are called commonwealths: the rulers and saviours of these begin their journey from here, and hither they return."

[6 (14)] Then, although I was frightened not so much by the fear of death, as by the thought of treachery on the part of my family, I asked whether he and Paulus my father, and the others who we thought were dead, were actually alive.

"Yes, indeed," he said, "it is these who are alive, having flown out from the bonds of the body, as if from a prison; and that which you call your life, is really death. Do you not see your father Paulus coming towards you?"

As I saw him, I let fall a flood of tears; but he put his arms round me and kissed me, and commanded me not to weep. [7 (15)] And as soon as I had suppressed my tears and was able to speak, I said to him, "Tell me, best and most revered of fathers: since this is true life, as I have just heard Africanus say, why do I remain on earth? Why should I not hasten to come here to you?"

"No," he said, "for unless that god, whose temple is this whole universe that you see, has freed you from that bodily prison, the way here cannot be open for you. For men were created on this condition, that they should watch over that globe, called the Earth, which you see in the centre of this heaven; and a soul was given them out of these eternal fires which you call stars and planets, each of which revolves with wonderful speed in its own circular orbit, being itself round and spherical and animated by a divine mind. Therefore both you, Publius, and all good men, must keep the soul in the prison of the body, and must not depart from human life without the command of him who gave your soul to you, lest you appear to desert the duty assigned to you by God. [8 (16)] But you, Scipio, as your grandfather here did, and as I who begot you have done, must practise justice and do your duty: your duty which is great towards parents and family, but greatest of all towards your country. By living thus you may find the way to heaven, into this gathering of those who have lived their lives, and being now freed

incolunt locum quem vides – " (erat autem is splendidissimo candore inter flammas circus elucens) " – quem vos, ut a Grais accepistis, orbem lacteum nuncupatis."

Ex quo omnia mihi contemplanti praeclara cetera et mirabilia videbantur, erant autem eae stellae quas numquam ex hoc loco vidimus, et eae magnitudines omnium quas esse numquam suspicati sumus. Ex quibus erat ea minima, quae ultima a caelo, citima a terris, luce lucebat aliena. Stellarum autem globi terrae magnitudinem facile vincebant; iam ipsa terra ita mihi parva visa est, ut me imperi nostri, quo quasi punctum eius attingimus, paeniteret.

[IV:9 (17)] Quam cum magis intuerer, "Quaeso," inquit Africanus, "quousque humi defixa tua mens erit? Nonne aspicis quae in templa veneris? Novem tibi orbibus, vel potius globis, conexa sunt omnia: quorum unus est caelestis, extimus, qui reliquos omnes complectitur, summus ipse deus arcens et continens ceteros, in quo sunt infixi illi qui volvuntur stellarum cursus sempiterni; cui subiecti sunt septem qui versantur retro, contrario motu atque caelum. Ex quibus unum globum possidet illa quam in terris Saturniam nominant; deinde est hominum generi prosperus et salutaris ille fulgor qui dicitur Iovis; tum rutilus horribilisque terris quem Martium dicitis; deinde subter mediam fere regionem Sol obtinet, dux et princeps et moderator luminum reliquorum, mens mundi et temperatio, tanta magnitudine ut cuncta sua luce lustret et compleat. Hunc ut comites consequuntur Veneris alter, alter Mercuri cursus, in infimoque orbe Luna radiis solis accensa convertitur. Infra autem iam nihil est nisi mortale et caducum, praeter animos munere deorum hominum generi datos; supra lunam sunt aeterna omnia. Nam ea quae est media et nona, Tellus, neque movetur et infima est, et in eam feruntur omnia nutu suo pondera."

[V:10 (18)] Quae cum intuerer stupens, ut me recepi, "Quid hic," inquam, "quis est qui complet aures meas, tantus et tam dulcis sonus?"

"Hic est," inquit, "ille qui intervallis coniunctus* imparibus, sed tamen pro rata parte ratione distinctis, impulsu et motu ipsorum orbium efficitur, et acuta cum gravibus temperans varios aequabiliter concentus efficit. Nec enim silentio tanti motus incitari possunt, et natura fert ut extrema ex altera parte graviter, ex altera autem acute sonent. Quam ob causam summus ille caeli stellifer cursus, cuius conversio est concitatior, acuto et excitato movetur sono, gravissimo autem hic lunaris atque infimus; nam terra nona immobilis manens una sede semper haeret, complexa medium mundi locum. Illi autem octo cursus, in quibus eadem vis est duorum, septem efficiunt distinctos

from the body, inhabit that place which you see – " (this was a circle of brilliant whiteness, shining out and surrounded by flames) " – which you have learnt from the Greeks to call the Milky Way."

And now, as I looked at everything around me, I saw (though the rest too seemed splendid and amazing) that there were stars which we have never seen from this country, and all the stars were of a size that we have never suspected; the smallest of all was that one which is nearest to earth and furthest from the heavenly sphere, shining with borrowed light; the globes of the stars far surpassed the earth in size, and now the earth itself seemed to me so small that I was ashamed of our empire, which reaches hardly more than a point on its surface.

[IV:9 (17)] As I looked at the earth more closely, Africanus said, "Tell me, how long will your thoughts be fixed down on the ground? Do you not see into what regions you have come? Look: the universe is interlocked in nine circles or rather spheres. One, the outermost, is the sphere of Heaven, embracing all the rest. It is itself the highest divinity, and it contains and holds in itself all the others. In it are fixed the eternal revolving courses of the stars. Beneath it are seven others, which turn in a retrograde direction, with contrary motion to that of Heaven. The first of these belongs to that star which on earth is called the star of Saturn. Then comes that luminary, bringing health and prosperity to the human race, which is called that of Jupiter. The next is red in colour, an object of terror for the earth; you call it the star of Mars. Under these the middle region is ruled by the Sun, the leader and chief and governor of the other lights, the mind and controlling force of the universe: it is of such magnitude that it illuminates and fills everything with its light. Here follow two orbits, one of Venus, the other of Mercury, as companions of the Sun. In the lowest circle, the Moon revolves, set alight by the rays of the Sun. Below this point there is nothing but what is mortal and transitory, except the souls given to mankind by the gift of the gods; above the moon all is eternal. The Earth, the centre and the last of the nine, does not move, and occupies the lowest place. Towards it all heavy objects fall by their own weight."

[V:10 (18)] I looked at these things in amazement; then I collected myself and said, "What is this loud and sweet sound that now fills my ears?"

"That," he said, "is the sound that is made by those very spheres, as they move and are driven onwards, producing varied harmonies smoothly by mixing high and low notes; it is composed of a series of unequal intervals which are nevertheless marked off from each other in a strict proportion. For it is not possible for such great movements to be produced in silence; and it is ordained by nature that the furthest parts at one extreme should sound at a high pitch, while the other extreme sounds at a low pitch. Thus the highest orbit, that of Heaven, carrying the stars, since its revolution is faster, moves with a high and lively note; the lunar sphere, the lowest, sounds the lowest note; for the earth, the ninth in order, remains immovable and is held constantly in one position, containing within itself the central point of the universe. In this way the eight orbits, of which two have the same effect, make seven distinct notes, separated by intervals; now

intervallis sonos, qui numerus rerum omnium fere nodus est; quod docti homines nervis imitati atque cantibus, aperuerunt sibi reditum in hunc locum, sicut alii qui praestantibus ingeniis in vita humana divina studia coluerunt. [11 (19)] Hoc sonitu oppletae aures hominum obsurduerunt, nec est ullus hebetior sensus in vobis; sicut ubi Nilus ad illa quae Catadupa nominantur praecipitat ex altissimis montibus, ea gens quae illum locum accolit propter magnitudinem sonitus sensu audiendi caret; hic vero tantus est totius mundi incitatissima conversione sonitus, ut eum aures hominum capere non possint, sicut intueri solem adversum nequitis, eiusque radiis acies vestra sensusque vincitur."

[VI:12 (20)] Haec ego admirans referebam tamen oculos ad terram identidem; tum Africanus, "Sentio," inquit, "te sedem etiamnunc hominum ac domum contemplari; quae si tibi parva, ut est, ita videtur, haec caelestia semper spectato, illa humana contemnito. Tu enim quam celebritatem sermonis hominum, aut quam expetendam consequi gloriam potes? Vides habitari in terra raris et angustis in locis, et in ipsis quasi maculis ubi habitatur, vastas solitudines interiectas, eosque qui incolant terram non modo interruptos ita esse ut nihil inter ipsos ab aliis ad alios manare possit, sed partim obliquos, partim transversos, partim etiam adversos stare vobis: a quibus exspectare gloriam certe nullam potestis. [13 (21)] Cernis autem eandem terram quasi quibusdam redimitam et circumdatam cingulis, e quibus duos maxime inter se diversos, et caeli verticibus ipsis ex utraque parte subnixos, obriguisse pruina vides, medium autem illum et maximum solis ardore torreri? Duo sunt habitabiles, quorum australis ille in quo qui insistunt adversa vobis urgent vestigia, nihil ad vestrum genus; hic autem alter subiectus aquiloni quem incolitis, cerne quam tenui vos parte contingat: omnis enim terra quae colitur a vobis, angustata verticibus, lateribus latior, parva quaedam insula est, circumfusa illo mari quod Atlanticum, quod magnum, quem Oceanum appellatis in terris; qui tamen tanto nomine quam sit parvus vides. [14 (22)] Ex his ipsis cultis notisque terris, num aut tuum aut cuiusquam nostrum nomen vel Caucasum hunc quem cernis transcendere potuit, vel illum Gangen tranatare? Quis in reliquis orientis aut obeuntis solis ultimis aut aquilonis austrive partibus tuum nomen audiet? Quibus amputatis cernis profecto, quantis in angustiis vestra se gloria dilatari velit. Ipsi autem qui de nobis loquuntur, quam loquentur diu? [VII:15 (23)] Quin etiam si cupiat proles illa futurorum hominum deinceps laudes uniuscuiusque nostrum a patribus acceptas posteris prodere, tamen propter eluviones exustionesque terrarum, quas accidere tempore certo necesse est, non modo non aeternam, sed ne diuturnam quidem gloriam adsequi possumus. Quid autem interest, ab eis qui postea nascentur sermonem fore de te, cum ab eis nullus fuerit qui ante nati sunt, qui nec pauciores et certe meliores fuerunt viri; [16 (24)] praesertim cum apud eos ipsos, a quibus audiri nomen nostrum potest, nemo unius

the number seven is crucial in virtually everything. All this, wise men have imitated with strings and voices, and have opened up for themselves a way back to this place, along with all those who with great powers of intellect have pursued divine studies in human life. [11 (19)] Filled with this sound, the ears of men have grown deaf to it, and of your bodily senses this is the dullest; just as, where the Nile rushes down from the mountain heights at the place called Catadupa, the tribe that inhabits that area, because of the volume of sound, has no sense of hearing. But this sound, caused by the extremely rapid circular motion of the whole universe, is so great that the ears of men cannot perceive it, just as you cannot look straight at the sun, and your sight and sense are defeated by its rays."

[VI:12 (20)] I wondered at this, but still kept turning my eyes back to earth again and again; whereupon Africanus said, "I see that even now you are watching the home and habitation of men. It appears small to you, and indeed it is small: so you must look always towards these heavenly things, and despise things merely human. What sort of fame, or what glory that is desirable, can you achieve through the talk of mankind? You can see that the earth is inhabited only in a few small areas. Even among those patches where men live, there are vast empty areas interposed. Those who inhabit the earth are not only so broken up that no commerce can flow between them from one place to another; some even stand at a different angle from you, some at right angles, and some even directly opposite to you. From those you can certainly not expect any glorious reputation. [13 (21)] Do you see, further, that this same earth is as it were girdled and surrounded by a number of belts? The two furthest apart of these, which are placed under the poles of the sky at either side, are frozen with ice; the central one, which is the largest, is burnt by the heat of the sun. Two of them are habitable; the southern one of these, where they stand with their footsteps opposite to yours, has nothing to do with your race; and as for this other one, over which the north wind blows, see what a small part of it is of concern to you! The whole of the land which is inhabited by your people is really a small island, narrow at the extremities and broader in the centre, surrounded by that sea which you on earth call the Atlantic, the great sea, or the Ocean; and you see how small even that is, despite its great name. [14 (22)] Furthermore, has either your name or that of any of us been able to travel from these well-known and civilised lands, so as to cross the Caucasus, which you see here, or to swim across the Ganges yonder? Who in the other countries of the East, or in the utmost West, or in those parts farther north or south, will ever hear your name? Cut these away, and you will clearly see what a narrow space it is, in which the glory of your people desires to spread itself abroad. Even those who do talk about us, for how long will they talk? [VII:15 (23)] Indeed, even if that generation of men yet to be born will be eager to hand on in turn to its descendants the praises of each one of us, which they have heard from their fathers, nevertheless, because of the floods and conflagrations of the world, which inevitably must happen at their appointed time, we cannot achieve glory that lasts for any length of time, let alone eternally. And what difference does it make to you, that there will be talk about you among those who will be born in the future, when there was none among those born before you, who were no fewer and certainly better men? [16 (24)] – especially since even among those who may come to hear our names, no man

anni memoriam consequi possit? Homines enim populariter annum tantummodo solis, id est unius astri, reditu metiuntur; cum autem ad idem unde semel profecta sunt cuncta astra redierint, eandemque totius caeli descriptionem longis intervallis rettulerint, tum ille vere vertens annus appellari potest, in quo vix dicere audeo quam multa hominum saecla teneantur. Namque ut olim deficere sol hominibus exstinguique visus est cum Romuli animus haec ipsa in templa penetravit, quandoque ab eadem parte sol eodemque tempore iterum defecerit, tum signis omnibus ad principium stellisque revocatis expletum annum habeto; cuius quidem anni nondum vicesimam partem scito esse conversam. [17 (25)] Quocirca si reditum in hunc locum desperaveris, in quo omnia sunt magnis et praestantibus viris, quanti tandem est ista hominum gloria, quae pertinere vix ad unius anni partem exiguam potest? Igitur alte spectare si voles atque hanc sedem et aeternam domum contueri, neque te sermonibus vulgi dedideris, nec in praemiis humanis spem posueris rerum tuarum, suis te oportet illecebris ipsa virtus trahat ad verum decus. Quid de te alii loquantur, ipsi videant, sed loquentur tamen; sermo autem omnis ille et angustiis cingitur his regionum quas vides, nec umquam de ullo perennis fuit; et obruitur hominum interitu, et oblivione posteritatis exstinguitur."

[VIII:18 (26)] Quae cum dixisset, "Ego vero," inquam, "Africane, si quidem bene meritis de patria quasi limes ad caeli aditum patet, quamquam a pueritia vestigiis ingressus patris et tuis decori vestro non defui, nunc tamen tanto praemio exposito enitar multo vigilantius."

Et ille, "Tu vero enitere, et sic habeto, non esse te mortalem, sed corpus hoc; nec enim tu is es quem forma ista declarat, sed mens cuiusque is est quisque, non ea figura quae digito demonstrari potest. Deum te igitur scito esse, si quidem est deus qui viget, qui sentit, qui meminit, qui providet, qui tam regit et moderatur et movet id corpus cui praepositus est, quam hunc mundum ille princeps deus; et ut mundum ex quadam parte mortalem ipse deus aeternus, sic fragile corpus animus sempiternus movet. [19 (27)] Nam quod semper movetur aeternum est; quod autem motum adfert alicui, quodque ipsum agitatur aliunde, quando finem habet motus, vivendi finem habeat necesse est. Solum igitur quod sese movet, quia numquam deseritur a se, numquam ne moveri quidem desinit. Quin etiam ceteris quae moventur hic fons, hoc principium est movendi. Principii autem nulla est origo; nam ex principio oriuntur omnia, ipsum autem nulla ex re alia nasci potest; nec enim esset id principium, quod gigneretur aliunde. Quodsi numquam oritur, ne occidit quidem umquam; nam principium exstinctum nec ipsum ab alio renascetur, nec ex se aliud creabit, si quidem necesse est a principio oriri omnia. Ita fit ut motus principium ex eo sit quod ipsum a se movetur; id autem nec nasci potest nec mori, vel concidat omne caelum omnisque natura et consistat necesse est, nec ullam

can achieve fame that lasts as long as a year? Men commonly measure a year only by the return of the sun to its place – that is, of one star; but when all the stars have returned to the place from which they started, and after a long interval have brought back the same configuration of the whole heaven, that cycle can truly be called a year, in which I hardly dare to say how many generations of men are contained. The sun once appeared to men to be eclipsed and extinguished when the soul of Romulus entered these very regions: and when the sun is eclipsed again in the same part of the sky and at the same time, then you may believe that the constellations and stars have all been called back to their starting-point, and the year completed; but of that year, you are to know that not yet a twentieth part has elapsed. [17 (25)] Wherefore, if you abandon hope of a return into this place, in which is the whole reward of great and eminent men, what is now the value of that mortal fame, which can hardly endure even for a small part of one year? But if you will look upwards and fix your thoughts on this habitation and eternal home, neither placing yourself at the mercy of the common talk of men, nor putting your hopes for the future in human rewards, then Virtue herself must draw you by her own enticements towards true glory. Let it be for others to decide what they will say about you; say it they will; but all that talk is confined by that small region which you see, nor has it ever been eternal about any man; it is buried when men die, and is extinguished in the forgetfulness of posterity."

[VIII:18 (26)] After he had said this, "Truly," I said, "Africanus, if, as you say, there is as it were a path to the gates of heaven for those who have deserved well of their country, although I have already from boyhood trodden in the footsteps of my father and in yours, and have not been a disgrace to you, nevertheless now that such a great reward has been shown to me, I shall strive with all the more vigilance."

And he said, "Strive on indeed, and remember this, that it is not yourself that is mortal, but only this body. For you are not that which your outward form declares: the mind of each man is his true self, not that shape which can be pointed out with the finger. Know then that you are a god, if it is right to call a god that which lives, which perceives, which remembers the past and foresees the future, which rules and governs and moves that body over which it is placed, as much as the supreme God does the universe: just as God who is himself eternal moves the world, which is in some part mortal, so the body, which can be destroyed, is moved by a soul which is everlasting. [19 (27)] For what is always in motion is eternal. What brings motion to another thing, and what is itself set in motion from elsewhere, when it ceases to move, must also cease to live. Therefore, only what moves itself, since it is never deserted by itself, also never ceases to move. Indeed, for other things which move, this is the fountainhead and beginning of movement. Now a beginning has no source; for all things have their source in a beginning, but the beginning itself cannot be born from any other thing, for if it were brought into being from something else, it would not be a beginning. But if it is never brought into being, it cannot ever cease to exist either; for a beginning which had ceased to exist could not itself be reborn from another thing, nor could it create anything else out of itself, supposing that it is necessary that everything must have its origin in a beginning. So it is that the beginning of motion comes from that which is moved by itself; but that cannot be born or die, or the whole heaven and all of nature would

vim nanciscatur qua a primo impulsa moveatur. [20 (28)] Cum pateat igitur aeternum id esse quod a se ipso moveatur, quis est qui hanc naturam animis esse tributam neget? Inanimum est enim omne quod pulsu agitatur externo; quod autem est animal, id motu cietur interiore et suo, nam haec est propria natura animi atque vis; quae si est una ex omnibus quae se ipsa moveat, neque nata certe est et aeterna est. [21 (29)] Hanc tu exerce in optimis rebus! Sunt autem optimae curae de salute patriae, quibus agitatus et exercitatus animus velocius in hanc sedem et domum suam pervolabit; idque ocius faciet, si iam tum cum erit inclusus in corpore, eminebit foras, et ea quae extra sunt contemplans quam maxime se a corpore abstrahet. Namque eorum animi qui se corporis voluptatibus dediderunt, earumque se quasi ministros praebuerunt, impulsuque libidinum voluptatibus oboedientium, deorum et hominum iura violaverunt, corporibus elapsi circum terram ipsam volutantur, nec hunc in locum nisi multis exagitati saeclis revertuntur."

Ille discessit; ego somno solutus sum.

necessarily collapse and come to a halt, nor would it find any force to set it moving in the first instance. [20 (28)] Since it is clear, therefore, that what is moved by itself is eternal, who would deny that this nature is granted to souls? Whatever is set in motion by an external impulse, is inanimate; whatever is living, is moved by its own internal movement, for this is the peculiar nature and power of a soul. But if it does indeed move itself – the only one of all things to do so – then certainly it was never born, and it is eternal. [21 (29)] Exercise it, then, in the best things!   What is best is to care for the safety of one's country. A mind occupied and exercised in these cares will more quickly fly on the journey here, to its proper home. And it will do that sooner still, if already while it is still confined in the body, it extends its gaze outwards, and takes itself away from the body as much as it can, in contemplating those things which are outside it. For the souls of those who have given themselves up to the pleasures of the body, and have made themselves as it were their servants, and have been driven to violate the laws of gods and men by desires that obey only the demands of pleasure, when they escape from the body, wander round the earth itself, and they do not return to this place until they have been tossed around for many generations."

He departed; I awoke from my sleep.

SOMNIUM SCIPIONIS: COMMENTARY

1 (= De Rep. VI.9). **When I arrived in Africa** Scipio refers to the beginning of the Third Punic War, 149 BC, when he served as a military tribune under Manius Manilius, consul in that year (who is one of the speakers in the *De Republica*). For "Manilius here", see textual appendix.

Massinissa Mas(s)inissa - the spelling varies - had been an ally of Scipio Africanus in the Second Punic War, and was made king of all Numidia under the terms of the peace treaty, 202 BC. He was a constant enemy of Carthage and ally of the Romans (cf. Sallust, *Jug.* 5.5). By 149 BC he was around ninety years of age, but still in remarkable health (cf. *Cato Maior* 34). The official occasion for the declaration of war against Carthage was when the Carthaginians (not, apparently, without provocation) attacked Massinissa during the previous year. There is difficulty in reconciling the information on Scipio's visit to Massinissa given in this passage with the other historical evidence. Historians have naturally assumed that Cicero is altering historical fact for the purposes of the dialogue, though it is possible that he represents a genuine rival historical tradition (or that he simply made a mistake). The other sources record a visit by Scipio to Massinissa in 150, before the commencement of hostilities against Carthage, and another visit to the Numidian court near the end of 149, after the Romans had already won some successes, by which time Massinissa himself was dead. See Appian, *Libyca* 105-6, Polybius 36.16.10, [Livy] *Epitome* 50; Astin, *Scipio* 271, Broughton, *MRR* I, 457 n. 2, J.Evrard-Gillis, "Historicité et composition littéraire dans le *Somnium Scipionis*: quelques observations", *Ancient Society* 8 (1977) 217-22. In any case, Cicero makes the visit he describes into an emotional occasion; he seems to imply that it is Scipio's first, although he places it after the outbreak of war in 149.

thanks *grates*, a grandiose alternative to the more ordinary *gratias*.

highest Sun *Summe Sol* is a phrase from Roman tragedy, Ennius *Medea* 234 Jocelyn; its use here is in tune with the grandiose style. Massinissa is represented as worshipping a pantheon of which the most important member is the Sun. This may reflect actual Numidian religion, of which something was presumably known to the Romans. Massinissa's solar religion has been seen as connected with the vision of the solar system in the *Somnium* itself (cf. Coleman, *PCPS* NS 10 [1964] 3), but this seems doubtful. Cf. A.Piganiol, *CRAI* 1957, 88-93.

before I depart this life Massinissa actually died around the end of the year 149. "Depart" represents Latin *migro*: the usual meaning of this is to change one's place of residence (cf. English "migrate"). It is used here instead of the more normal *decedo*, perhaps in order to imply that Massinissa believes in the afterlife (though perhaps simply to give a more elevated stylistic effect). Piganiol (p. 89 of article cited in previous note) sees here another connection with actual Numidian religion, as deduced from funerary monuments; whether or not this is the case, it certainly fits well with Cicero's ideas on the immortality of the soul.

in this house *his tectis*: lit. "under these roofs"; *tecta* in the plural, in the meaning "house", is poetic in style.

that best and most invincible of men The elder Scipio Africanus.

2 (10) deeper sleep The depth of sleep is conventionally emphasised in the narration of prophetic dreams, cf. Cic. *Div.* 1.59 (a dream of Cicero's own). The implication is also that Scipio usually slept lightly, an advantage for Roman generals who were traditionally praised for *vigilantia* (watchfulness).

I think ... it was because of what we had been speaking of This rationalist explanation of dreams is found at least as early as Herodotus (7.16.2), and was apparently endorsed by Aristotle, as Cicero says in *De Divinatione* 2.128, as also by the Epicureans (e.g. Lucretius 4.960ff.); cf. *Div.* 1.45. The effect of bringing it forward here is of a sort of irony like that of the Platonic Socrates when introducing a myth: Scipio makes no claims for the truth of his vision. Cf. F.Lucidi, *RCCM* 21-2 (1979-80) 57-75; H.Görgemanns, *WS* 81 = NF 2 (1968) 46-69; G.Maurach, *Hermes* 92 (1964) 299-313.

Ennius At the beginning of his epic, the *Annals*, Ennius recounted a dream in which Homer had appeared to him; Cic. *Acad.* 2.51 quotes his words *visus Homerus adesse poeta*; cf. Lucr. 1.123-5, Horace, *Epist.* 2.1.50, Persius 6.10-11; Skutsch, *Ennius* 164ff.

Africanus himself appeared Africanus enjoys posthumous immortality among the stars, of the kind described below, §5 (13). It is perhaps not coincidental that earlier in the *De Republica* (fr. incert. 6 Ziegler, ap. Sen. *ep.* 108.34) Cicero had quoted some lines of Ennius (*varia* 23-4 Vahlen²) which suggested that Scipio Africanus was deserving of deification, while in section 16 (24) below, the traditional Roman deification of Romulus is assimilated to the Platonic doctrine of astral immortality. But in any case, Africanus is a highly authoritative figure with something of a numinous aura about him; he was supposed to have cultivated the impression that he communed with the gods (cf. Maurach, *Hermes* 92 [1964] 299ff.).

from his effigy Noble Roman families kept effigies or portrait-masks (*imagines*) of those of their ancestors who had held curule office; see *OCD* s.v. *imagines*. What Scipio says here is a considerable understatement: he could hardly have remembered Africanus at all from real life, since the latest possible date given by the sources for Africanus's death is 183 BC (cf. on *Cato Maior* 19), when Scipio Aemilianus was two years old, so even if he was adopted as an infant he can hardly have had a clear memory of his adoptive grandfather.

3 (11) cast off your fear The recipient of a vision is usually frightened, and the first task of the supernatural being (angel or ghost, etc.) who appears is to calm him or her down and display kindly intentions. Cf. the angels in Luke 1.29-30 (the Annunciation) and 2.9-10 (the shepherds); Lucian, *Icaromenippus* 13. G.Wojaczek, *Würzburger Jahrbücher f.d. Altertumswissenschaft* NF 9 (1983) 123-45, though it is difficult to be convinced by the connection he alleges with initiation into the mysteries, accurately notes the progress of Scipio's reactions in the *Somnium*, from fear through wonder to resolution; cf. also G.Bretzigheimer, *WS* NF 19 (1985) 125-50.

Do you see that city Africanus prophesies the destruction of Carthage and Scipio's future career. The idea of a prophetic dream is universal; in Macrobius's classification of dreams (*SS* 1.3) a dream in which an august personage appears and delivers a prophecy is called an *oraculum* (oracle). Cicero refers to a number of such dreams in the *De Divinatione* (cf. e.g. 1.43).

cannot stay quiet This is very much the Roman side of the story; in fact Carthage was reluctant to go to war. Cf. Livy 30.44.8 (Hannibal's speech after his defeat in the Second Punic War) *nulla magna civitas diu quiescere potest*.

little more than a common soldier Scipio was (as said above) military tribune; this was of course a lowly office compared with the consulate which he was to reach only two years later, in 147 (cf. on *Lael.* 11).

Within these two years A slight exaggeration. Scipio became consul two years later, in 147, but Carthage was not destroyed until the following year, 146 (Scipio was then in fact proconsul, but this looseness of usage is not uncommon). Cf. Evrard-Gillis, article cited on §1 above.

the name i.e. Africanus. On the name, cf. Livy 30.45.6-7. It is unlikely, despite what Cicero says here, that Scipio Aemilianus used the name "as an inheritance" before his Carthaginian victory. Note the stylistic symmetries *ad quam tu oppugnandam nunc venis paene miles – hanc hoc biennio consul evertes*, and *id tibi per te partum – quod habes adhuc a nobis hereditarium*.

censor In 142 BC.

legate This embassy is usually supposed to have taken place in 141-139 BC, though Cicero in *Acad.* 2.5. mentions one before the censorship, which may however be a different one. Cf. also *Rep.* 3.48.

chosen consul a second time In 135; Scipio was elected consul for 134, in order to finish the war against the insurgents in Spain, which ended with the capture of their fortress of Numantia in the upper Douro valley. This is apparently the only evidence that Scipio's election to his second consulship took place in his absence (Evrard-Gillis art. cit.) Cf. *Lael.* 11; [Livy] *Epit.* 56.

ridden up to the Capitol i.e. celebrated another triumph. Numantia was captured in 133 BC, the year of Tiberius Gracchus's tribunate; Scipio returned for his triumph in 132.

my grandson Tiberius Gracchus, son of Cornelia, Africanus's daughter.

4 (12) Africanus Scipio's grandfather addresses him pointedly by this name, here and in §5 (13) below.

a fork in the road of destiny *ancipitem video quasi fatorum viam: anceps* etymologically means "two-headed" (*ambi-* + *caput*); the standard translation "doubtful" obscures the metaphor. Africanus prophesies, in oracular manner, two alternatives: either Scipio will die (as he in fact did) at the hands of his relatives (as was generally suspected), or he will attain an even more glorious political eminence. To prophesy his death unambiguously would have been too pessimistic for the present context; the effect of the passage as it stands is of a certain dramatic irony; cf. Macr. *SS* 1.7; R.Montanari Caldini, *Atene e Roma* 29 (1984) 17-41.

accomplished literally "turned" (*converterit*); there is perhaps a rhetorical echo between this word and *convertet civitas* "the state will turn" below.

eight times seven revolutions i.e. when Scipio was 56, in 129 BC, the year of the dialogue and of Scipio's death.

these two numbers, which are both for diverse reasons thought to be perfect There was no set definition of a "perfect" number (*plenus*, literally "full"). The Pythagorean tradition attributed a separate significance to all the numbers up to ten. The number eight was thought important because it is the first cube greater than unity, or because it is the number of the cosmic spheres (i.e. the sun and moon, the five planets anciently known, and the fixed stars; see below). Seven was considered important because it is the number of the planets (including the sun and moon) and for various other reasons; the curious may consult the numerological excursus in Macr. *SS* 1.5-6. A possibly relevant fact here is that the human lifespan was commonly divided into seven-year periods, a topic written about by Cicero's contemporary Varro (*Hebdomades*). The multiples of seven were held to mark the transitions from one stage of life to the next, and some of them were thought critical from a medical point of view (the so-called climacterics), though 56 was not normally supposed to be particularly important. But the real point is simply that Scipio was 56 when he died, and 56 = 7 x 8; a competent numerologist can find some magic significance in any number whatsoever.

the allies and the Latins cf. on *Lael.* 12.

can rest *nitatur*: some see an etymological play on the name *Scipio* (Σκηπίων in Greek), which means a "staff", i.e. a stick to rest or lean on, connected with Greek σκήπτομαι "lean".

dictator This is probably nothing more than Cicero's imagination; but see C. Nicolet, *REL* 42 (1964) 212-230, who argues (on the basis of this passage) that there was a real move to make Scipio dictator; against this, see R.Werner in *Festschrift für F.Altheim* I (Berlin 1969) 438. R.Montanari Caldini, *Prometheus* 10 (1984) 19-32 misguidedly attempts to use a passage of Firmicus Maternus (*Math.* 1.7.39) as evidence to support Nicolet's view, but that passage clearly enough derives from Cicero and is worthless as evidence.

re-establish the republic *rem publicam constituas*, echoing the official formula *dictator rei publicae constituendae*, the title taken by Sulla in 82 BC.

impious hands of your relatives On the suspicions regarding Scipio's death, see on *Lael.* 12. "Impious" refers particularly to the breach of *pietas*, family duty, involved in the killing of a relative.

Laelius ... the others For the cast of the *De Republica*, see Introd. §3. Scipio's jocular comment, "don't wake me from my sleep", has the effect of releasing the tension after the sinister prophecy just made.

5 (13) for all those who have saved ... their native land On Roman ideas of immortality in general, see F.Cumont, *After Life in Roman Paganism* (New Haven 1922), esp. 81-109 on astral immortality; id., *Lux Perpetua* (Paris 1949) 162ff. Cicero does not here reserve immortality for politicians only, as seems sometimes to be thought; it is said below (10 [18]) that there are philosophers and musicians in heaven as well. All that is said here is that there is a place reserved for statesmen (implying, presumably, that there are other places for other sorts of people); the passage echoes Plato, *Phaedo* 82a-b εἰς βέλτιστον τόπον ἰόντες οἱ τὴν δημοτικὴν καὶ πολιτικὴν ἀρετὴν ἐπιτετηδευκότες. Plato almost certainly, and Cicero probably, was thinking of the segregation of the virtuous in the mythical Elysian Fields (a special region of the underworld). Naturally statesmanship is emphasised in this context: on the relationship between the *Somnium* and the themes of the rest of the *De Republica*, see Introd. §5. **saved** recalls Cicero's own claim to have saved the Republic (as consul in 63); cf. *Rep.* 1.12; *Sest.* 138.

of all at least that is done on earth Macrobius (*SS* 1.8.12) interprets this as contrasting with the higher studies of philosophy, but for Cicero (one presumes) they too would count as "done on earth". It is more likely that Cicero had in mind the distinction between the imperfect and transitory nature of earthly things, and the perfect, eternal regularities of heaven.

that supreme God The Platonic universe here described is ruled by one supreme deity, a doctrine also held by the Stoics; Plato tended to refer simply to "the god", while the Stoics tended to identify God mythologically with Zeus and philosophically with Nature and Providence. Cf. below on §9 (17).

communities ... held together by law This echoes the definition of *res publica* in *Rep.* 1.39.

begin their journey from here, and hither they return Not only rulers, but all human beings were supposed by Plato to have pre-existent souls. In the *Timaeus* (41d-e) it is said that the soul descends from heaven at birth in order to be incarnated. Cicero refers to this doctrine of astral pre-existence also in *Cato Maior* 77, *Tusc.* 1.72 (referring to Plato's *Phaedo*), and *Pro Scauro* 4. That the soul belongs properly to heaven and will return there as if to its real home (cf. below, §17 [25]) is said in *Tusc.* 1.51, *Hortensius* fr. 115 Grilli, *Lael.* 14 and *Leg.* 1.26. Cf. also Virgil, *Aeneid* 6.730 *caelestis origo*; Sen. *Ep.* 86.17. The doctrine was much elaborated in Neoplatonism: the soul was supposed to come in a pure state from the highest sphere of heaven, and assume a series of qualities and accretions as it descended through the various spheres, ending with the physical body in the lowest sphere. Cf. Macr. *SS.* 1.9.10; 1.11.10-12; 1.12.13-15.

6 (14). the bonds of the body Cf. *Cato Maior* 81 *e corporum vinculis* (an intrusion of this image into a context otherwise taken from Xenophon; see my note ad loc.); *Tusc.* 1.75 *compedes corporis* (fetters of the body); *Lael.* 14; *Div.* 1.110; *Scaur.* 4. *Vincula* in itself simply means "bonds", with no necessary connotation of imprisonment, and Cicero may in some of these passages have been thinking primarily of the δεσμοί (bonds) which, in Plato *Timaeus* 42e, 44b and 81d, secure the soul within the body; cf. also *Phaedrus* 250c; Cic. CM 77 *inclusi in his compagibus corporis*. Macrobius (*SS* 1.11.3) refers to an etymological play on δέμας (a poetic word for "body") and δεσμός (bond), which however does not seem to occur in Plato. The idea of the body as a prison for the soul originated apparently with the Orphics: cf. Plato *Cratylus* 400c, *Phaedo* 67d and 82e, also perhaps 61d; *Gorgias* 492d; [Plato] *Axiochus* 365e, 370d; it is common in later authors influenced by Plato. Cf. also Virgil *Aen.* 6.734 and Austin ad loc.

that which you call your life, is really death Cicero seems to have thought that this was part of genuine Platonic doctrine, but in fact Plato never claims the idea as his own. In *Gorgias* 492d, Socrates attributes the idea to "the wise", not further specified, and quotes the famous lines of Euripides, *Polyidus* fr. 639 N², τίς οἶδεν εἰ τὸ ζῆν μέν ἐστι κατθανεῖν, | τὸ κατθανεῖν δὲ ζῆν; ("Who knows if life is death, and death is life?"), and the etymological pun on σῶμα and σῆμα (body/tomb); cf. *Cratylus* 400c. But Cicero, in *Tusc.* 1.75, appends the idea to a context otherwise largely derived from Plato's *Phaedo*, and he wrongly attributes it to the *Phaedo* itself in *Scaur.* 4. Macrobius (*SS* 1.10.6ff.) attributes the doctrine to "followers of Pythagoras and Plato". Cf. also Cic. *CM* 77 *eam quidem vitam quae est sola vita numeranda* (of the afterlife); Sext. Emp. *Pyrrh. hypot.* 3.230, claiming to quote Heraclitus; Augustine *Civ. Dei* 12.21 (probably echoing Cicero).

your father Paulus i.e. Scipio Aemilianus's natural father Aemilius Paulus; cf. *Lael.* 9. He had died in 160 BC.

7 (15). unless that god ... has freed you The prohibition of suicide occurs also in *Cato Maior* 73 (attributed there to Pythagoras), *Tusc.* 1.74 and 118, and *Scaur.* 5. The source is Plato, *Phaedo* 61d-62c and 67a. There, the authority of Philolaus (a

Pythagorean) is quoted for the prohibition; Socrates also refers to a "secret doctrine" (of the Pythagoreans) that men are ἔν τινι φρουρᾷ (either "on guard" or "under guard": see below) and must not release themselves from it or run away. Socrates says that he finds this hard to understand, but does believe that men are under the care and command of the gods, who would be displeased if a man were to kill himself without their permission, just as a man would be if one of his slaves, whom he did not wish to die, were to commit suicide. Cicero seems to mix the "secret doctrine" with Socrates's argument. In this passage, he also seems to combine the notions that men are "on guard", i.e. put on the earth to watch over it, and must not desert their post, and that they are "under guard", i.e. confined in the prison of the body. Regarding Plato's phrase ἔν τινι φρουρᾷ, it seems that the "under guard" interpretation was more current in the ancient tradition (see my note on *Cato Maior* 73); Macrobius *SS* 1.13.8 refers to the passage, and translates φρουρά as *carcer* (prison); for the doctrine of the body as prison, cf. above; see also F.Cumont, *REG* 32 (1919) 113ff. on Neoplatonic interpretation of the passage. The "on guard" interpretation tends to be favoured by modern commentators on Plato, who compare the passage in Plato's *Apology* (28d) where Socrates says that ceasing to philosophise would be like deserting a military post under divine command, but nothing is said there about suicide, and this cannot be taken as clear evidence for the interpretation of the *Phaedo*; some compare also *Crito* 51b where escape from a real prison is compared to military desertion, though the relevance of this is even more doubtful. It seems that Cicero was the only ancient writer to take the *Phaedo* passage this way: he did this much more clearly in the *Cato Maior* than here (*CM* 73 *vetatque Pythagoras iniussu imperatoris, id est dei, de praesidio et statione vitae decedere*). Here the notion of guard-duty may be extracted from *tuerentur* "watch over". On the other hand, *custodia* (here translated "prison) looks like an attempt to reproduce φρουρά (both literally mean "guard" or "guarded place"); the word *custodia* appears also in *Lael.* 14, and the "prison" interpretation of the *Phaedo* passage seems to be used also in *Tusc.* 1.74. All in all, therefore, it looks as though Cicero was trying to have the best of both worlds as regards the interpretation of this passage. Naturally, in the present context of the *Somnium*, the idea that life, and especially the statesman's life, was a sort of guard-duty imposed by divine authority, had a special appropriateness. The idea of life as imprisonment is reduced here to a vivid image for bodily existence; Cicero never explicitly states the logical corollary of the idea, which is that earthly life is a punishment, although that doctrine is certainly present elsewhere in the Platonic or Pythagorean tradition (cf. Euxitheus the Pythagorean quoted in Clearchus of Soli fr. 38 Wehrli = Athenaeus 4.157c, "the soul is bound in the body and in this life for the sake of punishment"; Philolaus ap. Athen. ibid.). On the philosophical views of suicide and their currency in Rome, see M.Griffin, *G. & R.* 33 (1986) 64-77 and 192-202, esp. 70-72.

men were created on this condition Cf. *Cato Maior* 77 *sed credo deos immortales sparsisse animos in corpora humana, ut essent qui terras tuerentur*; *ND* 2.99. Cf. Macr. *SS.* 1.14.1ff.

in the centre of this heaven *in hoc templo medium*. The central position of the earth is a cardinal doctrine of Platonic cosmology; the earth is the point around which all the heavenly bodies revolve. Virtually all Greek cosmologists believed this, except for Aristarchus (who proposed a heliocentric system) and some

Pythagoreans, who thought that the earth revolved around a "central fire" (invisible to us). Cf. below, §9(17); Cleomedes 1.9.47-9; Cic. *Tusc.* 1.40, 1.68, 5.69; *ND* 2.116; Plato *Tim.* 39b, *Phaedo* 108e. *Templum* is here translated "heaven" rather than "temple": a *templum* in the original Roman sense was an area of land or sky marked out for religious purposes, e.g. for augural observation of the flight of birds. Temples in our sense, i.e. sacred buildings, simply constituted a subclass of *templa*; there was nothing to prevent a *templum* from embracing the whole visible sky; and here, the whole of the universe is the *templum* of its presiding deity (cf. above "that god, whose temple is this whole universe that you see"). This idea was not unfamiliar; Ennius (*Ann.* 541 V2) called the sky *templum magnum Iovis altitonantis*, and the plural *templa* was used poetically of the sky (e.g. by Lucretius). Cf. also Cic. *Leg.* 2.26, and Sen. *Ep.* 90 (probably following Cicero). Though the Greeks did not have a word with a precisely equivalent range of meaning, they too compared the cosmos to a temple: Aristotle fr. 14 Rose, Dio Chrysostom, *Olymp.* 12, Festugière, *Révélation d'Hermès Trismégiste* II p. 238; Boyancé, *Études* p. 115. The blend of Greek and Roman is characteristically Ciceronian: Cicero takes advantage of the resources of native Latin religious and poetic language to convey what was originally a Greek philosophical idea.

a soul was given them out of those eternal fires cf. §13 above, "are sent from here"; Plato *Timaeus* 41d-e. That the material of which human souls are made was the same as that of the stars and planets was apparently believed by Aristotle, at least in the earlier part of his life, though he distinguished it, as "quintessence" or a fifth element, from fire (cf. Arist. *Cael.* 269a ff. on the material of the heavenly bodies; Cic. *Acad.* 1.26, etc.). The reference to fire here may be influenced by Stoicism, cf. *ND* 1.36, 2.41; *Tusc.* 1.19 *Zenoni Stoico animus ignis videtur* (though the more accurate Stoic definition was "heated breath" rather than "fire", Diog. Laert. 7.157). The doctrine that the soul has a fiery nature was attributed also to Heraclitus (cf. Plato, *Phaedo* 96b), Parmenides, Hippasus (Aet. *Plac.* 4.3.4), Hipparchus (Macr. *SS* 1.14.20). Note also Varro ap. Isid. *Etym.* 8.6.22, *Varro ignem mundi animum dicit, proinde quod in mundo ignis omnia gubernat, sicut animus in nobis* (cf. §18 [26] below): Varro was professedly a follower of the Stoically-influenced Platonism of Antiochus of Ascalon. Macrobius (*SS* 1.14.17-18) says that the fires are only the *bodies* of the stars and planets, whereas it is from their souls that the material of human souls comes; this subtlety arises from interpretation of Plato's *Timaeus*, but was probably unknown to Cicero. Note that the planets (included in the category of *stellae*: if one wanted to specify the planets precisely one would say *stellae errantes*; cf. Macr. *SS.* 1.14.21) are envisaged as fiery bodies, like the stars: the ancients knew that the moon shone by reflected light and had no luminosity of its own (cf. below, "shining with borrowed light"); but they did not realise that the same applies to the planets.

spherical Cicero uses *globus* for the Greek σφαῖρα, and *globosus* for σφαιροειδής; the equivalence is established in *ND* 2.47. The Greek word originally means simply a "ball", such as one plays with; in this sense the Latin equivalent is *pila* (doubtless too undignified a word to be used in this grandiose context), whereas the original meaning of *globus* was "round mass" or "conglomeration". Cf. Ronconi in *Studi Funaioli* (cited Introd. §5) 402. For the spherical shape of the stars cf. Plato *Tim.* 17, Diog. Laert. 7.144 (Stoics). It was believed in not because of direct observation, but partly by analogy with the known shapes of the earth, sun and moon, and partly because stars were supposed to be perfect, and the sphere was a perfectly regular shape. Of the heavenly bodies only the sun and moon could have been seen to be round; even Venus, Mars and Jupiter, which appear as discs through a telescope, appear only as points to the unaided eye, while no star, other than the sun, appears as a disc even through the largest telescope (if it seems to, there is something wrong with the telescope). We now believe in roughly spherical stars largely because of the theory of gravitation; and in fact it can be observed that the sun and planets are not perfectly spherical, since they are slightly flattened in the plane of their rotation.

animated by a divine mind The planets are animate and divine in Plato's *Timaeus*, 39a and 40b, and in *Laws* 896-7. Cf. also Alcmaeon of Croton, ap. Cic. *ND* 1.27 (Diels-Kranz I[6], p. 213); Zeno, *SVF* I, frr. 120 and 165; Cic. *ND* 2.43 and 54; Diog. Laert. 8.27; [Plato] *Epinomis* 982e.

must keep the soul in the prison of the body The Latin seems most naturally interpreted this way. Some (e.g. Ronconi) have tried to introduce the "on guard" image here as well (cf. note above); but it seems difficult to take *in custodiis corporis* to mean "on guard over the body"; additionally, it is (in this passage) not the body but the earth that we are meant to guard. Some have taken §26 *cui praepositus est* as a parallel to prove that the soul is conceived as guarding the body; but *praepositus* implies directing and ruling, not guarding.

8 (16). your duty Latin *pietas*, duty towards parents and country and towards the gods. Cf. *Rep.* I fr. 2 Bréguet; *Off.* 1.57.

this gathering cf. *Cato Maior* 84 *cum ad illud divinum animorum concilium coetumque proficiscar*, *Tusc.* 1.72, Sen. *Cons. ad Marc.* 25. This phrase, together with the fact that Paulus appears here as well as Africanus, emphasises that there is social life in the Platonic Heaven (as there was always supposed to be in the mythical Hades).

you have learnt from the Greeks The Latin *orbis lacteus* (lit. "milky circle") translates the Greek γαλαξίας, whence our word *galaxy*. Our "Milky Way" corresponds to *via ... lactea* in Ovid, *Met.* 1.168-9, who makes the Milky Way the gods' road to Jupiter's palace.

the Milky Way The idea that the Milky Way is the abode of the virtuous dead does not occur explicitly in Plato; it seems first to occur in Heraclides Ponticus, fr. 97 Wehrli (see Gottschalk, *Heraclides* 100ff.); Manilius has the idea (1.758ff.); in later times it seems to have been thought of as Pythagorean, cf. Macr. *SS* 1.4.5, 1.12.3, 1.15.1-7. Cf. also Proclus *Rep.* II.129 Kroll; Porphyry, *Antr. Nymph.* 28; Philoponus *in Ar. Met.* 8 p. 117; P. Capelle, *De luna, stellis, lacteo orbe animarum sedibus* (Diss. Halle 1917); A.B.Cook, *Zeus* (Cambridge 1925) II, pp. 37-45. After this point Paulus says no more; presumably he returns to his place among the stars.

there were stars which we never see from this country A natural deduction from the belief in the spherical universe. The ancients obviously knew that there were stars visible from Egypt (e.g. Canopus, the second brightest star in the sky) that were not visible from Greece or Italy, and it required merely a simple extrapolation to conclude that there were others still further south. There is no evidence that the Phoenicians who circumnavigated Africa kept any star-records (though they would have had the opportunity to see the southern polar stars). Cf. Macr. *SS* 1.16.3-7.

shining with borrowed light Apparently Thales was the first to realise that the moon had no luminosity of its own: Diels-Kranz I[6] p.78, cf. Cic. *ND* 2.119. The phrase reflects the words used by both Parmenides and Empedocles, ἀλλότριον (ἀλλότριος and *alienus* both literally = "someone else's"): Diels-Kranz I⁶ pp. 243 and 331. Cf. also Lucr. 5.574, Catull. 34.15.

the globes of the stars far surpassed the earth in size Ancient astronomers deduced the size of the stars and planets from their apparent brightness and a calculation of their distance; Cicero's statement would of course be endorsed by a modern astronomer, but no ancient scientist ever correctly estimated the true size and distance of the stars. Cf. Macr. *SS.* 1.16.8-13; Aristotle *De caelo* 2.14.298a; [Plato], *Epinomis* 983a; Cleomedes 2.3.94-100.

and now the earth itself seemed to me so small Note "and now": Scipio is now clearly at a higher altitude (cf. Introd. p. 127). The insignificance of the earth and of earthly glory is the theme of §§12-17 (20-25) below; cf. also *Rep.* 1.26; Introd. §5. It is not explicit in Plato, but occurs in Aristotle, *Meteorologica* 352a27 and in the pseudo-Aristotelian *De mundo*, I.391a.8ff.; cf. also Sen. *NQ* 1 praef. 8ff., Marcus Aurelius 4.3.8, 12.32; Cleomedes 1.11.56-65. This attitude to the earth's size contrasts rather paradoxically with the retention of the idea that the earth was supremely important in position, being the centre of the universe (cf. above), but both ideas are implicit in the astronomical system that Cicero adopts. See also Festugière, *RHT* II, pp. 449ff.

ashamed of our empire *Paeniteret:* the precise connotation is not quite what we mean by shame, but rather what the psychologists call "feelings of inadequacy". The application of this to a person's own past actions produces the later and common meaning of repentance or penitence (both these words are derived from *paenitere*); but the older meaning is found quite commonly in Republican and Augustan Latin, cf. E.Fraenkel, *Horace* (Oxford 1957) pp.5-6n. (on Hor. *Satires* 1.6.89 *nil me paeniteat ... patris huius*). Fraenkel's translation "to be dissatisfied" (which I followed in my notes on *CM* 19 and 84), as I now see, makes it too much of a judgement, not enough of an emotion.

9 (17). regions lit. "temples", cf. above.

nine circles or rather spheres This description of the structure of the cosmos as a sort of "Chinese box", with the Earth in the centre, the sun, moon and planets occupying successive (transparent) spheres, and the sphere of the fixed stars enclosing all the rest, is basically that of Plato's *Timaeus* (38b-39e). There is a similar, though more fanciful and less explicit, cosmic description in the Myth of Er at the end of the *Republic* (10.616b-617c). Plato simply described eight concentric spheres: the fixed stars, Saturn, Jupiter, Mars, Mercury, Venus, Sun and Moon. Cicero reflects genuine astronomy when he places the Sun next after Mars, and makes Mercury and Venus "follow" the Sun "as companions", though he does not say that they revolve round it (that would disturb the neat pattern of interlocked spheres). Heraclides Ponticus was apparently the first to realise, on the basis of the considerable variations in the brightness of Venus, that Mercury and Venus revolve round the Sun; the idea was accepted by Archimedes and Ptolemy. Cicero's order was also that of the "Chaldaeans" (the Babylonian astrologers); cf. *Div.* 2.91; Macr. *SS.* 1.19.1ff.; Plato's order was supposed to come from the Egyptians. This vision of the actual solar system mirrors the account of the Archimedean sphere, a mechanical model representing the movements of the heavenly bodies (what used to be called an "orrery"), in *De Republica* 1.21-2. Cicero in this context naturally retains the simplicity of Plato's version, without the elaborations introduced by astronomers, from Eudoxus onwards, in order to account for the actual movements of the planets (cf. S.Sambursky, *The Physical World of the Greeks* [London 1956] 58ff.).

the highest divinity   The sphere of the fixed stars, like those of the planets, is supposed to be animate and divine. Cicero seems here to identify the animating spirit of this outermost sphere with the supreme God that rules the universe; similarly the Stoics talked of the *aether*, or heaven, as the supreme god: cf. Cic. *Acad.* 2.126 *Zenoni et reliquis fere Stoicis aether videtur summus deus, mente praeditus, qua omnia regantur*; *Div.* 2.91; *ND* 1.34 and 37; the idea may be traced back in various forms to the Presocratics. On the other hand, Aristotle and later Platonists, following their own interpretation of the *Timaeus*, regarded the spirit of the starry sphere as being merely the "world-soul", to be distinguished from yet higher divinities in further spheres outside the observable universe (the so-called Primum Mobile and Empyrean).

In it are fixed the eternal revolving courses of the stars   The Latin *infixi*, "fixed", means literally "nailed" or "attached", rather than "immobile"; cf. Anaximenes, Diels-Kranz I[6], p.93; Cic. *ND* 2.54, Lucr. 4.391, Pliny, *NH* 2.28, Calcidius, *Tim.* 83. The stars are seen as attached to the outer sphere which revolves round the earth once in twenty-four hours (the optical effect of the earth's own rotation, of course). The stars do not apparently move relative to each other (in fact they do, but so slowly that the movements can only be observed with accurate instruments over a long period); but the supposed revolution of the whole sphere makes the stars appear each to follow a "revolving course" round the earth.

in a retrograde direction   The sun, moon and planets appear on the whole to move from west to east relative to the stars. Cf. Cic. *ND* 2.49; Plato, *Timaeus* 36d; Cleomedes 1.3.16; Macr. *SS* 1.17.6ff.; 1.18.1ff.

the star of Saturn   Cicero, following ancient convention, does not call the planets "Saturn", "Jupiter", etc., but "the star of Saturn", etc.: the planets are similarly described as belonging to their respective divinities e.g. by Plato in *Timaeus* 38d, and by Cicero in *ND* 2.52-3, cf. ibid. 2.119, *Div.* 2.91; [Plato], *Epinomis* 987b. Among the Greeks, the mythological names of the planets competed with names descriptive of their appearances: Phosphorus (Venus), Stilbon (Mercury), Pyroeis (Mars), Phaethon (Jupiter), Phaenon (Saturn), but the mythological ones eventually became standard. Cf. F.Cumont, *L'Ant. Class.* 4 (1935) 5-43 esp. 35.

bringing health and prosperity   Cicero here incorporates the astrological significances of the planets Jupiter and Mars (which have not changed in the least since ancient times); Mars is an "object of terror" because he brings war. Regarding Jupiter, some commentators refer to the ancient Latin popular etymology *Iuppiter* < *iuvare* "to help".

the middle region   Macrobius, *SS* 1.19.15-17 rightly explains (drawing attention to Cicero's phrasing *mediam fere regionem*, i.e. "more or less the middle region") that this means that the Sun occupies the middle position in the order of the planets, but not that it is exactly halfway in distance between the earth and the outermost sphere. It was understood that Jupiter, Saturn and the fixed stars were further from the Sun than the Sun is from the Earth, because of the long periods of revolution of the outer planets.

the mind and controlling force   Cf. *Tusc.* 1.66, *ND* 2.92, 2.49; Pliny *NH* 2.13 *mundi totius animum ac planius mentem*; Macr. *SS.* 1.20, id. *Sat.* 1.17.31. Cleanthes the Stoic (fr. 499 v.A.) believed that the sun contained the ἡγεμονικόν (the ruling rational spirit) of the universe: Cic. *Acad.* 2.126; Diog. Laert. 7.139; Plut. *comm. not. adv. Stoicos* 1075c; on the other hand, Posidonius placed this in the sphere of the fixed stars (*SVF* II, p.144). Cf. Boyancé, *Études* 78-104 and *REG* 65 (1952) 345ff. The doctrine seems to clash with the identification of the outermost sphere as the supreme deity, though it is possible that *summus* in that context only means "highest in position", or alternatively that the Sun's rule stops at the sphere of the fixed stars.

illuminates ... everything Cf. Cleomedes 2.1.84 πάντα τὸν κόσμον φωτίζει; Cic. *ND* 2.49, 2.119; Pliny *NH* 2.50.

there is nothing but what is mortal and transitory The moon's orbit is the boundary between the transitory (sublunary) world which we inhabit, and the heavens which are eternal. This idea became standard in later Platonism; cf. Macr. *SS* 1.11.6; Philo *De Monarchia* 1.1, *De Somniis* 1.34; Plutarch *Gen. Socr.* 22; Stobaeus 1.906; and it was very influential in the Middle Ages and Renaissance.

last of the nine cf. Eratosthenes 17 Hiller ἐνάτην ... γαῖαν.

does not move This was almost a universal belief in antiquity, but not quite; apart from the revolutionary Aristarchus, who thought the earth moved round the sun, one should recall also the views of Heraclides (see Gottschalk, *Heraclides* 58ff.), who supposed that it was the earth that moved, rather than the outermost sphere. Cf. Macr. *SS* 1.22.1ff.

Towards it all heavy objects fall Cf. *Tusc.* 1.40, Sallustius περὶ κόσμου, Aristotle *De Caelo* 2.14.296b15ff. The idea of gravitation towards the centre of the universe was used to explain the central position of the earth, which was supposed to consist of heavier material than anything in the heavens: *ND* 2.98, 2.116, *De Or.* 3.178, Plato *Phaedo* 108e, Arist. *Cael.* 297a8, Chrysippus fr. 646 v.A. = Plutarch *De Facie in orbe lunae* 923-4. What Newton discovered was not gravity as such, but the law of *universal* gravitation, i.e. that all massive objects gravitate towards *each other* with a force that may be mathematically defined.

10 (18). the sound that is made by those very spheres The idea of the Music of the Spheres was Pythagorean in origin, as Aristotle informs us in the *De caelo* (cf. W.Burkert, *Lore and Science in Ancient Pythagoreanism* [English ed., Cambridge, Mass., 1972] 350–5), and is referred to by Plato in the Myth of Er (617b). In Plato, each planet has a singing Siren attached to it. Cicero gives a much more mechanistic explanation, saying that the sounds were due to the motion of each sphere; this idea occurs also in Aristotle, *Cael.* 2.9.290b18; cf. Porph. *Vit. Pyth.* 30; Macr. *SS* 2.1ff. The notes were presumably imagined as being produced by the revolutions of the planets rather like the humming of a top. One may wonder precisely what sort of motion is in question. It can only be presumed that it is the apparent movement of the whole cosmic apparatus once in twenty-four hours, caused by the earth's rotation, rather than the actual movements of the planets in their orbits. The latter are, to the human observer, imperceptibly slow, and could hardly have given rise to such an idea. If this is true, then it is clear that all the heavenly bodies would be thought of as moving with *approximately* the same angular velocity, their movements relative to each other being slow enough to be ignored. Hence each of them would cover in twenty-four hours the circumference of a circle drawn around the earth. The distance covered would be proportional to the distance of the object from the earth, and so therefore would be the actual speed of **movement** (since the time taken would be the same in each case). Thus the planets would move faster the further they were from the earth. The speeds concerned would be very high even on ancient estimates of the distance of the sun, moon and planets, and movements at these speeds could easily be imagined as producing an appreciable noise (it would not be realised that the planets were not moving *through* any medium that could be agitated to produce or carry sound).

of which two have the same effect i.e. (according to the most reasonable interpretation of Cicero's words) the moon and the outermost sphere sound at the octave from each other; the moon has the lowest note because it moves slowest (having the shortest distance to cover), while the other spheres, being progressively further from the earth, produce the notes of an ascending seven-note scale. Cicero differs here from Plato, who said that the moon was the fastest and produced the highest note. Macrobius (*SS* 2.4.9) has a different interpretation of this passage: according to him, Mercury and Venus are the two that move at the same speed, and hence produce the same note; but this does not seem plausible. In Plato's *Timaeus* (36d, cf. *Rep.* 617b) there are *three* that move at the same speed (the Sun, as well as Mercury and Venus), and this accords roughly with observation. Cicero says that Mercury and Venus "follow the Sun as companions", i.e. never appear to go very far from the Sun; but clearly they occupy different spheres (otherwise the total of nine spheres would be wrong) and must be at different distances from the earth. It is possible that Macrobius took "as companions" to mean "as companions of each other", thus avoiding the conclusion that the Sun too produced the same note; but this interpretation would hardly accord with astronomical observation, and the Latin seems much more plausibly taken to mean "as companions of the Sun".

The doctrine of the Music of the Spheres occurs several times in later Roman writers; cf. Varro Atacinus fr. 14 Morel = 11 Büchner; Varius, *trag.* 265 Ribbeck; Pliny, *NH* 2.84; Censorinus, *Nat.* 13; Boethius *Mus.* 1.27; Mart. Cap. 2.169-99. Pliny the Elder (who follows Cicero, as interpreted above, in giving different notes to all the planets) actually specifies the intervals, which may be reproduced in modern notation as follows: C, D, D sharp, E, G, A, A sharp, B, C. There is apparently no way of avoiding the supposition that these notes were imagined as sounding continuously and simultaneously. A traditionally trained modern musician would regard this as inevitably cacophonous, and some scholars have accordingly tried to find alternative interpretations (such as supposing that the notes originally envisaged were not those of a scale but those of the harmonic series). But in fact, if one plays the notes given by Pliny together on one of the softer registers of an organ, the sound, though it can hardly be described as musical, is not unpleasant.

Cf. Boyancé, *Études* 104ff.; T.Reinach, *REG* 13 (1900) 432-49; G.Wille, *Musica Romana: die Bedeutung der Musik im Leben der Römer* (Amsterdam 1967) 438-42, with bibliography in n. 313, p. 439.

the number seven is crucial (literally "the knot of all things") Cf. above, §4 (12), on "perfect numbers".

wise men have imitated Because of the mathematical proportions involved in musical intervals, the Pythagoreans regarded music as a reflection of the heavenly order (and also a useful psychological therapy: Cic. *Tusc.* 5.113, Quintil. *Inst.* 9.4.12, Favon. Eulog. 25.5). The lyre had seven strings, apparently one for each note of the scale. Varro, *Menipp.* 351 Buecheler calls the universe the "gods' lyre". Cf. also Quintil. *Inst.* 1.10.12.

divine studies i.e. philosophy, astronomy, music and mathematics. Cicero uses the phrase of poetry and philosophy in *Cato Maior* 24.

11 (19) the ears of men have grown deaf This explanation of men's inability to hear the Music of the Spheres is referred to (and attributed to the Pythagoreans) by Aristotle, *De Caelo* 290b12ff.; cf. Censorinus 13.1. Porph. *Vit. Pyth.* 30 and Macr. *SS* 2.4.14 say simply that the sound of the Music of the Spheres is "too great" for our ears to perceive. Needless to say, both of Cicero's analogies are imperfect.

Catadupa A cataract on the Nile (either the first or the second), south of Syene (Aswan) which was at the southern border of ancient Egypt. The name comes from Greek καταδουπεῖν "to crash down". Cf. Herodotus 2.17, Pliny *NH* 5.54.

has no sense of hearing Cf. Pliny *NH* 6.181, Sen. *NQ* 4.2, *Ep.* 56, Philostr. *Vit. Apoll.* 6.18.23-6, Amm. Marc. 22.15.9, Macr. *SS* 2.5.

12 (20) despise things merely human This paragraph enlarges on the insignificance of worldly glory: cf. *De Rep.* 1.26-7, Introd. §5; also *Tusc.* 1.109, *Lael.* 86. It may owe something to writings *de contemnenda gloria*, to which Cicero refers in *Tusc.* 1.34 and Arch. 26. The theme recurs also in Cicero's *Hortensius* (fr. 78 and 80 Grilli), whence some have thought that it derived from Aristotle's *Protrepticus*, which is supposed to have been a model for the *Hortensius* (see A.D.Leeman, *Mnemosyne* 4.11 [1958] 138-51; H.Usener, RhM 28 [1873] 392-408, E.Bignone, *L'Aristotele perduto e la formazione filosofica di Epicuro* [Florence, ed. 2, 1973] I, 214-8 and II, 256-8; Büchner, *Ciceros Somnium Scipionis* 51-8, and Büchner's commentary on *De Republica*). The parallel with the *Hortensius*, in itself, proves 'nothing at all, except that Cicero re-used an idea which he had already expressed here in the *Somnium*; it tells us nothing whatever about the sources of the present work. (It might have been another matter if the *Hortensius* had been the earlier work of the two.) Nevertheless, the idea does indeed seem to have been present in Aristotle. A fragment attributed to the *Protrepticus* (B105 Düring) seems to allude to it; and the *De Mundo* (391a-b), which is doubtless not by Aristotle but may draw on Aristotelian material, makes very much the same point as Cicero does about the smallness of the inhabited world, and even employs similar language (cf. below); cf. also Arist. *Meteorologica* 352a27; A.J.Festugière, *Eranos* 44 (1946) 370ff. This sort of idea must, however, have been common enough in protreptic literature (i.e. exhortations to philosophical study) and elsewhere, and the search for a specific "source", here as elsewhere in the *Somnium*, is (at any rate given the limitations of the extant evidence) misconceived.

The geography of this section presumably derives simply from the received geographical wisdom of Cicero's time: one should distinguish between the facts or theories on the one hand, and the ethical use made of them on the other.

patches cf. [Aristotle] *De Mundo* 392b30.

stand at a different angle The natural meaning of the Latin here is (as Boyancé interprets) that those whose latitude or longitude differs from ours by an acute angle stand "obliquely" with respect to us; those whose latitude or longitude is exactly 90 degrees different from ours stand at right angles; while those who live at the Antipodes stand upside down with respect to us. But the passage has usually been interpreted differently, since according to Macrobius (*SS* 2.5.33) those who stand "obliquely" are the inhabitants of the southern hemisphere at the same longitude as ourselves (the nearest land to this point would be South Africa), while those who stand "transversely" are those who occupy the opposite longitude to ours in the northern hemisphere (i.e. on or around the International Date Line). This is an attempt to correlate Cicero's terminology with the Greek terms ἄντοικοι, περίοικοι, ἀντίποδες, but it seems less likely from a purely Latin point of view. Cf. *Acad. pr.* 2.123; *Tusc.* 1.68.

13 (21) belts The Latin is *cingula*, representing the Greek ζῶναι, from which derives our word "zone"; both words literally mean "belts" (in the sense of the article of clothing). The theory of the five zones approximately represents reality, and was common in ancient geographical thought; cf. Eratosthenes 18ff. Hiller, Cic. *ND* 1.24, *Tusc.* 1.45, Arist. *Meteor.* 2.362b; Virgil *Georgics* 1.232ff.; [Tibullus] *Panegyricus Messallae* 151-68; Ovid *Met.* 1.49; Strabo 1.94 (referring to Parmenides as inventor of the doctrine); Cleomedes 1.2.12-13; Diog. Laert. 7.155. The surface of the earth was, according to this theory, divided into two frigid (polar) zones, two temperate zones (northern and southern), and a torrid (equatorial) zone. The torrid zone was supposed to be bounded by the tropics (Macr. *SS* 2.7). According to Cicero's version here, only the two temperate zones were habitable, and the torrid zone could not even be crossed, so that the southern temperate zone was for ever inaccessible to the inhabitants of the northern hemisphere. This was not a universal belief; e.g. Posidonius (quoted by Cleomedes 1.2.15, 1.6.31-2) thought that the torrid zone could support human life.

stand with their footsteps opposite to yours A literal paraphrase of ἀντίποδες "Antipodes", i.e. "opposite-feet". Cf. Cic. *Acad. pr.* 2.123.

really a small island Cicero, in common with many ancient geographers, envisages Africa as stopping north of the Equator, and the whole of Europe, Asia and Africa as surrounded by water. One branch of "Ocean" was supposed to flow all the way round the Earth at the Equator. This geographical theory, which underestimates the size of the Eurasian and African landmass in proportion to the surface of the earth, suits Cicero's rhetorical purposes well. The idea is also found in *ND* 2.165, [Aristotle] *De Mundo* 392b20 σύμπασα μία νῆσός ἐστιν ὑπὸ τῆς Ἀτλαντικῆς καλεομένης θαλάττης περιρρεομένη; Aelian, VH 3.18.

narrow at the extremities and broader in the centre The ancients compared the shape of Europe, Asia and Africa, as they conceived it, to an outspread cloak: Strabo 2.5.6 and 14; 11.11.7; Macr. *SS* 2.9.8.

the Atlantic Used here as a name for the whole of the "Ocean" which is supposed to surround the habitable world. Cf. Polybius 16.29.6, [Aristotle] *De mundo* 392b, Avienus, *Ora Maritima* 402, Macr. *SS* 2.9.

14 (22) Caucasus ... Ganges The Ganges is often mentioned in ancient literature as the eastern boundary of the known world. The name 'Caucasus' in Latin may embrace mountain ranges further east than what we know as the Caucasus (see *OLD* s.v., 2).

the utmost West Included for symmetry, more than for any other reason; Scipio himself, when campaigning in Spain, travelled fairly near the Western end of Europe. Cicero may perhaps be thinking of reputed lands further west, but this is not certain, as there was no general belief in their existence.

15 (23) the floods and conflagrations of the world Commentators cannot resist seeing Stoic influence here, since the periodic destruction of the cosmos by fire was such a characteristic element in most Stoic cosmology (Zeno fr. 98 v. A., Chrysippus 596-632 v. A., Sen. *NQ* 3.29, Cic. *ND* 2.118; Long-Sedley II, 274); but this is doubtful. Cicero talks not of the whole cosmos but of *terrae*, i.e. the land-masses of the habitable world; he includes floods as well as fire, but floods were no part of Stoic thought on the subject; and the passage fairly clearly derives not from a Stoic source but from Plato, *Timaeus* 22c, πολλαὶ καὶ κατὰ πολλὰ φθοραὶ γεγόνασιν ἀνθρώπων καὶ ἔσονται, πυρὶ μὲν καὶ ὕδατι μέγισται, etc. It is possible that Cicero's statement that the floods and conflagrations happen at predetermined times may owe something to Stoicism (cf. Aristocles, *SVF* I, 98 κατά τινας εἱμαρμένους χρόνους), but even that is impl: cit in Plato, since he says that the disasters are caused by shifts in the position of the heavenly bodies (which, naturally, Plato believed to be regular and determined). In post-Platonic thought this was elaborated into an explicit correlation of the fires and floods with the "seasons" of the Great Year (the idea of which also came from the *Timaeus*): Cic. *ND* 2.51, *Fin.* 2.102, Lucr. 5.380ff., Cens. *Nat.* 18.11. Although Cicero mentions the Great Year doctrine immediately below, he does not make this connection here.

no fewer Cf. the proverbial *abiit ad plures* as a euphemism for death ("he has gone to join the majority", Petr. *Sat.* 42.5, cf. Plaut. *Trin.* 291, Ar. *Eccl.* 1073), and Lucretius 3.972f.

16 (24) last as long as a year The "Great Year" is defined in Plato's *Timaeus* (39d) as the period in which all the heavenly bodies return to the same positions. The period was sometimes defined by the so-called "Number of Plato" (*Republic* 546b); in rough terms, that gives a period of about 36,000 years. However, many authorities gave shorter periods; Cicero himself in the *Hortensius* (frr. 80-81 Grilli, = Tacitus, *Dialogus* 16 and Serv. *Aen.* 1.269) gave a figure of 12,954 years. Macr. *SS* 2.11.11 estimates 15,000 years. Other figures are given by Censorinus 18.11ff. Cf. Boyancé, *Études* 160ff.

when the soul of Romulus entered these very regions ("regions" = *templa*: see note above on this word.) The Roman deification of Romulus is assimilated here to the Platonic belief in astral immortality. The eclipse of the sun that is supposed to have accompanied Romulus's ascent to heaven was also referred to by Cicero in *Rep.* 2.17, but from a rational and sceptical point of view; also in the *Hortensius* (fr. 82 Grilli = *Aug. Civ. Dei* 3.15). The traditional date for Romulus's death was 716 BC; 567 years had elapsed between that date and the date of Scipio's dream (149 BC), which is certainly less than a twentieth of Cicero's figure for the length of the Great Year.

17 (25). this habitation and eternal home Heaven is the true home of the soul (cf. above, §5[13]). Cf. *Hortensius* fr. 115 Grilli *haud paulo meliorem domum*, [Plato] *Axiochus* 372a.

Virtue ... by her own enticements Cicero perhaps has in mind the Choice of Hercules, Xen. *Mem.* 2.1.21ff.

say it they will In other words, Scipio will after all achieve fame on earth (as, of course, he did).

18 (26). the mind of each man is his true self Cf. *Tusc.* 1.52. The idea occurs in Plato *Phaedo* 115cd, *Laws* 12.959b, but the classic statement of this doctrine is in the *First Alcibiades* (130b), a dialogue attributed to Plato, but generally considered spurious. Cf. also [Plato] *Axiochus* 365e; Cleanthes, *SVF* I, fr. 538, p. 123 v. A.; P.Boyancé, *L'Ant. Class.* 11 (1942) 16-22; J.Pépin, *REG* 82 (1969) 56ff.

Know then that you are a god If the belief that a man is his soul (or mind) is combined with the regularly Platonic or Aristotelian doctrine that the soul is divine (cf. Plato *Laws* 10.899d, *Rep.* 10.611e, *Phaedo* 80a, Aristotle *NE* 10, *Protr.* fr. 61

Rose, etc.), this is the logical result. Cicero argues for the divinity of the soul in *Tusc.* 1.52 and 1.65, and alludes to the idea in many passages (*Fin.* 2.114, *Lael.* 13, *Hort.* frr. 114-5 Grilli, *Leg.* 2.55, *ND* 1.31, *Off.* 3.44, *Tusc.* 5.70). The soul is said to be an emanation from the divine mind in *Cato Maior* 78, *Tusc.* 5.38, *ND* 1.27, *Div.* 1.110, and in Cicero's preface to his translation of Plato's *Timaeus* (4); in the *Timaeus* itself, individual souls are created from the world-soul. In *Tusc.* 1.65, Cicero says that the soul is divine, but disclaims the idea that the soul is actually a god; for this view he refers to Euripides (cf. fr. 1018 N²). Cf. C.Josserand, *L'Ant. Class.* 1935, 141ff. For a curiously misguided attempt to emend the passage, see E.Kapp, *Hermes* 87 (1959) 129-32; *contra*, G.Müller, *Mus. Helv.* 18 (1961) 38-40.

if it is right to call a god ... The argument from the capacities of the soul to its nature was used by Cicero more fully in *Tusculans* I. It also occurs in the pseudo-Platonic *Axiochus* (370b-c), in Philo of Alexandria (*Det. Pot. Insid.* 87), and in the *Didascalicus* ascribed to Albinus or Alcinous (25). In Cicero it takes three forms. In *Tusc.* 1.22 Cicero quotes Aristotle as arguing from the capacities of the soul to the conclusion that it cannot consist of any of the four material elements. (This presumably refers to the lost early works of Aristotle; cf. περὶ φιλοσοφίας 3, fr. 26 Rose; his extant *De Anima* puts forward a rather different view of the soul from that reproduced by Cicero.) In *Tusc.* 1.56-70, Cicero (quoting his own *Consolatio*) argues for the divinity and immateriality of the soul from its capacities. The analogy between the soul's control of the body and God's control of the world appears there, as here, but in that instance simply as an analogy; it does not play an essential part in the argument there, while here in the *Somnium* it is really the main point. Finally, in *Cato Maior* 78, Cicero argues for the immortality of the soul on the same grounds; this is the form of the argument that is found in the *Axiochus*, in Philo and in Albinus. These arguments seem to be part of popular Platonic tradition, deduced from Plato (particularly the *Timaeus* and *Phaedo*) rather than actually found explicitly in his writings.

19 (27). For what is always moved is eternal ... 20 (28) it was never born, and is eternal This passage is literally translated from Plato's *Phaedrus*, 245c-e. The translation is reproduced almost verbatim in *Tusculans* 1.53-4 and attributed there to its source (as, for obvious reasons, it could not be here: the spirit of the dead Africanus must know these things from first-hand experience, not from reading Plato); the argument is also summarised in *CM* 78. A later Latin translation was made by Calcidius and included in his commentary on the *Timaeus* (57, p. 104 Waszink). The passage has a mystical grandeur that makes it appropriate enough for this final revelation, and Cicero's Latin (despite R.Poncelet, *Cicéron traducteur de Platon* [Paris 1957]) does full justice to Plato's original. The passage itself contains echoes of other Platonic doctrines and arguments. The argument that, since the soul moves itself and never abandons itself, it never ceases to move, is similar to one used in the *Phaedo* (105d): the soul is what keeps the body alive; a body is alive if it contains a soul, and death is simply the abandonment of the body by the soul; but the mere fact of leaving the body should not affect the soul's status as a vital principle. For the doctrine of the soul's self-movement cf. also *Timaeus* 89a, Aristotle *De anima* 1.406a; the idea is attributed to Thales (Diels-Kranz I⁶, p 79) and Alcmaeon of Croton (ibid. p. 213: cf. J.Barnes, *The Presocratic Philosophers* [London 1979] I, 114-20). The argument about "beginnings" fits ir with the Platonic doctrine of the pre-existence of souls. It is really a conflation o two different thoughts: (a) that there must be such a thing as a first cause, in order to avoid an indefinite chain of causation; and (b) that since the soul is moved by itself, and does not acquire its motion from elsewhere, it must therefore be such a first cause of motion. (Cf. Arist. *De Anima* 1.406a; Anaxagoras, D.-K. II p.29.) The next section rests on the idea (familiar from the *Timaeus*) that the cosmos has a universal soul that is the source of its movement; this soul must have existed before the universe, in order to set the universe in motion, and it must continue to exist in order to keep the universe in motion. Then Plato shifts from the world-soul to individual souls, saying that self-movement is characteristic of whatever is alive. On the *Phaedrus* passage, see, in addition to the commentators, R.W.Sharples, *LCM* 10 (1985) 66-7; P. Boyancé, "Sur l'exégèse hellénistique du *Phèdre*", *Miscellanea di studi alessandrini in memoria di A. Rostagni* (Turin 1963) 43-53.

The reader may exercise his mind in the search for logical flaws in this whole argument. Aristotle concentrated his attack on the proposition that the soul moves itself: he maintained that the soul (both the individual soul and the vital principle in the universe) may cause motion in other things (e.g. bodies) but does not itself move at all: see Arist. *Physics* 8.3.253a-54b; *De anima* 406a ff.; [Plutarch], *Plac. Philos.* 4.6.899b; Macr. *SS* 2.14; D.J.Furley, "Self Movers", in G.E.R.Lloyd and G.E.L.Owen ed., *Aristotle on Mind and the Senses* (Cambridge 1975) 165-80. The first Platonic argument mentioned above could virtually be paraphrased as "If man has a soul that can survive death, then he has a soul that can survive death", since the idea of surviving death is built into the idea of a "soul" that leaves the body at death. Plato never properly proves the validity of the deduction that if something has always existed, it must always continue to exist. There is a constant confusion between a "beginning" as a cause of motion and a "beginning" as a cause of existence. It is assumed without proof that motion and existence both cease if their causes are removed. (To be fair to Plato, we should remember that in our ordinary observation of events, it does seem that motion needs something to keep it going; the Newtonian principle, that a body continues in uniform motion unless a force is applied, was unknown to the Greeks.) There is no account of the nature of the relationship between the world-soul and individual souls: are they simply instances of the same type, or does the one somehow include the others? All in all, it is perhaps better not to think about these philosophical difficulties when reading the passage, for one may then miss the impressiveness of the passage as a statement of the Platonic faith in immortality.

21 (29). to care for the safety of one's country The theme of statesmanship is reverted to, as is appropriate in the last paragraph of the *De Republica* (cf. *Rep.* 1.2; Introd. §5). But Cicero adds the Platonic doctrine (from the *Phaedo*, 67a, cf. *Timaeus* 47c, Cic. *Tusc.* 1.43, 72 and 75; *Hortensius* frr. 114-5 Grilli) that the soul's journey to heaven is facilitated by philosophic contemplation and contempt for earthly things. Cf. also Macr. *SS* 1.13.10; 2.17.

those who have given themselves up to the pleasures of the body Those who have been intemperate in pleasures, or have sinned in other ways because of the temptations of their bodily nature, are unable to ascend to heaven, because they have become as it were stuck on a lower level; they are thus condemned to wander round the earth (as ghosts or *daemones*) until their sins are purged. This doctrine comes from Plato, *Phaedo* 81c. In some later writers, e.g. Plutarch, the unvirtuous dead inhabit the region beneath the Moon's orbit: this was perhaps an attempt to reconcile the doctrine of the *Phaedo* with the cosmology of the *Timaeus*, the moon's orbit being regarded as the boundary between heaven and earth (cf. above, §9 [17]). [Plato] *Axiochus* 371b places Hades in the lower hemisphere of the Earth's atmosphere (assuming, of course, that the earth is immobile and that we are on the top half of it). Cf. also Macr. *SS* 1.9.4-5; 1.13.10; Porph. *Abst.* 2.47; F.Cumont, *Lux Perpetua* (Paris 1949) 209.

servants cf. *Phaedo* 66d and 81b.

for many generations Perhaps influenced by the idea in the *Republic* (615a ff.) that the dead are reincarnated after a thousand years; cf. also *Phaedrus* 248c-9a.

I awoke from my sleep Almost all commentators are agreed that this was the end of the whole dialogue; Büchner dissents (commentary pp. 440-1), thinking that the ending as it stands is too abrupt. But it is certainly very difficult to imagine what Cicero could have written after this without spoiling the effect.

APPENDIX: NOTES ON THE TEXT

Laelius

Title Both elements of the title are attested in MSS (LGVS); cf. Cic. *Off.* 1.31 *de amicitia alio libro dictum est qui inscribitur Laelius* (there is no good reason to doubt the text of this passage), Gellius 17.5.1, Jerome *In Mich.* 2.7, Charisius p. 205 Keil. *Laelius* alone is found in Char. p. 114 K., *de amicitia* alone in Gell. 1.3.11, Char. p. 234 K., Nonius pp. 206, 426 and 440 Mercier, and in numerous MSS and medieval library catalogues. K.A. Neuhausen in his edn. tries to show that only *Laelius* was intended as the title, and apparently sees literary significance in this, but the balance of evidence seems to be against him.

6. esse coniectos: unum te This punctuation is triply supported (against *coniectos unum: te*) by the MSS PAQR, by the rhythm of $\overline{esse}\ \overline{con}\overline{iec}\overline{tos}$ (one of the commonest clausula rhythms, as opposed to the awkward *coniectos unum*), and by the position of *te*, which comes second in its clause as a (relatively) unemphatic personal pronoun, by what is called Wackernagel's Law.

11. indicatum This, the reading of some later MSS, is to be preferred to *iudicatum*, which is in all the early MSS. "It was judged by the mourning of the citizens how dear he was" does not make much sense: one would expect "it could be judged from the mourning" (*ex maerore iudicari poterat*) but that would involve too great a change in the text. Far easier to suppose that *n* and *u* have been confused! Fedeli, *RhM* 1972, 161-2, compares Cic. *Rab. Post.* 48 *indicat tot hominum fletus quam sis carus tuis*. It is true that the rhythm of *funeris iudicatumst* is a marginally commoner Ciceronian clausula than *funeris indicatumst*, but this carries little weight compared with the argument from the sense.

19. aequitas Lambinus's conjecture for *aequalitas* (all MSS.); "fairness" is clearly the sense required. Cf. Fedeli, *RhM* 1972 p. 162.

sintque (recc.) for *sitque* (all earlier MSS): the sentence runs much more smoothly if the subject is kept the same, and *magna constantia* is taken as descriptive ablative.

22. denique Perhaps *deinde* ("further", rather than "after all") should be read?

23. nec agri quidem So all manuscripts; the change to *ne ... quidem* is not necessary. On *nec ... quidem* see my note on *Cato Maior* 27.

34. perduxissent should be retained (understanding an indefinite subject "they" and *amores* as object); cf. my note on *CM* 60. Meissner's conjecture *perducti essent*, supported by Fedeli, *RhM* 1972, 164-5, is unnecessary.

35. non inveteratas modo The word order *inveteratas non modo* in some later MSS is clearly wrong. Earlier MSS have *inveterata* for *inveteratas*, as if agreeing with *querela*; this was accepted by Madvig, but it seems far more natural to talk of long-established friendships being broken by these people's accusations, than of friendships (in general) being broken by long-established accusations; further, we expect *amicitias* to have an adjective to balance *sempiterna* with *odia*.

38. sapientia si simus G. Canter, for *sapientia simus* (or *sumus*) *si* (all MSS), an easy correction; the MS reading does not give satisfactory logic; most probably *si* has been omitted and subsequently re-inserted in the wrong place. It would be possible, but hard, to make the reading of the MSS mean "we should have to be persons of perfect wisdom if all fault in this matter is to be avoided".

41. Publio Nasica The MSS are divided between *P. Nasica(m) Scipione(m)* (QGVHSB) and *P. Scipione(m)* (POL). Presumably the case should be ablative ("in the matter of") rather than accusative. There may indeed be doubt whether Cicero refers here to Nasica or to Aemilianus, but the reading *P. Scipione* is not really satisfactory whichever is meant. If Aemilianus were meant, Laelius would surely not use the formal *praenomen* here any more than he does elsewhere in referring to his friend. On the other hand, the mere addition of the *praenomen* would hardly be a sufficient means of specifying Nasica, since Aemilianus's *praenomen* was also Publius. The normal way for Cicero (or Laelius) to refer to Nasica in a context like this would be *Publius Nasica* (cf. §101, *Phil.* 8.13, *Off.* 1.76). Add to this that if *Nasica* in some MSS. is not a correct reading, it must be a gloss by someone acute and knowledgeable enough (a) to see from the mere presence of the *praenomen*, and/or from the context, that someone different from Scipio Aemilianus was meant, (b) to know that Scipio Nasica had supposedly suffered at the hands of the supporters of Tiberius Gracchus. I do not know whether there were such people involved with the production of medieval manuscripts of the *Laelius*, but it is much more likely that, given an original reading *P. Nasica*, someone should have glossed *Nasica* by *Scipione*, and that the latter reading should have ousted the former from the text in one half of the tradition. The context, involving the events that took place immediately after Tiberius Gracchus's death, supports Nasica (the killer of Gracchus) against Aemilianus. The insistence on Gracchus's "tyranny" functions as justification of Nasica's action in killing him. Aemilianus's death was discussed at greater length earlier in the dialogue, and Laelius did not in that passage expressly commit himself to the theory that Gracchus's followers were responsible for it; for him to be so much more explicit here would be strange.

quoquo modo potuimus ... sustinuimus This is the reading of some later MSS (12th century onwards), and makes reasonable sense. Of the readings of the MSS, the only other one that could make sense is *quoque modo potuimus* (PO[1]): the meaning would be the same ("in whatever way we could"), but *quoque* for *quoquo* or *quocumque* would be an archaism. The remaining MSS insert *quem* between *quoque* (which they all read) and *modo*, and change *potuimus* to *posuimus* or *possumus*. This was clearly a bungling attempt to emend a passage not understood, *quŏque* having been confused with *quŏque* "also". Cf. Fedeli, *RhM* 1972, 166.

diem e die This, or something like it, seems to me to be unavoidable as a correction for MSS *deinde* (*denique* K). *Deinde* normally means "then" or "next", but in older Latin it could mean "from now on" or "from then on". This latter meaning might be thought to be just possible here, on the assumption that Cicero was using the word in a sense obsolete in his own time, as part of the stylistic characterisation of Laelius. Yet on closer inspection, even that seems unlikely. Laelius is not saying that the evil is starting to grow *from Gaius Gracchus's tribunate onwards*, (which is what that would strictly mean); Gaius Gracchus's tribunate is still in the future, and a great deal of damage has (according to Laelius) already been done by Tiberius Gracchus and his supporters.

The required sense is that the evil is growing continuously all the time, i.e. from day to day.

42. in magna aliqua re   Ernesti; *in magnam aliquam rem* O[2]; *in magna aliqua re p<ublica>* PO[1]; *in magnam aliquam rem p<ublicam>* LQGV(?)HSB.   The ablative is clearly right, not the accusative.   It is strange that so many editors still retain *publica* after *re*, as if *magna aliqua re publica* could mean anything other than "in some great commonwealth".   But most early MSS simply have *rep.*, and the *p* is clearly enough a dittography of the *p* of *peccantibus*; *publica* in later MSS. results from a mistaken expansion of this *p* as if it had been an abbreviation (*rep.* is a very common abbreviation for *re publica*).

44. consilium vero dare   The emphatic particle *vero* (in L alone of the MSS known to me) is desirable here, while it is quite unnecessary to say that we should not hesitate to give *true* advice, however well attested *consilium verum* may be in that meaning (cf. Fedeli, *RhM* 1972, 166-7).   Who would need a ruling on whether the advice given by friends to each other should be good or bad?

48. si qua   It is possible that the reading here should be *si quasi* (*qua* OKMRV[2]; *quasi* PLQGV[1]HSB);   the change either way would be extremely easy before the *si* of *significatio*.   In either case, the effect is to qualify the metaphor of *significatio ... eluceat*, and the most natural English translation is "as it were". (Cf. Reid.)

50. immanis   Earlier MSS all read *immunis*, retained by a surprising number of editors: it is difficult to see what sense in this context could possibly be extracted from that word, which means "exempt from duty". Fedeli *RhM* 1972, 167, proposes to correct to *immanis* from later MSS., and this is clearly right; cf. *Planc.* 81, *Pro Sulla* 7.

51. atqui haud sciam   The logic requires that *atqui* "and yet" (proposed by O.F.Kleine, progr. Wetzlar 1854) should be written instead of the MS reading *atque* "and (also)";   the two words are easily and constantly confused, and the triple negative in the next sentence, together with the tricky idiom *haud sciam an*, could well have added to the confusion.   *Haud sciam an* is equivalent not to English "I am not sure whether..." but to "I am not sure whether ... not".   So the literal equivalent of this sentence would be "And yet I am not sure whether it is not the case that it is not even desirable for nothing ever to be lacking for friends".   The reader will forgive the less literal version which I have adopted in the translation;   there is nothing obscure or awkward in the Latin.

56. deligendi (PS[1], cf. *delegendi* GV) is more appropriate here than *diligendi* (OKLQ etc., adopted by many editors and taken as genitive qualifying *fines et quasi termini*).   *Diligendi* would be otiose as a qualification of the *fines et termini*; and what follows is an examination of various philosophical attempts to define the scope of friendship (cf. below, §§58 *definit amicitiam*, and 59 *finis verae amicitiae*), not to define the scope of "loving" within friendship (which, if it meant anything at all, would presumably be hardly distinguishable from the question already dealt with above in §§36ff. *quatenus amor in amicitia progredi debeat*).   The false reading has in fact led some commentators to take §§56 ff. as merely continuing the discussion of §§36-44; but the two sections are on quite different topics, and the difference ought to be explicit.   In addition, the word order *qui sint ... fines ... deligendi* is eminently natural and Ciceronian, with the gerundive at the end as complement of *sint.* (The reading of M, *dirigendi*, is perhaps also worth considering: *dirigo* "to direct, lay out" is idiomatic with *fines* "boundaries".)

60. deligendo (P only). Here again a part of *deligere* must be read, not *diligere*. Cicero means, clearly, "if we have been unfortunate in *choosing* [our friends]", not "unfortunate in loving them" - whatever that might be supposed to mean. Since *diligere* refers above all to attentive or affectionate *behaviour*, it would not be the proper word in such a context. One can be unfortunate in friendship or in love, but that means after all that one is unfortunate in one's friend or lover; one can hardly be unfortunate in one's own friendly behaviour.

63. est igitur prudentis sustinere, ut currum, sic impetum benevolentiae; quo utamur quasi equis temptatis, sic amicitia aliqua parte periclitatis moribus amicorum. *currum* OMKRLQ: *cursum* PGVHSB. *temptatis* edd.: *temperatis* O²RVHSB, *temperantis* Q¹ (*temperatis* Q²), *tempestatis* PO¹KML¹G. *amicitia* RO²V²H²S²: *amicitias* PO¹KMLQGV¹H¹S¹B. This sentence presents considerable difficulty, although the general meaning is clear enough. The variants *currum/cursum* and *temptatis/temperatis/ tempestatis* need not detain us; "chariot" is preferable to "course", and *temptatis* "having been tried out" is obviously correct. Neither does *aliqua parte* (all MSS.) present a major problem: editors have often changed to *ex aliqua parte*, but there is nothing wrong with *aliqua parte* = "in some respect", "in some area"; *ex a. p.* would mean "to some extent", and is to my mind not so appropriate. The chief difficulty lies in the syntax of *quo utamur ... amicorum*. *Quo* looks at first sight like a relative pronoun, referring back to *impetum* (or just possibly *currum*). But this will not work with the rest of the sentence as it stands. Even if *equis temptatis* and *aliqua parte periclitatis moribus amicorum* are both ablative absolute, we are still left with two conflicting objects for *utamur*, i.e. *quo* and *amicitia* (supposing that *amicitia* is read: the alternative *amicitias* is even more clearly ungrammatical). There are really two alternatives. One alternative is to delete *amicitia(s)*, which could possibly be an intrusive gloss (as proposed by Strelitz, ed. 1884). The sentence would then mean "... to restrain the rush of benevolence, in order that we may use it (i.e. the rush of benevolence) after trying out the characters of our friends in some respect, as if after trying out a team of horses."   However, it seems rather odd to talk of restraining the rush of benevolence in order that we may later make use of the very same rush of benevolence. The other alternative is to abandon the idea that *quo* is a relative, and take it instead as a conjunction equivalent to *ut*, "in order that"; this would be a mild archaism, possibly chosen to suit the stylistic characterisation of Laelius, and to avoid the cacophony of *ut utamur*; although it must be granted that it is confusing, since the proximity of *impetum* creates a strong expectation that *quo* will be relative. Nevertheless, on this assumption, *utamur* is now free to govern *amicitia*, and we arrive at the sense which I have translated; a literal version would be: "... in order that we may, as if after trying out a team of horses, use friendship having in some respect tried out the characters of our friends." It would also be possible to take *equis temptatis* as object of another implied *utamur* in the clause of comparison, rather than as ablative absolute, but that would spoil what symmetry the sentence has. In either case, the syntax is certainly elliptical and confusing, but can perhaps just be accepted. If Cicero did not write this, we do not know what he wrote; and any reader who is still dissatisfied is welcome to pencil an obelus in the text at the appropriate point. Cf. also W.A.Camps, *AJP* 101 (1980) 443-4.

67. veterrima quaeque... esse debent (*debent* all MSS.) There is no reason to change *debent* to *debet* (Beier's conjecture, supported by Madvig). The meaning is "in the case of friendships, as in the case of wines, the oldest [things] should be the pleasantest".

68. nec vero in hoc, quod est animal (all MSS.) There is no need to add *solum* or *modo*: it may be understood, as in the passages cited by Kühner-Stegmann, *Lateinische Grammatik* II, p. 66 Anm. 2.

69. per se ipsos esse I have substituted this for *per se posse esse*, the reading of all the MSS; *posse* seems otiose, and was deleted by Halm; while some emphasis on *per se*, such as is provided by *ipsos*, seems desirable. It is just possible that Cicero wrote not *per se ipsos* but *per sepse*, which would explain the corruption very easily Compare *Cato Maior* 82 and my note.

72. opere Reid prefers *opera* (M only), "by the application of effort".

74. eos habere necessarios (all MSS.) We must understand *oportet*; there is no reason to insert it in the text, as did some older editors. Cf. Fedeli *RhM* 1972 p. 169, Madvig on *Fin.* 2.103.

sed alio quodam modo est ... aliter All editors have assumed here that *est* is corrupt, and have tried to emend it in various ways; e.g. *aestimandi* Mommsen. Among the MSS, R expunges *est* (adding a gloss *diligendi sunt*); while Wolfenbüttel, Aug. 51.12 and Vatican, Reg. Lat. 1574 (both twelfth century) anticipated Mommsen's type of conjecture by writing *amandi*. But no single-word substitution for *est* has produced a satisfactorily logical text. "Otherwise firm friendships cannot last" presupposes a preceding sentence specifying the conditions under which firm friendships *can* last. It makes no sense to say that firm friendships cannot last unless we value the people concerned in some other way than the way we normally value friends. The only reasonable conclusion is that something has dropped out of the text. It may have been one line, or five, or a whole page; there is no way whatsoever of telling. Nor, if one accepts that this is the case, is there any way of telling whether *est* is sound or corrupt; *alio quodam modo est ...* is simply not a complete sentence; one could imagine ways of completing it while retaining *est*, e.g. *sed alio quodam modo est talis necessitudinis ratio comparanda*. (This is merely an example, not a suggestion as to what Cicero wrote.)

77. graviter ac moderate I have accepted Reid's emendation, which seems to me both the most apt in sense and palaeographically the easiest, for the manuscripts' nonsensical reading *graviter auctoritate*. Madvig and Halm deleted *auctoritate* altogether; H^2 reads *gravi auctoritate* - a worthy medieval attempt at sense, accepted by Clark and others, but not ideal in context.

81. volucribus nantibus agrestibus, cicuribus feris (all MSS.) The text has been doubted by Meissner and Fedeli (*RhM* 1972, 171), but there is nothing unsatisfactory in the grouping of three followed by two; indeed it is natural and inevitable that an enumeration of classes of animal should embrace both tame and wild, and the three habitats of land, sea and air.

88. sublevanda (POM^{2}L^{2}V^{2}H: in *sublevanda* L^{1}G^1, in *sublevando* QG^{2}V^{1}SB, *sublevando* K - none of these readings makes sense.) *Sublevanda* is to be retained, since it fits with *elevare* in the previous sentence. Facciolati, Madvig and Reid altered to *subeunda* "to be undergone".

89. ratio [et] diligentia All MSS previously known read *et* here: I had already decided to delete it when I discovered it already omitted in R^1. No editor seems to have seen the real shape of this sentence, that is to say, *OMNI- (igitur) hac-in-re habenda-ratio -DILIGENTIA est,* "WITH-ALL-DILIGENCE, therefore, account-is-to-be-taken in-this-matter". The order *omni igitur hac in re* is strange, if *omni* really qualifies *re*; the collocation *habenda ratio et diligentia est* is strange, since one *adhibet diligentiam*, not *habet*; omit *et*, and all is well, including the elegant (and not at all unusual) hyperbaton *omni ... diligentia*.

96. non comitem (all MSS) was omitted by Gernhard and Meissner, because of its difficulty (see the commentary); but the omission leaves the sentence rather bald and not much less puzzling, since one then has to wonder in what sense the phrase *ducem populi Romani* is to be taken.

100. ductum (POKLR[1]) is preferable to *dictum* (MR[2]QGVHSB) for the sense "derived".

101. alia <ex alia> Orelli's supplement seems necessary; the MS reading *alia* does not make satisfactory sense.

Somnium Scipionis

1 (9).   hoc Manilio consule   Most editions read *Manio Manilio consuli* after Sigonius. But the MSS all read *consule*; A reads *hoc*, while the other MSS give Manilius an erroneous praenomen (*A.Man(i)lio* or *Anicio Manlio* - the latter clearly interpolated by somebody who was thinking of Boethius's first two names Anicius Manlius!). There is nothing at all wrong with the reading of A, the oldest manuscript, and it should be accepted. "When Manilius here was consul" suits the dialogue setting, which had clearly been forgotten both by the writers of the other MSS and by the editors who follow Sigonius. See R.Montanari Caldini, *Prometheus* 10 (1984) 224-40.

7 (15). munus assignatum The medieval MSS have *munus humanum assignatum*, but *humanum* is omitted by Macrobius and deleted by the second hand of A; it seems better to omit it, since it performs no useful function in context.

10 (18).   intervallis coniunctus imparibus   The tradition divides between *coniunctus* and *disiunctus*. The latter is to be rejected since it does not contrast sufficiently with *ratione distinctis*. *Coniunctus* is the Latin equivalent of the Greek technical musical term συνημμένος. The octave can be envisaged either as a series of discrete points (the notes of the scale) divided from each other by gaps (intervals), or as a continuous line divided into sections (intervals) by points marked on it (the notes). The latter is the more natural picture for those who primarily use stringed instruments (whose strings can be stopped at any point at the will of the performer) and pipes (in which holes can be bored at any point by the manufacturer). It is therefore natural that the ancients should have inclined towards thinking about music in this way. *Coniunctus* refers to the "joining" of successive intervals of the scale, each one added to the last, to produce the complete octave. Those who favour *disiunctus* here presumably have the other model in mind; but our modern tendency to see the octave as a series of discrete notes is probably to be accounted for by the prevalence of the pianoforte. Cf. G.Alberti, *SIFC* 33 (1961) 163-84.

INDEX